By Susan Elnicki Wade and Bill Wade

www.crabdecksandtikibars.com

This book is dedicated to

My Father & Uncle Joe,
For teaching me the joy of travel and adventure.
You are with us every step along the way.

Max & Nicholas,
For being our greatest love and inspiration.

ISBN: 978-1-5121-1116-3

Authors: Susan Elnicki Wade and Bill Wade
Photographs by Susan Elnicki Wade
Maps by Bill Wade
Cover Design by Joe Barsin at Citizen Pride
Web Site Design by Zach Howard at Exton Edge

Printed in the United States of America

Crab Decks & Tiki Bars of the Chesapeake Bay
2916 Northampton Street, NW
Washington, DC 20015
(202) 531-7135
susan@crabdecksandtikibars.com
bill@crabdecksandtikibars.com

For additional copies of this book or info about the Virginia edition, visit
www.crabdecksandtikibars.com

Table of Contents

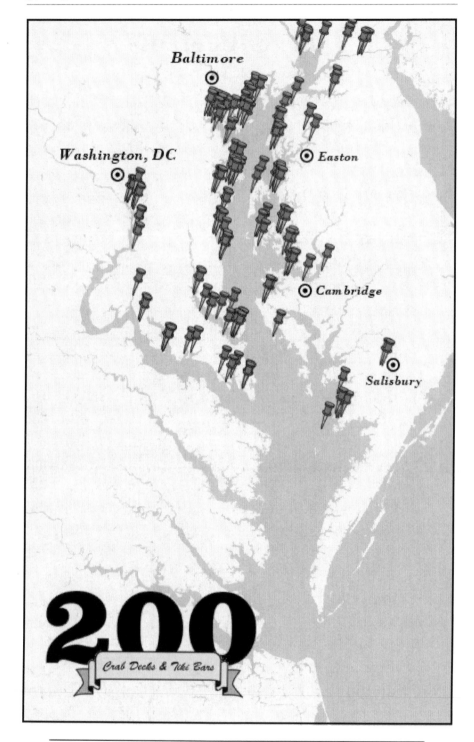

Baltimore

Washington, DC

Easton

Cambridge

Salisbury

200

Crab Decks & Tiki Bars

Introduction

The 2015 Maryland edition of *Crab Decks & Tiki Bars of the Chesapeake Bay* marks the fourth travel guide we've published in the past five years. Like the three before it, writing this book had its ups and downs, but there was never a dull moment or a lack of unforgettable events.

We traveled the shores of our favorite estuary, enjoying the Bay's unique charms and unrivaled beauty from hidden coves in the headwaters to rolling farmlands in southern Maryland and dramatic skylines in its urban pockets. Watermen, waitresses, and restaurant owners welcomed us with Chesapeake hospitality.

Every research trip felt like a mini-vacation – but not the kind of getaway where one leisurely rests on a beach with a blender drink in hand. Our excursions are more like The Great Race – whirlwind road trips to hit checkpoints and distant places and then rush back home in time to watch our sons' soccer games or piano recitals.

However, we did eat like we were on a cruise ship vacation. Our family's high consumption of fresh Maryland seafood was unwavering: 11 gallons of crab soup, 300 oysters, 85 crab cakes, 40 pounds of mussels, 25 rockfish, 200 steamed shrimp, and a few beers and Orange Crushes. Trekking around with a pair of hungry teens certainly put a dent in the Bay's seafood population.

Travel research always presents unexpected challenges, and this year's big hurdle was The Cold. To get current data, we  usually hit the road in the early spring, wearing light jackets and encountering an occasional rain shower. But 2015's late and record-breaking arctic weather battered us with snow squalls and frozen harbors. Watching brave watermen take axes to icy waters and pull out oyster flats silenced our complaints about the cold.

Yet, it was a unique experience trying to take photos of sandy beaches and Adirondack chairs when they were covered with snow, or getting a shot of the Bay's gentle waves when the water was frozen solid. Bill remembered The Great Freeze of 1977 when frigid temperatures turned the Bay into a massive ice-skating rink. His parents took him to Sandy Point State Park to witness the phenomena. Wearing a wool Redskins jacket, he walked across the waters where he had been swimming with his brother and sister the summer before.

One of the best perks about updating this book is discovering new crab decks and tiki bars, and we found some winners for this edition. For example, after years of wishing Betterton had a good restaurant near the beach, a new place named Barbara's on the Bay answered the call. Southern Maryland can now pair local craft beer with crabs pulled fresh from local creeks at the Ruddy Duck Seafood & Ale House near St. George Island. And palm trees are taking root up north in Port Deposit along the Susquehanna River to announce the arrival of a new eatery called

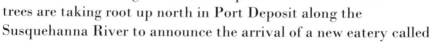

Lee's Landing Dock Bar, which features classic Chesapeake cuisine, hefty crab cakes, half-shell oysters, and ice-cold beer.

On the flip side, we sadly report the loss of some iconic establishments on the Bay. Phillips Seafood has packed up its mallets and closed locations in Annapolis and Washington, DC. John Steven was shuttered in Fells Point after being a staple on the water since 1911. And St. Mary's County will miss the crab cakes and charter fishing at Scheible's Crab Pot.

One final note: Our crabby friends will surely notice that this new book has a new look. Same goes with our web site. We'd like to express our appreciation to Joe Barsin at Citizen Pride in Annapolis for his exceptional artwork and Zach Howard at Exton Edge in San Diego for his mad skills and patience in designing our new web site. We hope you like their work as much as we do.

As we put the finishing touches on another edition and reflect on our Chesapeake adventures, we realize that the constantly changing nature of the Bay makes it a dynamic destination. Everyone's welcome in this patchwork world, with crabs, oysters, rockfish, and tiki cocktails leading the way.

Have fun with our book and take time to explore the treasures of the Bay. To see photos, get updates, or read the blog of our Chesapeake adventures, visit us on Facebook or Pinterest, or go to **www.crabdecksandtikibars.com**.

— Susan Elnicki Wade

About this Edition

Crab Decks & Tiki Bars of the Chesapeake Bay, 2015 Maryland Edition is the fourth in a series of destination guides to seafood restaurants, crab shacks, and tiki lounges. The 200+ authentic eateries chosen for this book must be located on or close to the Chesapeake Bay and its tributary rivers and creeks. We believe if you are not near the water, you don't get the full Bay experience. Restaurants must serve local crabs to make the cut for this book.

The book is divided into 13 regions. Each entry starts with contact information (address, phone, and web site), followed by:

- County in Maryland where it's located,
- When It's Open (year-round or seasonal),
- Latitude/Longitude,
- Body of Water,
- Dockage (yes or no), and
- Distance from Major Cities.

Every crab deck and tiki bar profile includes a map and photograph taken on-site. Our one-of-a-kind Atmosphere Meter rates the ambience, ranging from casual to formal on a scale of one to 10 (frosty beer mugs to crisp martinis).

Crab Decks & Tiki Bars of the Chesapeake Bay, 2015 Maryland Edition provides in-depth descriptions that paint a vivid image of each restaurant's décor, atmosphere, cuisine, and specialties, letting you know what to expect before you arrive. Many profiles include bonus info: colorful history, folklore, attractions, culture, and traditions unique to each neck of the Bay.

At the back of the book, three indexes are provided to help locate the seafood houses you want to visit: Bodies of Water, Cities, and Restaurant Names. A personal Tiki Tracker encourages you to document your own Bay adventures.

Meet the Authors

 Bill Wade was born and raised in Maryland. His father is a former DC firefighter who hadn't intended to be a waterman — until Bill's mom entered a jingle-writing contest for a local car dealership and won a boat. Their wooden cabin cruiser was built on the Bay and docked at Kent Narrows. Summers were spent cruising around the remote coves of the Bay and catching crabs with chicken necks. Bill can pick a crab faster than most workers at a Phillips processing plant.

 Susan Elnicki Wade grew up in a small town in western Pennsylvania and has worked at restaurants in Pittsburgh, New York, and Washington, DC. She leans more toward tiki and picking crabs doesn't come easy to her, but she can whip up a mean batch of fried oysters and bake a fine Smith Island cake. After visiting every county on the Chesapeake Bay over the past two decades, she's written travel articles for publications such as *MarinaLife Magazine* and *Washingtonian Magazine*.

Bill and Susan live in Washington, DC, with their two sons, Max and Nicholas. The Wades each have more than 20 years experience in the publishing industry and hope to make enough money on this book to buy a boat.

They have sold thousands of copies of their Maryland and Virginia Chesapeake Bay travel guides across the mid-Atlantic region. Books are available at retail locations or on their web site.

Please contact the authors on Facebook, Pinterest, email, or **www.crabdecksandtikibars.com**

More Crab & Tiki Online

Now that you have a copy of *Crab Decks & Tiki Bars of the Chesapeake Bay, 2015 Maryland Edition*, please visit our companion web site, **www.crabdecksandtikibars.com.** We added new features to make this book more useful and your Bay getaway more fun.

- **Crab Deck Updates** report on Chesapeake seafood houses that just opened or closed their doors after the book when to press.

- **Captain's Blog** chronicles our adventures as we keep cruising around the Bay to investigate new crab decks and tiki bars.

- **Photo Gallery** features restaurants in this book and gives you a clear picture of where you're headed.

- **Social Media,** such as Facebook and Pinterest, helps you link into our crabby community and get news about the region.

 # Know Before You Go

At times on our trips around the Bay, we felt like seasoned explorers successfully navigating Maryland's back roads and hidden creeks without a hitch. Other times, we made mistakes that took a little wind out of our sails. To make your trips run smoothly:

- **Call first.** Most destinations are family-run businesses that can have irregular hours, especially in the off-season. Give them a ring to see if they're open and if they have available dockage.

- **Use every navigation tool.** Grab a map, your GPS, nautical charts, and charge up your smart phone. Many crab decks are located off the beaten path where roads are poorly marked.

- **Plan ahead but be flexible.** The unexpected is bound to happen, such as waiting for boats to pass under a drawbridge or getting stuck on a road behind a dilapidated chicken truck. That's the Bay's charm, and it adds color to your travel tales.

- **Eat food in season.** Crabs bought off-season are rarely local. Ask servers what's fresh, even if your heart was set on a special dish. Each season offers delicacies that are worth the wait.

CRAB DECKS & TIKI BARS OF THE CHESAPEAKE BAY

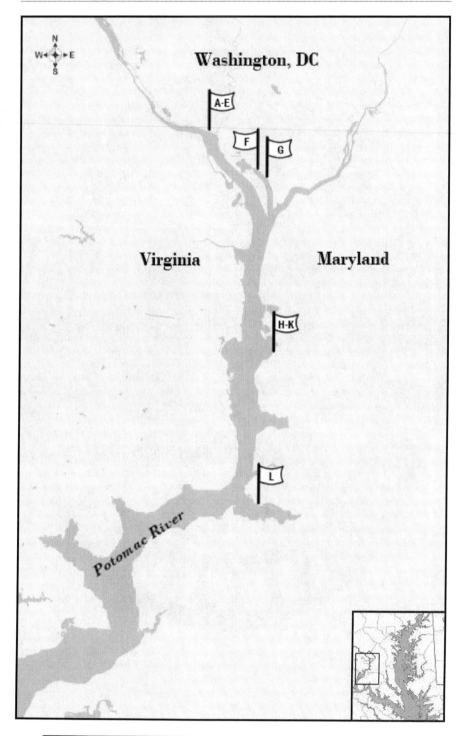

Upper Potomac River

Nick's Riverside Grill

3050 K Street, NW
Washington, DC 20007
(202) 342-3535
www.nicksriversidegrill.com

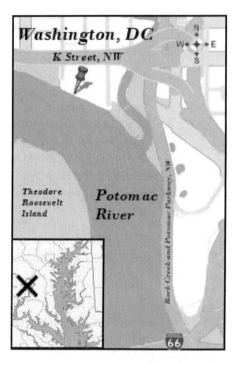

Location: Washington, DC

Open: Year Round

Dockage: Yes

Latitude: N 38° 54' 5"

Longitude: W 77° 3' 38"

Body of Water: Potomac River

Driving Distance:
   Baltimore 43 miles,
   Annapolis 36 miles,
   Easton 74 miles

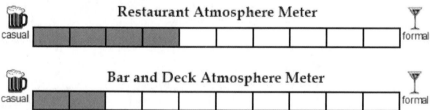

Restaurant Atmosphere Meter
casual ——— formal

Bar and Deck Atmosphere Meter
casual ——— formal

Georgetown Waterfront used to be a commercial wharf with sea-faring vessels and austere industrial buildings. Plans to develop the waterfront as a dining destination began in the 1960s. Since the 1980s, restaurants have been popping up along the Potomac's shores offering seafood for every palate and mood. Nick's Riverside Grill entered the scene in 1992. It's a family-run restaurant, owned by D.C. locals who proudly took part in their hometown's riverside revival.

In the afternoon on the outdoor patio, you can watch ducks paddle around and crew teams practice strokes on the water without hearing a honk of city traffic behind you in Georgetown. On summer weekend evenings, this place gets packed with boaters, college students, hipsters, and locals loving life along the water's edge. The restaurant has an inside bar and dining area with a contemporary yet comfortable décor accented with vibrant modern artwork and fireplaces imbedded in the walls.

The cooks roll out a menu that's loaded with tasty snacks and seafood. Among the starters are Bay favorites such as crab and artichoke dip, clam chowder, crispy fried calamari, and steamed mussels. Maryland crab cakes, grilled Atlantic salmon, swordfish steak, fish and chips, and Cajun BBQ shrimp are first-rate. Burgers, grilled chicken, pork chops, bison tacos and salads offer viable options to landlubbers.

Orange Anchor Dock Bar

3050 K Street, NW
Washington, DC 20007
(202) 802-9990
www.orangeanchordc.com

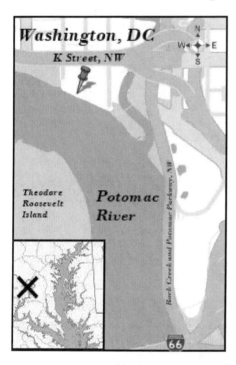

Location: Washington, DC

Open: Year Round

Dockage: Yes

Latitude: N 38° 54' 5"

Longitude: W 77° 3' 37"

Body of Water: Potomac River

Driving Distance:
Baltimore 43 miles,
Annapolis 36 miles,
Easton 74 miles

Atmosphere Meter

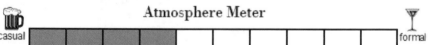

casual ——— formal

The most recent restaurant to test the waters in Georgetown is the Orange Anchor, which arrived in time to experience the bitter winter of 2014. Even though it's tucked behind the harbor's towering fountain, it's easy to find this new eatery. Just look for the bright orange awnings and ropes stretched between wooden pylons to mark off the patio. The tasteful nautical décor features wallpaper and matching seat cushions with tiny white anchors on a navy blue fabric, a few buoys and oars on the walls, and a ship's steering wheel serving as the hostess stand.

Its motto, "Where everyone is treated like a captain," should also say that "anyone can drink like a pirate," because the craft bar holds an impressive list of rums from Jamaica, Barbados, Nicaragua, and other countries around the globe. Specialty cocktails include the rum-enriched Georgetown Riviera, Anchor's Away! vodka shooter, and Sex on the Boat afloat with coconut rum, pineapple and cream.

A basket of Old Bay seasoned popcorn greets you at the table while you inspect the menu from a scratch kitchen that rejects prepackaged foods. Oysters Four Ways (on the half shell, grilled, fried, or filled with champagne) is an excellent starter, along with the ahi tuna roll, garlic sautéed shrimp, or clams casino. Crab fritters in beer batter and the duck confit corn dogs are unique crispy treats. Noteworthy entrees: mussels steamed in hard cider, shrimp and lobster roll, pecan trout, and chicken cooked in a brown ale and butter sauce.

Farmers Fishers Bakers

3000 K Street, NW
Washington, DC 20007
(202) 298-8783
www.farmersfishersbakers.com

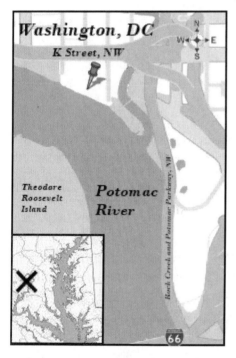

Location: Washington, DC

Open: Year Round

Dockage: No

Latitude: N 38° 54' 6"

Longitude: W 77° 3' 36"

Body of Water: Potomac River

Driving Distance:
Baltimore 43 miles,
Annapolis 36 miles,
Easton 74 miles

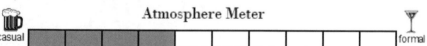

Atmosphere Meter

casual   formal

In 2008, Farmers Fishers Bakers came to Georgetown waterfront and introduced a new dining concept that's catching on like wildfire. It's all about eco-friendly cooking, sustainable ingredients, and farm-inspired "true" food. The restaurant is owned by the North Dakota Farmers Union, and everything that appears on your plate is made "with seasonal ingredients from abundant and healthy sources." That means you don't need to worry about putting preservatives, chemicals, or endangered species in your mouth.

So, it protects the environment, but does it taste good? Farmers delivers for both the planet and your palate. The chefs have worked up an extensive menu with vibrant flavors to bolster regionally-inspired dishes.

Stars of the seafood section include seafood Chesapeake jambalaya, shrimp scampi, littleneck clams, crab cakes with veggie succotash, and pots of mussels cooked eight different ways from coconut curry and cucumber to bacon basil bleu cheese. If you want to graze on local cows and pigs, order Danish BBQ pork ribs or steaks with corn pudding tamale. Also available are pizzas with organic mozzarella and tomatoes, hamburgers, and meatless entrees for vegetarians.

The location is as unique as the food. Patio diners sit next to the iconic water fountain in warm weather and feel toasty heat from a fire pit in the fall. The spacious dining room is divided into sections called "microclimates" that represent themes like baking, ranching, and fishing. Next to the bar is a larder (pantry) displaying mason jars filled with colorful fruit.

Tony & Joe's Seafood Place

3000 K Street, NW
Washington, DC 20007
(202) 944-4545
www.tonyandjoes.com

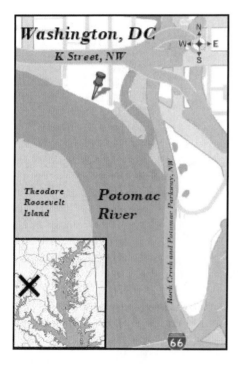

Location: Washington, DC

Open: Year Round

Dockage: Yes

Latitude: N 38° 54' 5"

Longitude: W 77° 3' 35"

Body of Water: Potomac River

Driving Distance:
    Baltimore 43 miles,
    Annapolis 36 miles,
    Easton 74 miles

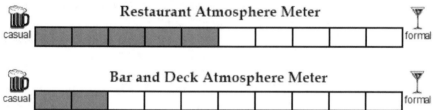

Restaurant Atmosphere Meter
casual / formal

Bar and Deck Atmosphere Meter
casual / formal

At Tony & Joe's, you can get a mini-tour of Washington without leaving your table. From the waterfront patio, the historic Watergate Hotel, Kennedy Center, Roosevelt Island, Key Bridge, and the Potomac River are headliners along the panoramic view. And they're all within easy walking distance if you choose to get up close to these landmarks.

The restaurant, which has been a dining institution here for decades, is owned by D.C. natives and is part of a family of local eateries that includes The Dancing Crab and Nick's Riverside Grill just a stone's throw away. Those names and the big red crab on the logo send a message that this place makes seafood a top priority.

The raw bar is exceptional with a daily list of fresh Chesapeake oysters and a pricey chilled seafood tower of lobster, oysters, clams, salmon, shrimp, and crab meat. For starters, you can dip bread into longneck clams steamed with garlic butter or savor a smoked salmon salad. Dinner entrees take seafood to a whole new level. The Chesapeake Steamer Pot — packed with shrimp, mussels, clams, and crab claws with sweet corn and Old Bay — looks like an edible postcard from the Bay. Maryland crab cakes are brimming with flavor. Sure winners with meat eaters: grilled lamb chops, roasted half chicken, and boneless short ribs. Live jazz brunch features champagne, mimosas, oysters, and smoked trout.

Sequoia

3000 K Street, NW
Washington, DC 20007
(202) 944-4200
www.arkrestaurants.com/sequoia

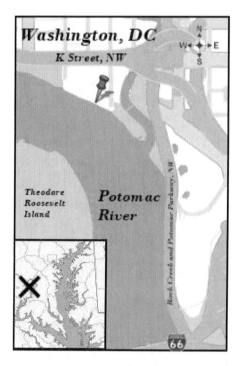

Location: Washington, DC

Open: Year Round

Dockage: Yes

Latitude: N 38° 54' 4"

Longitude: W 77° 3' 35"

Body of Water: Potomac River

Driving Distance:
  Baltimore 43 miles,
  Annapolis 36 miles,
  Easton 74 miles

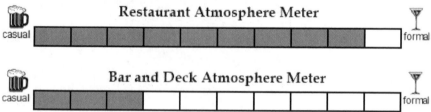

For almost 90 years, if you heard someone say "Sequoia on the Potomac," it meant the presidential yacht was cruising along the river. The glamorous ship was built in 1925 by Annapolis naval architect John Trumpy, and it ferried around players who changed American history. Herbert Hoover used it for fishing trips, John Kennedy celebrated his last birthday on board, and Richard Nixon had a powwow on the water with Brezhnev. Today when people say Sequoia at the Georgetown waterfront, they're talking about a national treasure for fine dining. It attracts Washington's A List, because it's one of the most gorgeous restaurants in town. The three-tiered veranda, with trees wrapped in tiny white lights, presents a superlative view. The restaurant's lofty ceiling is draped in elegant white curtains. The upstairs bar is modeled after the wooden deck of the Commander-in-Chief's boat.

The menu has an international flare, showcasing seafood from the Chesapeake region and around the globe. The raw bar features a dazzling array of seafood including oysters from the Atlantic and Pacific coasts, as well as a tower of assorted shrimp, lobster, jumbo crab and more. Maryland crab cakes share table space with Chilean sea bass. Crab-stuffed mushrooms and coconut mussels introduce plates laden with sesame tuna steaks or day boat scallops. Seared chicken breast and filet mignon are accompanied by creamy polenta or house-cut fries.

Maine Avenue Fish Market

1100 Maine Avenue, SW
Washington, DC 20024
(202) 484-2722

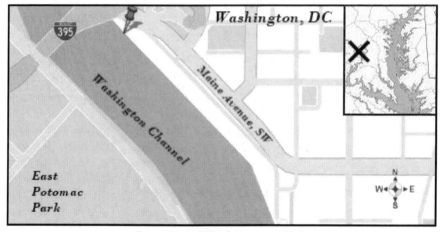

Location: Washington, DC
Open: Year Round ⚓ Dockage: No
Latitude: N 38° 52' 51" ➤ Longitude: W 77° 1' 41"
Body of Water: Potomac River
Driving Distance: Baltimore 41 miles,
Annapolis 34 miles, Easton 73 miles

Atmosphere Meter

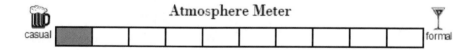

Cast away preconceived notions that Washington is all about black-tie events and five-star restaurants. You can discover the down-to-earth side of D.C. at the Maine Avenue Fish Market. It's located at a modest marina under the I-395 overpass bridge, and it sells the freshest seafood in town. The Market began in 1805 — about 17 years before New York's Fulton Market — and it's the oldest continuously working fish market in the United States. The original building was torn down in the 1960s to clear space for an urban development project, but the vendors refused to get pushed aside and cited a clause in their contract that permits them to stay for 99 years. That legal loophole saved D.C.'s most authentic seafood port.

The Market has a festival atmosphere and an eclectic cross section of locals surveying the wares. The city's top chefs barter with watermen, church ladies order bushels of steamed crabs for Sunday cookouts, and little boys dare each other to touch the eye of a gaping dead barracuda.

Floating barges link together and are tied up at the pier. The aroma on a hot day can be pungent, but it's well worth the visit because almost every imaginable type of seafood is on display. On trays packed with ice, you see piles of oysters, shrimp, crabs, mussels, clams, squid, and fish from the waters of the Chesapeake Bay and Atlantic seaboard. Most get wrapped up for preparing at home, but several vendors cook your selection for eating on the premises at a rustic seating area along the water. You might have to shoo away a persistent seagull, but you'll be glad you came to this one-of-a-kind seafood circus.

Cantina Marina

600 Water Street, SW
Washington, DC 20024
(202) 554-8396
www.cantinamarina.com

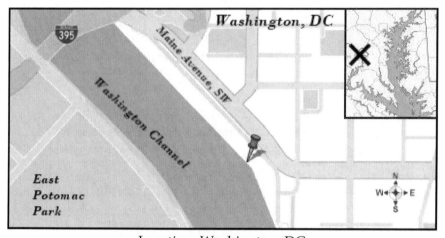

Location: Washington, DC
Open: Seasonal ⚓ Dockage: Yes
Latitude: N 38° 52' 36" ⬌ Longitude: W 77° 1' 20"
Body of Water: Potomac River
Driving Distance: Baltimore 40 miles,
Annapolis 34 miles, Easton 72 miles

Atmosphere Meter

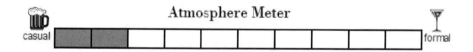

casual   formal

Cantina Marina is an inside the Beltway getaway where the atmosphere feels like a fiesta and Coronas come cold and fast. When it opened in 2003, it was the one of the first places to invest in the up-and-coming Southwest Waterfront and the only restaurant in town built on top of the Potomac River. It's also one of the few spots where you can take a picture of the Washington Monument with a palm tree in the foreground.

The two-story cantina floats among the boats at the Gangplank Marina with a 360-degree riverfront view that's hard to beat by day or at night. Its bright blue and yellow walls are plastered with mounted sharks and trophy fish, surfboards, beer and tequila signs, and other party artifacts. Strings of white lights crisscross over the deck, and a bare-chested mermaid statue winks at the festivities below. Bands play in the summer, and in August sailboats race in the annual Cantina Cup to raise money for a local charity.

The menu is an amiable fusion of Tex-Mex, Cajun, and Chesapeake Bay cuisines. Specialty grilled tacos wrap warm tortillas around fish, shrimp, chicken, or steak, and the savory pork tamales are handmade. The kitchen gives a nod to the Bay with dishes such as crab nachos, crab cake sandwich, fried shrimp, and clam strips with fries. Chicken and sausage gumbo and Texas chili add heat to a cool night. And don't forget the house cocktails featuring six kinds of icy margaritas, piña coladas, and Stoli blueberry lemonade.

McLoone's Pier House

141 National Plaza
Oxon Hill, MD 20745
(301) 839-0815
www.mcloonespierhousenh.com

County: Prince George's
Open: Year Round ⚓ Dockage: Yes
Latitude: N 38° 47' 9" 🐟 Longitude: W 77° 1' 0"
Body of Water: Potomac River
Driving Distance: Baltimore 44 miles,
Washington, DC 11 miles, Easton 76 miles

Atmosphere Meter

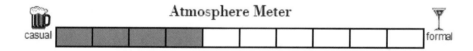

casual ... formal

McLoone's believes that every sunset deserves a celebration, so they hung a big digital clock at the bar to count down the minutes until the sun goes down. They also built one of the largest decks at National Harbor where you can watch the sky turn crimson above a remarkable view of the Woodrow Wilson Bridge, Potomac River, downtown

Washington, Old Town Alexandria, and fleets of boats pulling into the marina. The atmosphere along the waterfront is energetic and fun.

This location marks the first out-of-state restaurant for the New Jersey franchise, and it has adapted well to its new home. Bold blue colors on the walls, umbrellas, and even the wine glasses match the waves on the Potomac. Models of wooden sailboats, ships' flags on the ceiling, and nautical artwork prove these folks are ready to be part of the Bay. A row of round fish tank windows that looks like portholes underscores the sea-faring theme.

The cooks select oysters harvested from Maryland and Virginia shores, and an entire section of the menu is dedicated to local crab specialties. The Bay's favorite crustacean is a major player in dishes such as crab cakes, crab cobb salad, crab mac and cheese, and seafood crab imperial. Fresh fish dominates the dishes, but meat eaters find plenty of options with juicy steaks, tender chicken, grilled pork chops, veal osso buco, and thick burgers.

McCormick & Schmick's Harborside

145 National Plaza
Oxon Hill, MD 20745
(301) 567-6224
www.mccormickandschmicks.com

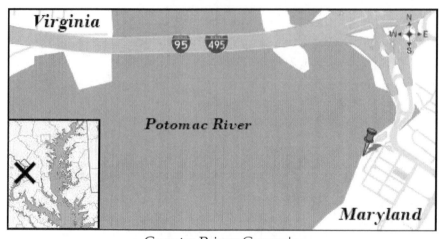

County: Prince George's
Open: Year Round ⚓ Dockage: Yes
Latitude: N 38° 47' 7" 🐟 Longitude: W 77° 1' 0"
Body of Water: Potomac River
Driving Distance: Baltimore 44 miles,
Washington, DC 11 miles, Easton 76 miles

Atmosphere Meter

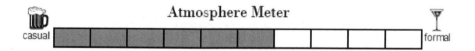

casual | | formal

For decades, McCormick & Schmick's has been part of the D.C. restaurant scene. Even though this surf-and-turf chain has expanded to 80 U.S. locations, it's still the local go-to place for a first-rate meal. When it dropped anchor at the National Harbor in 2010, M&S scored a prime location along the waterfront in the center of all the activities.

Under the iconic green awning, a wraparound deck offers an ideal vantage point to watch boats dock at the marina and tourists buy tickets for the water taxi across the harbor. You also get a bird's eye view of "The Awakening," a five-piece cast iron sculpture of a bearded giant breaking free from the earth. It's a fantastic piece of art and a great place for kids to crawl around and work up an appetite for dinner.

Inside the restaurant, the atmosphere is comfortable and not too formal. The rooms are decorated with a mixed theme of American politics and the sea. The bar displays photos of former presidents and vintage campaign posters, while dining rooms are adorned with trophy fish and pictures of crabs and other nautical life.

Entrees are split between creatures that swim in the sea or live on the land. Seafood standouts include the fresh oyster bar, shrimp stuffed with jumbo lump crab, and live Maine lobster. Steaks are the signature dish, but you can satisfy other carnivorous whims with parmesan crusted chicken, grilled burgers, or beef medallions with roasted potatoes.

Crab Cake Café

140 National Plaza
Oxon Hill, MD 20745
(240) 766-2063
www.crabcakecafe.com

County: Prince George's
Open: Year Round ⚓ Dockage: Yes
Latitude: N 38° 47' 9" 🐟 Longitude: W 77° 0' 59"
Body of Water: Potomac River
Driving Distance: Baltimore 44 miles,
Washington, DC 11 miles, Easton 76 miles

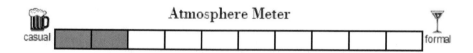

Atmosphere Meter

casual   formal

    As hoards of major restaurant chains claim space at
National Harbor, it's refreshing to see a family-owned eatery
willing to run with the big corporate players. Crab Cake Café
began outside of Annapolis but moved its operations in
August 2014 to this new location on the Potomac. It doesn't sit

directly on the river and it lacks a waterfront deck, but the place is so totally crabby that it rightfully belongs in this book.

Huge photos of crab cakes, exposed brick walls, and shiny chrome accents create a clean, casual décor. Old Bay shakers await on each of the wooden tabletops. Orders are placed at the counter, and glass refrigerators hold chilled sodas and bottled water instead of beer and wine.

The menu is all about the crab. Traditional Maryland crab cakes are outstanding – jumbo lump and almost no filler. You can also experiment with crab cakes by choosing new twists such as Hawaiian with crushed pineapple and coconut crust, New Orleans with andouille sausage and okra, or Tex Mex with chipotle and adobo. Hand-cut fries or Old Bay cheddar corn muffins come on the side. Soups, salads, and roasted chicken breast sandwiches round out the menu. To make the most of a sunny day, get everything to go and relish a splendid meal of local crab down by the water near the boats. For dessert, you could take a spin on new Ferris wheel.

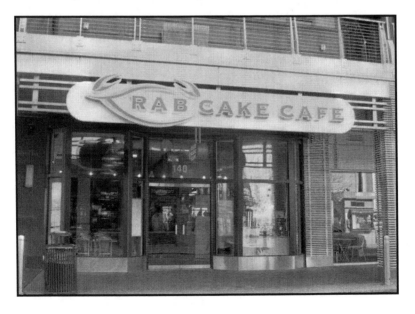

Sauciety...An American Grill

171 National Plaza
Oxon Hill, MD 20745
(240) 766-3640
www.westinnationalharbor.com

County: Prince George's
Open: Year Round ⚓ Dockage: Yes
Latitude: N 38° 47' 7" 🐟 Longitude: W 77° 1' 3"
Body of Water: Potomac River
Driving Distance: Baltimore 44 miles,
Washington, DC 11 miles, Easton 76 miles

Atmosphere Meter

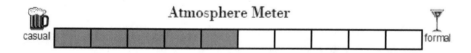

casual ———————————————— formal

National Harbor is the new jewel on the Washington Beltway crown. It opened in 2008 after claiming 300 acres of waterfront land and planting more than 70 shops, restaurants and hotels. The price tag was a cool $2.1 billion, but piece of Maryland shore is now home to a deluxe American-themed carousel, a towering Ferris wheel, and venues for sports, arts, and other entertainment. Even Cirque du Soleil performs here when the acrobats tumble into town.

Sauciety is located in the Westin Hotel, just off the beaten path of the throngs of tourists and shoppers. Its sophisticated contemporary design projects simple elegance through calm pastel colors and modern art hung around the walls. A massive chandelier of glass balls looks like bubbles in the water rising to the surface. Tall windows beneath a high vaulted ceiling afford an exquisite riverfront view. The dining room is spacious and serene, and the bar upstairs offers a casual climate for cocktails and snacks. Designers built a glass wall between the kitchen and tables, which lets you watch the chefs at work without all the heat and noise.

The cooks offer a refreshing approach to American cuisine by adding new flavors to classic favorites. Crisp cornmeal fried oysters come with a spicy remoulade, and crab cakes are served with Old Bay aioli. Cream of crab soup is a bowl of silky decadence. Local rockfish comes in a bouillabaisse broth, and seared scallops are served with wilted spinach and dried tomatoes. If you're in the mood for meat, the menu has plenty of options including roasted chicken, filet mignon, lamb chops, and grilled veal paillard.

Proud Mary Restaurant

13600 King Charles Terrace
Fort Washington, MD 20744
(301) 292-5521
www.proudmaryrestaurant.com

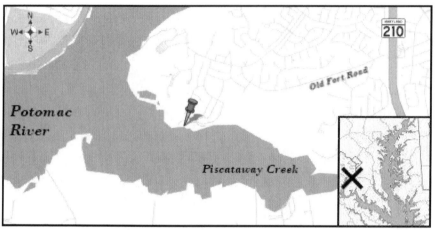

County: Prince George's
Open: Year Round ⚓ Dockage: Yes
Latitude: N 38° 42' 10" 🐟 Longitude: W 77° 1' 33"
Body of Water: Piscataway Creek off the Potomac River
Driving Distance: Baltimore 53 miles,
Washington, DC 19 miles, Easton 84 miles

Atmosphere Meter

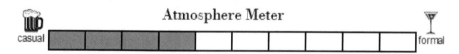

casual   formal

    Far upstream from the mayhem of the city waits a sweet crab deck outpost called Proud Mary Restaurant. This hidden gem is tucked away at the Fort Washington Marina overlooking the Potomac River and offers a lovely destination for enjoying life and taking time to unwind.

The restaurant has three distinct sections to fit your mood. The outdoor deck and tiki bar is where you start rolling on the river by watching boats sail across the water and sipping specialty frozen cocktails or cool treats from the expanded martini list. A snack or two can get you warmed up for a hearty meal inside.

Proud Mary's main dining area is a comfortable room, and the service is warm and welcoming. Colorful artwork and subtle music work like appetizers before a terrific meal. The menu marries Bay seafood with Southern Cuisine, and hot buttered sweet corn cake muffins are simply irresistible. Seafood standouts include award-winning jumbo lump crab cakes, a dozen jerk shrimp over rice, and honey teriyaki grilled salmon. The golden fried chicken and home-style pork chops are amazing, and steaks can be grilled or blackened.

The back room is a dining space and more. Photographs of singers like Aretha Franklin, Diana Ross, Tina Turner, Sam Cook, and Duke Ellington pay homage to American music legends. After dessert plates are cleared from the tables, live jazz musicians fill the air with soulful song.

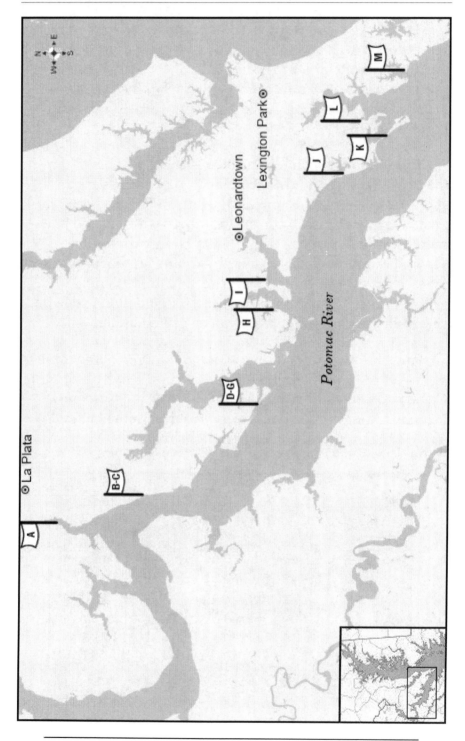

Lower Potomac River

Port Tobacco Restaurant

7536 Shirley Boulevard
Port Tobacco, MD 20677
(301) 392-0007
www.porttobaccorestaurant.com

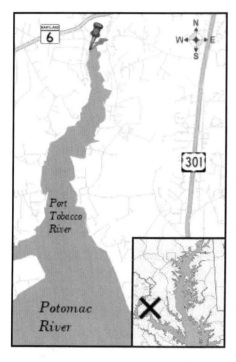

County: Charles County

Open: Year Round

Dockage: Yes

Latitude: N 38° 29' 52"

Longitude: W 77° 1' 36"

Body of Water: Port Tobacco
River off the Potomac River

Driving Distance:
Baltimore 69 miles,
Washington, DC 35 miles,
Easton 91 miles

Atmosphere Meter

casual 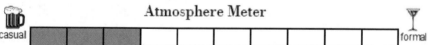 formal

Grab a map and keep your eyes on the GPS when you drive to Port Tobacco Restaurant. It's easy to get lost, and you don't want to miss this tucked-away treasure. Your reward for successfully navigating through scenic southern Maryland and the petite town of Port Tobacco (population 13) is a spectacular view and fun destination. Marshlands create a serene backdrop as boats chug along the river and herons pluck a dinner of minnows or baby crabs from the water's edge. The tiki bar and two-tiered decks that wrap around the restaurant overlook a picturesque waterfront. The atmosphere inside is cozy and friendly. Knotty pine walls are decorated with nautical items: crabs, fish, waterfowl, mermaids, pirates, and more. Big-screen TVs help you catch the score of a Nationals or Redskins game.

In 2012, the county dredged the river to create a deep water marina, and the restaurant changed hands from the former Crabby Dick's. The new owners spruced up the location and designed a fresh, seafood-driven menu. Crabs appear in crab dips, pretzels, soups and more. Fried oysters edge their way into the food roster while steamer pots turn up the heat on mussels, crabs and shrimp. Burgers, tacos and pasta are also available.

History buffs are flocking to Port Tobacco. It was the original county seat of Charles County (moved to La Plata in 1895). Until the end of the Revolutionary War, it was Maryland's second largest river port (first was St. Mary's City). The harbor gradually silted up due to excessive tree cutting and crop planting, particularly tobacco, so river trade became restricted to small boats. To learn more, visit Port Tobacco Historical Society and see the archaeological dig.

Captain Billy's Crab House

11495 Popes Creek Road
Newburg, MD 20664
(301) 932-4323
www.captbillys.com

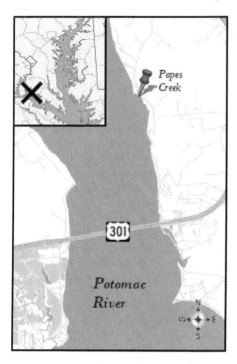

County: Charles County

Open: Seasonal

Dockage: Yes

Latitude: N 38° 23' 53"

Longitude: W 76° 59' 28"

Body of Water: Popes Creek
off the Potomac River

Driving Distance:
Baltimore 75 miles,
Washington, DC 43 miles,
Easton 97 miles

Atmosphere Meter

casual 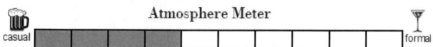 formal

As you stand on the shore at Captain Billy's Crab House, imagine a pair of unrelated historical events taking place near this spot. To escape capture after shooting President Lincoln, John Wilkes Booth looked at those waters hoping to cross the river into Virginia, where he thought he'd be heralded as a hero of the Confederacy. He wasn't.

Fast-forward about a century to a time when electricity had just arrived in Popes Creek, mail was delivered by boat, and construction had started on the Potomac River Bridge. A boy named Billy Robertson caught his first crab and started selling them around town. When Billy grew up, he became a waterman and eventually opened this restaurant, viewed by locals as a staple along the water.

For 60 years, a giant neon crab sign out front has pointed the way for diners who come to enjoy regional seafood and waterfront views from the outdoor deck or the air-conditioned comfort of the spacious indoor dining area.

Chesapeake seafood dominates the menu with steamed crabs, oyster stew "straight from the tongs," crab cakes, shrimp baskets, fried rockfish, and steamed clams — accompanied by homey touches such as hush puppies or corn fritters with honey. Landlubbers can opt for BBQ ribs, steak, burgers or chicken if they want, but when place mats give instructions for picking crabs, you might want to stick to what Captain Billy's family has been doing for decades — serving seafood with warm southern Maryland hospitality.

Gilligan's Pier

11535 Popes Creek Road
Newburg, MD 20664
(301) 259-4514
www.gilliganspier.com

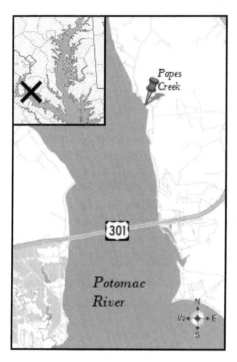

County: Charles County

Open: Seasonal

Dockage: Yes

Latitude: N 38° 23' 47"

Longitude: W 76° 59' 17"

Body of Water: Popes Creek
off the Potomac River

Driving Distance:
Baltimore 75 miles,
Washington, DC 43 miles,
Easton 97 miles

Atmosphere Meter

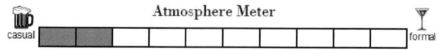

casual   formal

What do you get when you spread four truckloads of sand and plant 34 palm trees on the banks of the Potomac River? A tropical paradise called Gilligan's. You might be tempted to blink your eyes to make sure it's real, not a mirage. Tucked in amidst southern Maryland's rural landscape of farms, cornfields, and old tobacco barns is an oasis of tiki island pleasure. The restaurant and decks are surrounded with plush tropical plants, and a boat run aground serves chilled orange crushes. Live bands rock-and-roll at night, while specialty drinks are poured at the tiki bar. The summertime vibe is energetic, beachy fun.

Volleyball players rub on sunscreen before slamming a ball over the net. Children build sandcastles and dabble in the water along the 1.5 acre beach (a rare find along the Potomac). Recreational vessels tie up at the wooden pier, and a pontoon boat shuttles in folks who want to join the festivities. You can even rent an island for events! The scenic Route 301 Bridge in the background adds a special Chesapeake charm to sunsets.

Inside, the ceilings are draped with fishnets, crab bushels serve as lampshades, and brown paper on the tables catches shell carnage from bushels of hot steamed crabs. The food is good — fresh and plentiful with local seafood, salads, fish tacos, sandwiches, steaks, and steamers. Creamy seafood dip with shrimp and crab is poured into a sourdough bread bowl. Fried baskets hold hand-breaded oysters, shrimp, rockfish, and scallops. Picking crabs here on a breezy afternoon is a divine Bay experience.

Captain John's Crabhouse

16215 Cobb Island Road
Newburg, MD 20664
(301) 259-2315
www.cjcrab.com

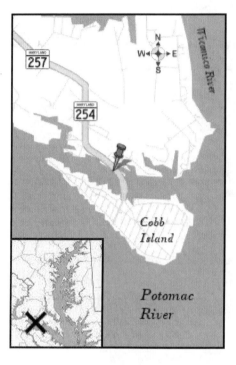

County: Charles County

Open: Year Round

Dockage: Yes

Latitude: N 38° 16' 4"

Longitude: W 76° 51' 5"

Body of Water: Neale Sound
between the Wicomico River
and the Potomac River

Driving Distance:
Baltimore 87 miles,
Washington, DC 55 miles,
Easton 109 miles

Atmosphere Meter

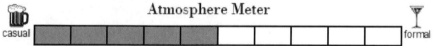

casual   formal

Deep in Charles County on the last stretch of mainland before the bridge to Cobb Island are a pair of family-owned restaurants that represent the best of Chesapeake seafood traditions: Captain John's and Shymansky's (see p. 38).

Captain John's is located on the western side of the road overlooking Neale Sound and a busy marina. Built in 1963 by John Shymansky and currently run by his grandchildren, this place continues a 50-year legacy of home-style cooking. Heartwarming vintage family pictures — including a robust portrait of the captain himself — hang on the walls. A string of lights made of red and white fishing bobbins brightens the outside waterfront deck.

During a recent visit, a 30-year veteran waitress pulled down a collage of before-and-after Hurricane Isabel photos that showed extensive flood damage and how hard the family and community worked to keep the business going.

A market in the back sells seafood brought in daily by local watermen. The famous seafood buffet offers a cornucopia of fresh Bay specialties: steamed or fried shrimp, crabs, clams, oysters, rockfish, and mussels. Hush puppies, onion rings, fries, or corn fritters come on the side. The fried flounder sandwich is colossal, and the hot roast beef sandwich comes with mashed potatoes and gravy. Crispy fried chicken gets high approval ratings from any southern Maryland native who takes a bite. No matter what you order, you won't leave hungry or disappointed.

Shymansky's Restaurant

16320 Cobb Island Road
Newburg, MD 20664
(301) 259-0300

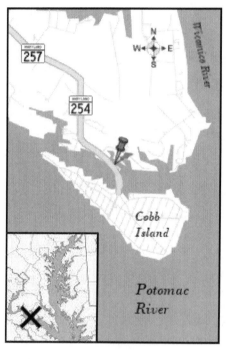

County: Charles County

Open: Year Round

Dockage: Yes

Latitude: N 38° 16' 2"

Longitude: W 76° 51' 0"

Body of Water: Neale Sound
   between the Wicomico River
   and the Potomac River

Driving Distance:
   Baltimore 87 miles,
   Washington, DC 55 miles,
   Easton 109 miles

Atmosphere Meter

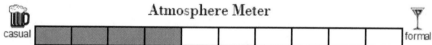

casual _____ formal

At the tip of Charles County where the Potomac and Wicomico Rivers meet, a southern Maryland family works hard to keep Bay traditions alive. On the eastern side of the road just before you reach Cobb Island is Shymansky's Restaurant and Marina (Captain John's across the street is owned by other family members. See p. 36).

The one-story white building was bought by Bruce Shymansky in the 1950s, and his clan has been serving Chesapeake visitors ever since. The restaurant's dining room and bar have a homey casual feel that make you want to linger a while at your table and gaze out at the expansive waterfront view.

Plump steamed crabs are delivered daily and couldn't get any fresher. The menu features local seafood selections of shrimp, oysters, rockfish, mussels, and clams. The stuffed soft-shell crab dinner is a sure winner, and the all-you-can-eat shrimp and crab legs special is a seafood lover's dream. Hearty sandwiches, seafood baskets and juicy burgers come with sides such as potato salad and hush puppies. The Sunday Breakfast Buffet Bar runs from 8:00 a.m. until noon and offers eggs, bacon, and other savory delights that are guaranteed to get your day started right.

If you're willing to leave terra firma and experience some of the best fishing in the region, walk over to Shymansky's full-service marina. They'll set you up with boat rentals, bait and tackle, tips, take-out food or gas — everything you need for a perfect day on the Bay.

Crab Decks & Tiki Bars of the Chesapeake Bay, 2015 Maryland Edition

The Scuttlebutt Restaurant

12320 Cobb Island Road
Cobb Island, MD 20625
(240) 233-3113

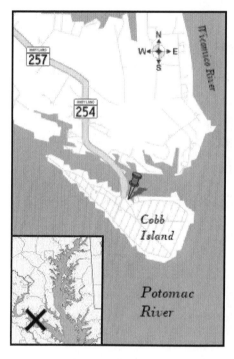

County: Charles County

Open: Year Round

Dockage: Yes

Latitude: N 38° 15' 50"

Longitude: W 76° 50' 58"

Body of Water: Neale Sound
between the Wicomico River
and the Potomac River

Driving Distance:
Baltimore 88 miles,
Washington, DC 55 miles,
Easton 110 miles

Atmosphere Meter

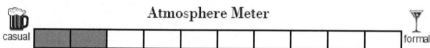

casual   formal

The word "scuttlebutt" originally referred to a fountain or cask on a ship that held the day's supply of drinking water. It's kind of like the office water cooler or village well, where people gather to gossip about the latest buzz around town. It's the perfect name for the Scuttlebutt Restaurant on Cobb Island. This cozy little restaurant has a special charm that makes you want to stay for a while and hear local residents and watermen tell tales about life in their island community.

Bright yellow exterior walls are decorated with palm trees on a beach with red crabs and a blue heron. Rosy pink impatiens overflow the edges of stone planters near the front door. On a warm summer evening, the outdoor deck at the water's edge gives you a front-row seat to crimson sunsets. The lighthouse mural behind the bar pays tribute to the island's maritime traditions. Good food at affordable prices features delicious soups of the day, oyster stew, pizza, burgers, and fresh seafood caught nearby. Crab cakes, rockfish, shrimp … they're all on tap and cooked nicely.

When you leave the Scuttlebutt, be sure to take a spin around Cobb Island. Don't worry; it won't take long. This tiny piece of land (only 290 acres) offers big natural beauty and a placid community where the Potomac and Wicomico Rivers meet. You won't see a sprawling shopping mall or high-rise buildings. Instead, you'll pass a post office, market, and quaint cottages interspersed with newer homes among old oak trees. The 1,166 residents own more boats than cars. They gather for bingo night, oyster and ham dinners, or the Friday fish fry at the fire hall. It's a slice of pleasant Bay living that you won't want to miss.

The Rivah Restaurant & Bar

12364 Neale Sound Drive
Cobb Island, MD 20625
(301) 259-2879
www.piratesdenmarina.com

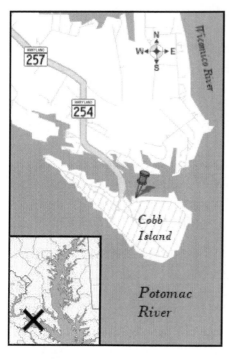

County: Charles County

Open: Year Round

Dockage: Yes

Latitude: N 38° 15' 50"

Longitude: W 76° 50' 51"

Body of Water: Neale Sound
between the Wicomico River
and the Potomac River

Driving Distance:
Baltimore 88 miles,
Washington, DC 56 miles,
Easton 110 miles

Atmosphere Meter

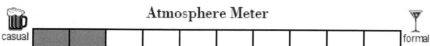

casual — formal

When you visit southern Maryland, you hear people talking about going to "the rivah," instead of "the river," because they're ready to relax. Then they start looking for waterfront dock bars to further that kicked-back state of mind. Maybe that's why The Rivah is such a perfect name for this spot overlooking Neale Sound. It's got an easy feel and a deck that makes you want to spend lazy summer afternoons chatting with buddies over a few cold ones and watching boats from Pirate's Den Marina cruise under the bridge to Cobb Island.

The Rivah's newly renovated dining room has salmon colored walls with wood-framed pictures of sea creatures and shares space with Ledo's Pizza. A good jukebox and an amiable bartender set a pleasant mood. The menu features regional dishes with the catch of the season leading the charge. Steamed oysters, mussels and shrimp are keystone appetizers. Soft-shells and crab cakes are delicately delicious. Roasted Cornish game hens and steaks are a meaty treat. Burgers and sandwiches share the plate with hand-cut fries.

So, have you wondered where Neale Sound and Cobb Island got their names? In 1642, the island was owned by James Neale, a ship captain who was notorious for capturing Spanish treasure ships in the West Indies and returning home with his stolen bounty. The large Spanish coins that Neale confiscated were cut into pieces called "cobbs" and used as coins by the early colonists.

Morris Point Restaurant

38869 Morris Point Road
Abell, MD 20606
(301) 769-2500
www.morris-point.com

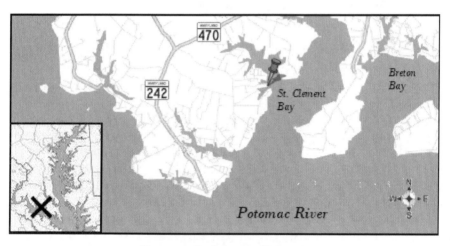

County: St. Mary's County
Open: Year Round ⚓ Dockage: Yes
Latitude: N 38° 15' 8" ➤ Longitude: W 76° 43' 57"
Body of Water: Canoe Neck Creek off St. Clements Bay
off the Potomac River
Driving Distance: Baltimore 91 miles,
Washington, DC 59 miles, Easton 113 miles

Atmosphere Meter

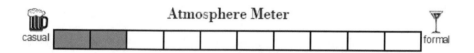

casual | | | | | | | | | | | formal

Frank Morris Point is an ideal destination for adventurers seeking an authentic Bay experience. It's a wisp of a place, more deck than building. The restaurant is in a remote part of St. Mary's County surrounded by working boats, modest houses, and mobile homes. It rests on pylons above Canoe

Neck Creek and offers a dazzling view of the water. On this spot in 1885, Stewart Morris ran a general store and oyster packing house. Years later, it was converted into a restaurant called the Ebb Tide (which burned down), and eventually waterman Frank Morris built his eatery here.

Everything about it says "Classic Chesapeake," but a few surprises make this place special. The front yard is landscaped with the standard oyster shells, pea gravel, and foliage, but unique abstract stone statues of human figures are arranged around the lawn. The décor inside is casual and comfortable with enough space for a dozen oilcloth-covered tables neatly arranged in the dining room. Homey blue curtains with a sailboat pattern line the top of the windows, and colorful nautical flags add a dash of cheer.

The menu is anchored in family tradition, proudly serving Grandma's chili, made-to-order oyster stew for two in an iron pot, and hand-dipped fried shrimp with homemade tartar sauce. Seafood feasts featuring fresh catch from the Patuxent and Potomac Rivers are memorable. Pleasant surprises include the smoked trout platter, homemade lasagna, and linguine with fresh clams in a smooth tomato sauce. All this located near four state parks creates a wonderful southern Maryland getaway for families and friends.

Fitzie's Restaurant & Pub

21540 Joe Hazel Road
Leonardtown, MD 20650
(301) 475-1913
fitzies.homestead.com

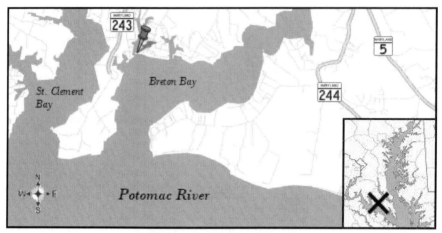

County: St. Mary's County
Open: Year Round ⚓ Dockage: Yes
Latitude: N 38° 15' 33" ➤ Longitude: W 76° 41' 42"
Body of Water: Breton Bay off the Potomac River
Driving Distance: Baltimore 90 miles,
Washington, DC 58 miles, Easton 112 miles

Atmosphere Meter

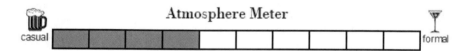

casual   formal

Is it kosher to mix tiki and crabs with shamrocks? In
that "anything goes" Chesapeake spirit, the odd combo works
well at Fitzie's. It's a large building, newly renovated and
expanded after Hurricane Isabel damaged the original
structure in 2003. Its cream-colored siding with kelly green
accents provides a contrasting backdrop for three thatched

tiki huts standing guard in the sand near the water. The view of Breton Bay is expansive and spectacular, and there's plenty of space for parking or docking.

Inside, an Irish theme plays throughout. The lounge, equipped with a pool table, pinball machines, and a wooden bar, is decorated with flags from the Emerald Isle, hand-stitched shamrock craft art, and a lighted palm tree. Above the brick fireplace, green needlepoint testifies that Fitzie's was established in 1993. Two stories accommodate dining needs: the top floor is reserved for special events and the lower level provides regular service. Walls of windows let in ample light to brighten the main dining area where tables are covered with pale green oilcloths.

The menu takes traditional Bay dishes and dresses them up with a little Gaelic flair. Entrees include Leprechaun's Dream (char-broiled New York strip with steamed shrimp), and the Shillelagh (crab cake, scallops and fried shrimp). The Kelly Girl presents fresh local scallops broiled or fried. Jumbo lump crab cakes are legendary, and sandwiches are robust and filling. So, go figure ... at the Bay, it's perfectly fine to enjoy hot red crabs with cold green beer.

Reluctant Navigator

18521 Herring Creek Road
Tall Timbers, MD 20690
(301) 994-1508
www.talltimbersmarinasomd.com

County: St. Mary's County

Open: Seasonal

Dockage: Yes

Latitude: N 38° 10' 37"

Longitude: W 76° 32' 38"

Body of Water: Herring Creek
off the Potomac River

Driving Distance:
Baltimore 97 miles,
Washington, DC 70 miles,
Easton 113 miles

Atmosphere Meter

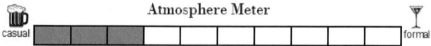

casual / formal

If Reluctant Navigator claims to be the best kept secret on the Potomac, then why is it packed with scores of fishermen, boaters, and locals having a good time on the water?

After over 50 years of service, they welcome early bird patrons who like to jump-start their morning with what the bar calls, "The Best Damn Bloody Mary" at the Sunday breakfast buffet and Miss Claudia's omelet bar. The cook lays out a mighty spread of biscuits with creamed chipped beef, bread pudding, spiced apples, pancakes, cheesy eggs, grits, corn beef hash, and breakfast burritos.

Other guests hold out until later in the day for a frosty beer with their favorite dish on the regular menu. Steamed shrimp, crab cakes, rockfish, and the catch of the day are fresh treasures. Oysters come from the Double T Oyster Ranch nearby. Burgers, chicken, steaks, homemade meatloaf with mashed potatoes, and prime rib are a landlubber's delight.

Some folks have so much fun at Reluctant Navigator that they forget to take their personal belongings. The owners hold what's left behind in safe keeping at "The Museum." From top to bottom, this room overflows with an astonishing collection of oddities such as wooden oars, boat motors, duck decoys, old signs, fishing poles, rusty tools, knotted ropes, oyster tongs, beaded necklaces, and banged-up kids' toys. It's a hoarder's heaven that boggles the imagination. When you're done surveying the long-forgotten artifacts, head out to the deck to watch boats glide into the marina and raise a glass to the wonderfully quirky ways of the Chesapeake Bay.

Ruddy Duck Seafood & Alehouse

16800 Piney Point Road
Piney Point, MD 20674
(301) 994-9944
www.ruddyduckbrewery.com

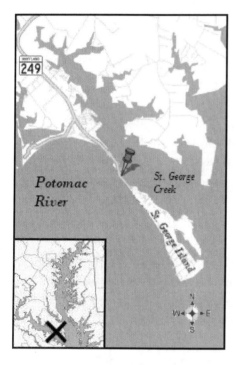

County: St. Mary's County

Open: Seasonal

Dockage: Yes

Latitude: N 38° 7' 48"

Longitude: W 76° 29' 39"

Body of Water: between
  St. George Creek and the
  Potomac River

Driving Distance:
  Baltimore 99 miles,
  Washington, DC 72 miles,
  Easton 114 miles

Atmosphere Meter

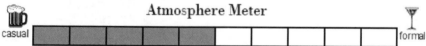

casual

formal

Ruddy Duck is the type of destination that Chesapeake enthusiasts dream about when planning a bay getaway. It's located on the narrow causeway that leads from the mainland to St. George Island. Fishermen cast their lines from barriers made of huge white rocks, while armadas of swans, ducks and other waterfowl paddle through the waves. The view from the deck and inside the restaurant is strikingly beautiful.

Ruddy Duck opened in 2013 with a passion for local seafood. Oysters are pulled from sustainable aquaculture reefs next to the restaurant, and the crab meat is never frozen. Seafood treasures include sesame crusted tuna, seared salmon and crispy fried calamari. Meat options: steaks, meatloaf, BBQ ribs, and pizza. Bratwurst might inspire you to sample the list of award-winning craft beers from Ruddy Duck Brewery. Live music adds to the upbeat and friendly atmosphere.

While you're here, explore the region's two famous islands. St. George Island was host to the first battle on Maryland soil in the Revolutionary War. In the War of 1812, the British claimed it as home base for raiding along the Bay. St. Clement's Island is a short jaunt away. In 1634, a pair of British ships called the *Ark* and *Dove* brought Maryland's first English-speaking settlers and celebrated the first Catholic mass in the colonies. A museum at Coltons Point chronicles the story and offers water taxi service to the island, where you can hike trails that lead to restored Blackistone Lighthouse and a 40-foot cross erected in memory of the Catholic settlers.

Riverside Bistro

46555 Dennis Point Way
Drayden, MD 20630
(301) 994-2404

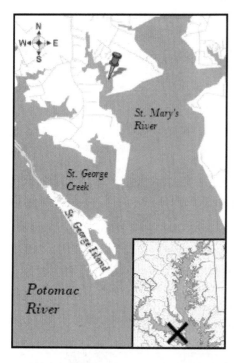

County: St. Mary's County

Open: Seasonal

Dockage: Yes

Latitude: N 38° 9' 25"

Longitude: W 76° 28' 8"

Body of Water: Carthagena
　　Creek off the St. Mary's
　　River off the Potomac River

Driving Distance:
　　Baltimore 96 miles,
　　Washington, DC 70 miles,
　　Easton 111 miles

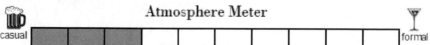

Atmosphere Meter

casual | | | | | | | | | | | formal

When summer rolls around, plenty of people think about going camping. There's just something about sleeping under the stars near the water that makes the experience extra special. When you start looking for destinations for picking crabs while enjoying fresh air and the great outdoors, put Riverside Bistro on your list.

It's located at Dennis Point Marina and Campground, where even those who prefer urban life can find fun things to do. You can pitch a tent, park your RV, or lodge in a cabin on 50 acres of waterfront property. They've got nature trails, a dock for crabbing and fishing, bike rentals, volleyball, and horseshoes. Osprey, eagles, and waterfowl captivate bird watchers. The Flip Flop Bar next to the swimming pool is decorated with colorful footwear stapled to the rafters.

The restaurant switched hands 2014 and hired a new chef, who will cook the rockfish or bluefish you catch if you eat it at the restaurant. It's a cozy place, and the menu favors local seafood mixed with classic southern Maryland cuisine. Crab comes in robust cakes or on top of pizza with Old Bay. Blackened mahi mahi has plenty of zing. Hush puppies, fried pickles, and collard greens are perfect sides for crispy Southern fried chicken. Carnivores can dive into plates laden with meatloaf, burgers, pasta, and chicken marsala. A thoughtful kids menu covers the essentials: hot dogs, grilled cheese, peanut butter and jelly, and chicken fingers. It all boils down to family fun and good memories on the Bay.

Courtney's Restaurant & Seafood

48290 Wynne Road
Ridge, MD 20680
(301) 872-4403
www.courtneysseafoodrestaurant.com

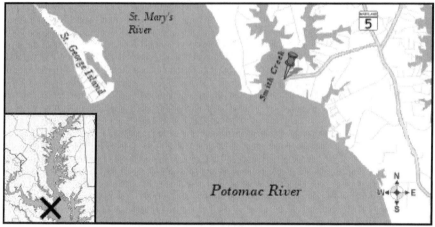

County: St. Mary's County
Open: Year Round ⚓ Dockage: No
Latitude: N 38° 6' 34" ⟩⟩ Longitude: W 76° 24' 21"
Body of Water: Smith Creek off the Potomac River
Driving Distance: Baltimore 102 miles,
Washington, DC 75 miles, Easton 117 miles

Atmosphere Meter

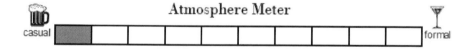

casual ▮▮▮▮▮▮▮▮▮▮ formal

If you want to get away from city noise and traffic, Courtney's is the answer. When you see the restaurant's red stenciled sign planted next to a rusty propane tank and a six-pack of mobile homes, you know you're as far from urban life as you can get. Courtney's is all about simple country living — no fuss and very rustic. The white cinder block building's low ceiling looms over wood-paneled walls decorated with a hodgepodge of old photos, nautical artifacts, and beer signs. A radio, almost tuned in to the local country station, plays staticky tunes by Elvis, Hank, and Patsy. Shelves are stacked with dusty vintage knickknacks.

Tables lined up on a time-worn wooden floor are covered with red cloths and paper place mats that disclose fun facts about the Bay. You'll probably be seated and served by the owner or his wife, who also do the cooking. When a patron asks for ketchup or another condiment, they grab one from an old refrigerator in the back of the dining room, next to the salad bar and a pair of black fat-belly pots that keep the soup-of-the-day warm. Likely candidates inside the cauldrons would be clam chowder, vegetable crab soup, or creamy oyster stew.

What Courtney's lacks in fancy décor, it makes up in home-style food at good prices. Crab cakes are fresh, huge, and a third the price of their urban counterparts. Fried oysters, rockfish, shrimp, and other local seafood taste like they just got pulled from the Bay. Meat lovers can choose fried honey-dipped chicken, steaks, or cheeseburgers. If you venture out early, Courtney's serves up a hearty country breakfast with eggs, pancakes, chipped beef, scrapple, grits, corned beef hash, creamed sausage, and biscuits.

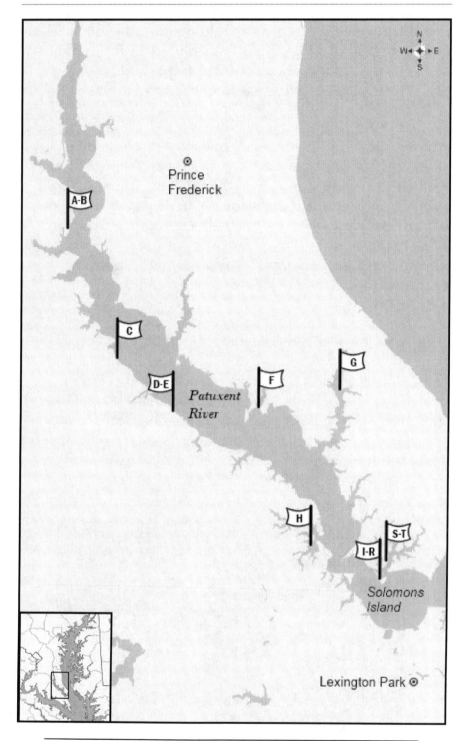

Prince
Frederick

A-B

C

D-E

*Patuxent
River*

F

G

H

S-T

I-R

*Solomons
Island*

Lexington Park ⊙

Patuxent River

Ray's Pier Restaurant

18170 Desoto Place
Benedict, MD 20612
(301) 274-3733

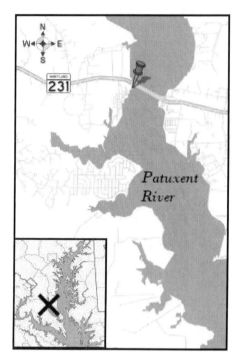

County: Charles County

Open: Year Round

Dockage: Yes

Latitude: N 38° 30' 46"

Longitude: W 76° 40' 34"

Body of Water: Patuxent River

Driving Distance:
  Baltimore 67 miles,
  Washington, DC 40 miles,
  Easton 83 miles

Atmosphere Meter

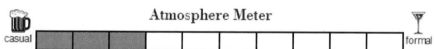

casual   formal

There's a timeless feel to Ray's Pier, where old and new blend together in a seamless continuum of life connected to the water. Maybe it's the hard work behind a family-owned business that gives Ray's a rustic, comfortable atmosphere. You feel instantly at home when you walk inside the weathered one-story white building. Decorative lobsters, crabs, geese, fish nets, and pictures of boats garnish the walls.

A giant blue and silver marlin with slightly chipped paint hangs from a string above the doorway. Table-to-ceiling windows open up to a grassy lawn with tall trees and picnic tables near the water's edge. The smell of hot steamed crabs and shrimp gets your taste buds excited for an authentic Chesapeake feast.

Crab cakes and rockfish are fried to perfection — crisp on the outside yet moist and tender inside. Country-fried steak is blanketed in velvety smooth gravy. Homemade cole slaw and potato salad are freckled with a dash of Old Bay. And the tireless waitress — who patiently juggles the tasks of serving patrons and steaming crabs in the kitchen — makes everyone feel right at home.

Ray's location adds to its unique charm. The tiny town of Benedict was established in 1683 and was originally named Benedict-Leonardtown after the 4th Lord Baltimore, Benedict Leonard Calvert. It was a fishing village in the late 17th century and grew into a shipbuilding port that constructed a vessel for George Washington in 1760. Steamboats, tomato-processing plants, and seafood-packing houses once stood on its shores. Today Benedict is a pastoral home to watermen, farmers, sports fishermen, and duck hunters.

River's Edge Restaurant

7320 Benedict Avenue
Benedict, MD 20612
(301) 274-2828
www.riversedgebenedict.com

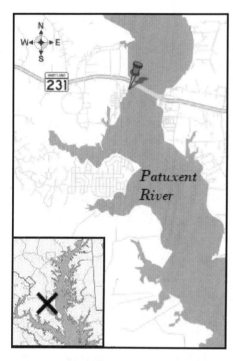

County: Charles County

Open: Year Round

Dockage: Yes

Latitude: N 38° 30' 37"

Longitude: W 76° 40' 41"

Body of Water: Patuxent River

Driving Distance:
  Baltimore 67 miles,
  Washington, DC 40 miles,
  Easton 83 miles

Atmosphere Meter

casual 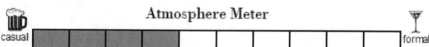 formal

At River's Edge, you can enjoy a memorable experience on the waterfront in the quiet town of Benedict. It's a cozy restaurant above the water on a wooden deck with a spectacular view of the Patuxent River.

Seafood dominates the menu from appetizers to entrees, with local crab, rockfish, and oysters at the helm of the dishes.

Bacon-wrapped scallops, fried calamari, and steamed mussels are good starting points. Special soups: vegetable or cream of crab soup and oyster stew. Golden-brown crab cakes the size of baseballs are served with hush puppies. Also from the kitchen come steaks, chicken, salads, and hefty sandwiches.

All of that would make your trip worthwhile, but there's more to this spot than meets the eye. In this region of the Bay, events occurred that changed the course of American history. In August 1814, after fierce battles with U.S. naval forces, British ships sailed up the Patuxent and unloaded soldiers near the location where River's Edge stands today. Those English troops marched north to Washington where they burned and looted the White House and Capitol.

But wait, there's more. Benedict, MD, also played a role in the Civil War. In 1863, Camp Stanton was built on this site to train Maryland's 7th Regiment and help squelch Southern aggression. The 19th Regiment of Colored Troops also trained at this location. It was comprised of slaves, whose freedom was bought by the U.S. government, enabling them to join the Union cause.

Drift Inn

6240 Delabrooke Road
Mechanicsville, MD 20659
(301) 884-3470

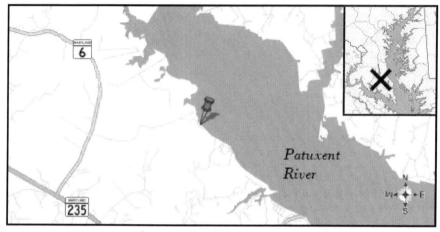

County: St. Mary's County
Open: Seasonal ⚓ Dockage: Yes
Latitude: N 38° 26' 21" ➤ Longitude: W 76° 38' 44"
Body of Water: Patuxent River
Driving Distance: Baltimore 79 miles,
Washington, DC 47 miles, Easton 101 miles

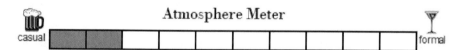

Finding Drift Inn by boat is no big deal, but arriving by car presents some interesting challenges. Even if you lock in your GPS and bring along a map, the roads aren't particularly well marked, so it's easy to lose your way.

But it's well worth the adventure. Winding through these scenic rural back roads is like an appetizer to an authentic Bay experience. Some say Drift Inn is the oldest crab house in operation in southern Maryland. For about 50 years, it has been run by generations of the Copsey family who have deep roots in the community and longstanding traditions with Chesapeake seafood.

You'll know you successfully reached your destination when you see the big hand-painted sign with bright red letters and plastic seagulls perched on top. A red tin roof sits on top of the one-story white cinderblock building. Red and blue crabs point the way to the entrance.

It's only open Friday, Saturday, and Sunday from May to October, so you might run into a crowd during peak dining hours. But that's okay. The wait gives you a chance to gaze down the long wooden pier that stretches out into the Patuxent River and witness the kaleidoscope of colors from a summer sunset reflected on the water.

When the waitress places a tray of hot steamed crabs, shrimp, fried soft-shells, oysters, rockfish and homemade sides on your table, you'll be glad you took the time to discover this authentic treasure on the Bay.

Sandgates Inn

27525 North Sandgates Road
Mechanicsville, MD 20659
(301) 373-5100

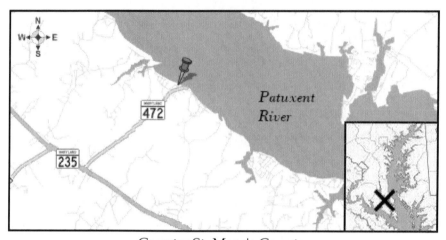

County: St. Mary's County
Open: Seasonal ⚓ Dockage: Yes
Latitude: N 38° 24' 48" Longitude: W 76° 36' 32"
Body of Water: Patuxent River
Driving Distance: Baltimore 82 miles,
Washington, DC 50 miles, Easton 104 miles

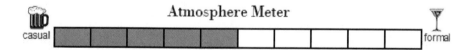

Atmosphere Meter

casual   formal

At Sandgates Inn, pictures of Chesapeake crabs seem to be everywhere — on the doors, the walls, the front sign, the windows, and the menu. Even a red crab made of lights shines brightly outside near the roof.

The endearing crab infestation underscores the top priority for this traditional Maryland seafood house. But the crabs that merit your full attention are the hot steamed ones piled high on the table in front of you.

They're cooked to order with a special house seasoning that enhances their delicate flavor and makes them a favorite dish for locals and tourists alike. Also worth a try are the jumbo lump crab cakes, creamy seafood chowder, steamed shrimp, fried oysters, and tender clams. Hearty sandwiches and exceptional fried chicken are big crowd pleasers.

The décor inside the red brick building is casual nautical, and the atmosphere is laid-back. You can eat inside with a lively crowd of families and watermen or venture out to the waterfront deck that reveals a gorgeous view of the Patuxent River and rolling lawns of the neighborhood.

After a splendid seafood meal, take a stroll on the wooden pier that stretches out on the water or sit back to relish a summer evening on the porch. You might even want to play a game or two of horseshoes next door. It's all about easy living in southern Maryland.

Seabreeze Restaurant & Crab House

27130 South Sandgates Road
Mechanicsville, MD 20659
(301) 373-5217

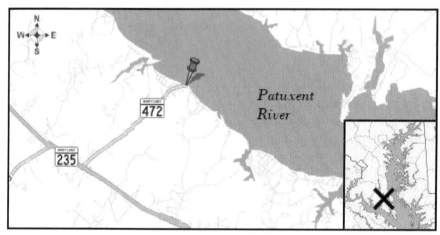

County: St. Mary's County
Open: Year Round ⚓ Dockage: Yes
Latitude: N 38° 24' 47" ➤ Longitude: W 76° 36' 26"
Body of Water: Patuxent River
Driving Distance: Baltimore 82 miles,
Washington, DC 50 miles, Easton 104 miles

Restaurant Atmosphere Meter
casual ▏formal

Tiki Bar Atmosphere Meter
casual ▏formal

Don't eat and run when you visit Seabreeze. Stay awhile
and enjoy everything this crab house has to offer. There's
easy docking for boaters and ample parking for cars and

motorcycles. The one-story blond-brick building houses a lounge and dining room with table-to-ceiling windows that open up to a fantastic view of the Patuxent River.

Seabreeze specializes in hot crabs and cold beer — good, no-frills Maryland cooking at reasonable prices. Special starters include creamy crab flatbread, fried pickles, and butterfly shrimp. The steam feast for two creates an ultimate platter of crabs, shrimp, clams, fries and cole slaw. Pizza, quesadillas, subs, steaks, burgers, chicken, and oysters arrive with crispy corn fritters on the side.

After you picked your fill of crabs, head over to Swampy's Tiki Bar. It's a simple wooden structure with beer posters plastered all over its walls and Harleys lined up in front. Bartenders hand out cool cocktails and frosty mugs to a mixed crowd of friendly bikers, thirsty boaters, and suntanned fishermen who meander out to the deck or pick up a game of darts inside. The fishing pier and horseshoe pits keep folks busy for hours. When the bands start to play on Friday and Saturday nights, you'll be tempted to dance on the beach under the moonlight. Go ahead. The dress-down feeling is contagious at the water's edge.

Stoney's Broomes Island Seafood House

3939 Oyster House Road
Broomes Island, MD 20615
(410) 586-1888
www.stoneysseafoodhouse.com/broomesisland

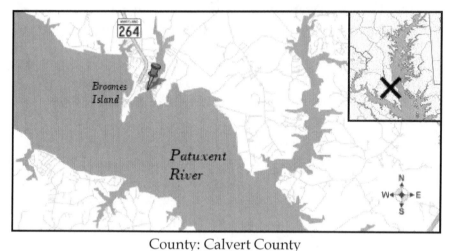

County: Calvert County
Open: Seasonal ⚓ Dockage: Yes
Latitude: N 38° 24' 46" 🐟 Longitude: W 76° 32' 43"
Body of Water: Island Creek off the Patuxent River
Driving Distance: Baltimore 72 miles,
Washington, DC 54 miles, Easton 87 miles

Atmosphere Meter

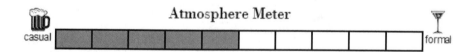

casual — formal

Whether you arrive by boat or car, it's hard to imagine a more pleasant location to spend a summer day than at Stoney's Broomes Island. Tucked away in a lovely residential neighborhood on a narrow road appropriately named Oyster

House Road, this charming place has been serving good Maryland seafood for almost 20 years.

As a sister restaurant of Stoney's Kingfishers, Clarke's Landing, and Solomons Pier, jumbo lump crab cakes are the house specialty, made with a half pound of meat and only a hint of filler. Clams, steamed shrimp, and oysters are local and fresh, and the rockfish basket has the right mix of crunch and flavor. Steaks, sandwiches, salads, wings, burgers, and soups expand your options.

The indoor dining rooms offer a unique display of waterfowl replicas and aquatic wildlife dangling from the rafters. Floor-to-ceiling windows open up to a panoramic view of Island Creek and Solomons Bridge. If you're seeking an outdoor Bay experience, give in to the temptation to walk through the back doors. Along the water's edge, decks with round wooden picnic tables are lined up like an archipelago of crab-covered islands. Boaters and landlubbers alike belly up to the tiki bar for icy rum cocktails or beer. Keep strolling the grounds and you'll discover a waterfall surrounded by lush green landscaping and a beach that beckons you to take a cooling dip in the water.

Vera's Beach Club Restaurant & Marina

1200 White Sands Road
Lusby, MD 20657
(410) 586-1182
www.verasbeachclub.com

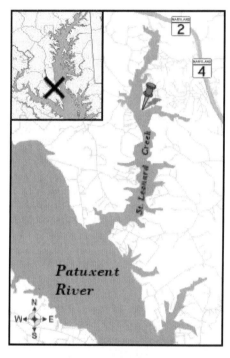

County: Calvert County

Open: Year Round

Dockage: Yes

Latitude: N 38° 25' 16"

Longitude: W 76° 29' 12"

Body of Water: St. Leonard
Creek off the Patuxent River

Driving Distance:
Baltimore 74 miles,
Washington, DC 56 miles,
Easton 89 miles

Atmosphere Meter

casual 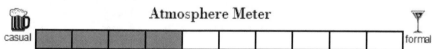 formal

It all started over a half-century ago when an adventurous young woman named Vera left her small town in Montana for the bright lights of Hollywood. Vera never found fame as a movie star but she married optometrist Effrus "Doc" Freeman. The couple explored the world aboard his yacht, visiting exotic ports-of-call from India to Indonesia. Crates filled with mementos from their journeys came to rest at their home in southern Maryland among the farmers and watermen. After WWII when tiki became the rage, Vera and Doc opened a restaurant showcasing their Polynesian art and collectibles.

Celebrities from around the globe came to this tropical kingdom where Vera held court. In 2006, when Vera reached her nineties and the upkeep became too challenging, she relinquished her tiki throne and sold the place. After major renovations, it reopened with a beach party style steeped in tiki tradition. Upon arrival, you're welcomed by a massive granite statue of Poseidon and a huge Easter Island stone head stands guard over the boats in the marina below. Vera's home next door is now a villa hotel filled with her fab tiki collection.

In the restaurant, dark tiki masks stare out from bamboo walls, faux leopard-skin stools encircle the bar, and seashells add a splash of color to the dining rooms. On the menu, casual fare is mixed with more ambitious dinner entrees. Steamed shrimp, sandwiches, chicken tenders, and fried rockfish in baskets rest on tabletops next to steaks, crab cakes, and oysters. All-you-can-eat steamed crabs are local. A glamorous portrait of Vera hangs on the wall. Perched on top of her golden hair is a tall seashell headpiece, while she wears a dress made of peacock feathers and jewelry laden with oyster shells and emeralds. That alone is worth the trip.

Stoney's Seafood at Clarke's Landing

24580 Clarke's Landing Lane
Hollywood, MD 20636
(301) 373-3986
www.stoneysseafoodhouse.com/clarkeslanding

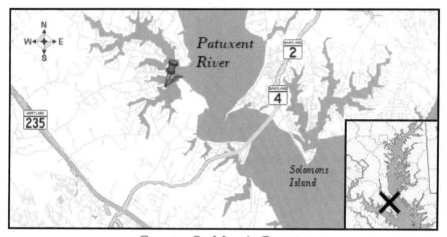

County: St. Mary's County
Open: Year Round ⚓ Dockage: Yes
Latitude: N 38° 20' 33" ⤞ Longitude: W 76° 30' 13"
Body of Water: Cuckold Creek off the Patuxent River
Driving Distance: Baltimore 88 miles,
Washington, DC 58 miles, Easton 103 miles

Atmosphere Meter

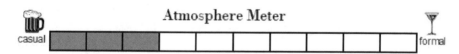

casual   formal

On one side of the Gov. Thomas Johnson Bridge is busy bustling Solomons; on the other side, life is more laid-back. The epitome of this easy southern Maryland living and cuisine is Stoney's Seafood at Clarke's Landing.

It joined the Stoney's restaurant group in 2014 and underwent renovations that give it an updated and open look. The one-story building is newly painted sky blue on bottom and white on top with matching striped awnings. Umbrellas protect diners from the summer sun on the deck. Inside, new wood cabinets behind the bar and enlarged vintage photos of oyster shuckers and watermen send a clear message that this place is very Bay-centric.

Right off the bat, the menu wows with a raw bar of local boutique oysters such as Chincoteagues and Island Creeks. Then it presents an all-star cast of essentials for a Chesapeake seafood feast. Crab dip, rockfish bites, and smoked bluefish lead the charge for appetizers. Steamer pots of fresh caught crustaceans present crab legs, mussels, lobster tails, shrimp, and other seasonal seafood. Delicious kabobs of jumbo shrimp, scallops and vegetables are grilled to perfection, and rockfish gyros appear with cucumber yogurt sauce, lettuce, and feta cheese. Meat eaters get a few choices: steaks, burgers, grilled cheese sandwiches, and filet mignon.

Isaac's Restaurant & Pub

155 Holiday Drive
Solomons, MD 20688
(410) 326-6311
www.isaacsrestaurant.com

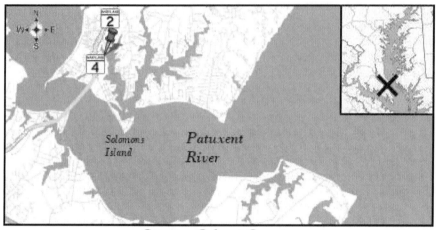

County: Calvert County
Open: Year Round ⚓ Dockage: Yes
Latitude: N 38° 20' 14" ➤ Longitude: W 76° 27' 47"
Body of Water: Back Creek off the Patuxent River
Driving Distance: Baltimore 80 miles,
Washington, DC 63 miles, Easton 95 miles

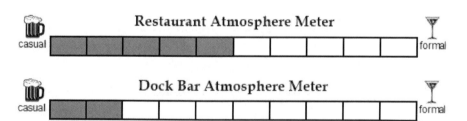

Even though it's located in a Holiday Inn, there's a lot to
like about Isaac's. Its marina location hums with boaters and
families enjoying a Bay getaway. The bustling dock bar is

stationed between a swimming pool and waterfront that's packed with a fleet of recreational vessels.

The restaurant, which is surrounded by more windows than walls, offers a glorious view of the creek. Beer is a hot commodity, with local brews ranging from Flying Dog to Heavy Seas Loose Cannon. The extensive menu is seafood-driven with starters such as creamy crab dip, crab pizza, steamed shrimp, and mussels. Sautéed rockfish is topped with crab imperial and a sweet ginger sauce. Fried green tomatoes reflect southern Maryland roots. A trio of crab entrees is irresistible: jumbo lump crab cakes, chicken Chesapeake with crab imperial, and crab mac & cheese. Chicken, steaks, and burgers are also on tap.

The life-sized crabbing skiff boat plopped in the middle of the dining room pays tribute to the man for whom this restaurant and the island are named. Isaac Solomon was a Baltimore businessman who bought 80 acres of what was called Sandy Island in 1865 when the area was little more than tobacco farms and marshland. Hoping to join the economic boom from oyster reefs nearby, Isaac built a seafood cannery, shipping company, and housing for his workers that helped turn the rural outpost into a vibrant town.

Angler's Seafood Bar & Grill

275 Lore Road
Solomons, MD 20688
(410) 326-2772
www.anglers-seafood.com

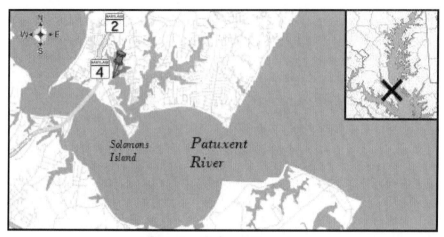

County: Calvert County
Open: Year Round ⚓ Dockage: Yes
Latitude: N 38° 19' 56" 🐟 Longitude: W 76° 27' 41"
Body of Water: Back Creek off the Patuxent River
Driving Distance: Baltimore 80 miles,
Washington, DC 63 miles, Easton 95 miles

Atmosphere Meter

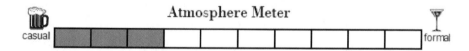

Don't be alarmed when you see a hotel chain next door to Angler's Seafood. The two are separate businesses. When new owners took the helm of the seafood house in 2014, they crafted a new menu, gave the restaurant's interior a fresh coat of paint, and brightened up the atmosphere. The outdoor deck didn't need much work, because it already offered a great view of boats drifting in and out of the marina and provides a lovely spot to spend time at the waterfront.

The restaurant serves hearty meals with regional Chesapeake flare. The kitchen opens for breakfast to accommodate early morning risers and hungry watermen. You can start your day with dishes such as crab omelets, pancakes, or biscuits and gravy. Lunch and dinner menus read like a fishing guide to the Bay's aquatic favorites: crab cakes, oysters on the half shell, smoked bluefish, and steamed shrimp. Rockfish stuffed with crab imperial and pan-fried soft-shell crabs are delightful. Meat eaters can choose among a variety of entrees such as country fried steak, chicken parmesan, prime rib, pasta alfredo, and liver and onions. Salads, sandwiches, wraps, and a kids' menu ensure everyone at the table leaves with a full belly.

In addition to food, Angler's dishes out plenty of fun with trivia nights, karaoke, live bands, and TVs tuned into local sporting events. It's a good neighborhood watering hole with staff that warmly welcomes guests to their slice of the Bay.

The Dry Dock Restaurant

251 C Street
Solomons, MD 20688
(410) 326-4817
www.zahnisers.com/restaurant-2

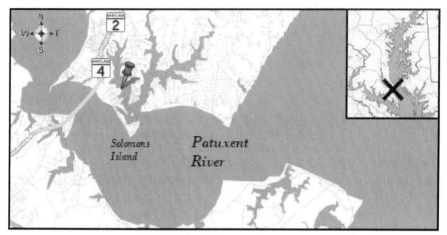

County: Calvert County
Open: Year Round ⚓ Dockage: Yes
Latitude: N 38° 19' 43" ⟶ Longitude: W 76° 27' 31"
Body of Water: Back Creek off the Patuxent River
Driving Distance: Baltimore 80 miles,
Washington, DC 63 miles, Easton 95 miles

Atmosphere Meter

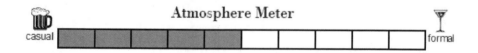

casual   formal

The primary pleasure at Dry Dock is easy living. It's part of Zahnisers Yachting Center, which has committed decades to helping folks enjoy time on the water. You can dine inside and gaze out the bay windows at the creek. The slate green building's upper balcony gives a magnificent view of the marina where sailboats sway with the waves and boaters tie up at the dock. Children do cannonballs into the swimming pool next door, while parents unwind with a cool beverage in hand. The scene is charming and relaxing.

The menu takes classic Chesapeake cuisine up a notch and promises "to use as much sustainable seafood and local produce as possible." You can jumpstart a farm-to-table meal with creamy crab soup, jumbo shrimp with Amaretto glaze, fried oysters, Ducktrap River smoked salmon, or petit crab cake sliders.

Standout seafood entrees include grilled salmon with sundried tomato and pesto salad or shrimp, mussels, and scallops in a creamy marinara sauce. Imaginative cooking also extends to land dishes: crispy duck breast comes with wild rice pilaf, beef tenderloin is accompanied by sautéed spinach and crimini mushrooms, and vegetarian Florentine tosses linguini with pesto and fresh vegetables.

At Dry Dock, the dynamic combo of fine dining and phenomenal scenery is sure to make you want to come back as soon as the trade winds blow you in that direction.

Stoney's Kingfishers
Seafood House

14442 Solomons Island Road South
Solomons, MD 20688
(410) 394-0236
www.stoneysseafoodhouse.com/kingfishers

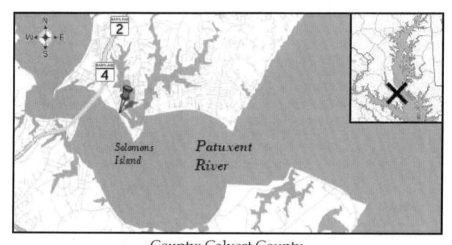

County: Calvert County
Open: Year Round ⚓ Dockage: No
Latitude: N 38° 19' 26" 🦐 Longitude: W 76° 27' 37"
Body of Water: The Narrows off Back Creek off the Patuxent River
Driving Distance: Baltimore 80 miles,
Washington, DC 63 miles, Easton 95 miles

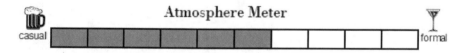

🍺 **Atmosphere Meter** 🍸
casual ▢ formal

When you see a bait and tackle shop next door, signs for charter fishing boats inside, and locally harvested oysters on the menu (baked, raw, or fried), you know you're in the right place for Chesapeake seafood. Sandwiched between the

Patuxent River and Back Creek, Stoney's Kingfishers has Bay heritage written all over it.

Murals on the walls are accented with hand-crafted wood carvings of Maryland estuary life including geese, eagles, ducks, herons, and osprey. The atmosphere is casual-nice: the kind of place where you'd feel comfortable meeting colleagues after work, rather than the gritty crab shacks where you worry about feisty seagulls swooping down to steal your french fries. Seating is available on the patio and an outdoor bar upstairs. Established in 2012, this is a sister restaurant of Stoney's at Clarke Landing, Broomes Island and Solomons Pier.

The food is fresh, well-prepared, and seafood-centric. A steaming bowl of crab soup (tomato-based or creamy) with a salad is enough to fill you up. Sandwiches give a token nod to chicken and beef but focus more on crab, tuna, and rockfish. Burgers are made with a whopping half-pound of cow. The seafood entrees are where Stoney's Kingfishers really shines: crab in cakes or creamy imperial, seared scallops with brussels sprouts, Neptune platters with mixed delicacies from the Bay, and fried oysters and shrimp with a crispy outside coating. Live music on weekends adds to the dining experience.

The Striped Rock at Solomons

14470 Solomons Island Road South
Solomons, MD 20688
(410) 449-6059
www.thestripedrock.com

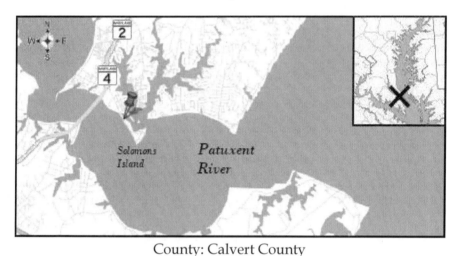

County: Calvert County
Open: Year Round ⚓ Dockage: Yes
Latitude: N 38° 19' 22" ➤ Longitude: W 76° 27' 36"
Body of Water: The Narrows off Back Creek off the Patuxent River
Driving Distance: Baltimore 80 miles,
Washington, DC 63 miles, Easton 95 miles

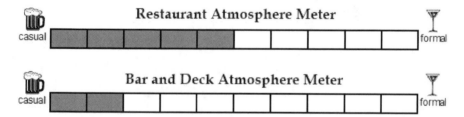

Ingredients from local farmers, co-ops, and fisheries await at The Striped Rock. In the summer of 2013, it filled the space left behind by Catarmarans, and everyone has welcomed it warmly to Solomons restaurant row.

The restaurant's name and logo are derived from a beloved Chesapeake swimmer — the rockfish, which is also known as the striped bass because of the dark lines that run the length of its body. It has the honor of being designated Maryland's official state fish, and its delicate flavor makes it a popular dish. Unfortunately rockfish have suffered the same fate as Bay oysters and crabs. Overfishing, pollution, and disease decimated the population by the 1980s, forcing a fishing moratorium that lasted to the 1990s. With strict limits on the number and size you can catch, rockfish have rebounded, so you can eat it guilt-free.

Staying true to its name, The Striped Rock specializes in Chesapeake seafood, especially striped bass entrees. You'll also find plates of fried oysters, crab cakes, tarragon shrimp, flash-fried calamari, conch fritters, crab nachos con queso, and mussels in a garlic cream sauce. Overstuffed sandwiches, fresh salads, and savory BBQ pork provide casual fare. And all this is served in a newly renovated building with a double-deck view of the water.

Island Hideaway

14556 Solomons Island Road South
Solomons, MD 20688
(410) 449-6382
www.islandhideawaysolomons.com

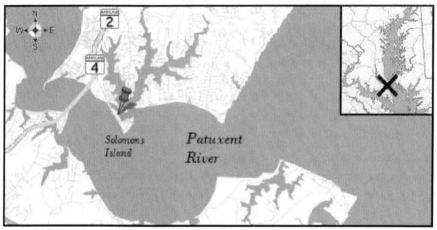

County: Calvert County
Open: Year Round ⚓ Dockage: Yes
Latitude: N 38° 19' 19" Longitude: W 76° 27' 28"
Body of Water: The Narrows off Back Creek off the Patuxent River
Driving Distance: Baltimore 80 miles,
Washington, DC 63 miles, Easton 95 miles

Atmosphere Meter

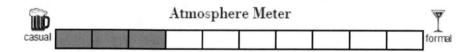

casual | | | | | | | | | | formal

A sign that looks like a treasure map heralds the arrival of a new restaurant on Solomon's main drag. In 2014, Island Hideaway replaced Di Giovanni's Italian cooking with classic Chesapeake fare and a wink of subtle pirate motif. The one-story building is spruced up with new colors and décor, and the deck out back continues to delight guests seeking a front-row seat to the boats and water.

The menu features traditional Maryland seafood: crab cakes, broiled scallops, stuffed shrimp, flounder packed with crab imperial, and fried oysters. Steaks, sandwiches, honey fried chicken, and burgers round out the dining options.

The restaurant gives a nod to the maritime tradition of pirates. For centuries, buccaneers roamed these waters and preyed on ships crossing the Atlantic. They were tolerated, even courted, by colonists who wanted to thumb their noses at the British and buy black market goods. A trio named Davis, Wafer and Hinson stole a king's fortune in the South Seas and plundered the entire Bay. They were captured and thrown in a Jamestown jail for a year. The deal for release stated that they had to return the loot and pay 300 pounds, which would later establish the College of William and Mary. The most infamous pirate to roam these waters was Edward Teach (a.k.a. Blackbeard), who repaired his ships in the isolated necks of the Bay and raided towns en route to the ocean. His reign of terror ended in 1718, when Robert Maynard attacked the pirate's ship and fatally shot the scoundrel. Maynard severed Blackbeard's head and mounted it on the ship's bow.

Stoney's Solomons Pier Seafood House

14575 Solomons Island Road South
Solomons, MD 20688
(410) 326-2424
www.stoneysseafoodhouse.com/solomonspier

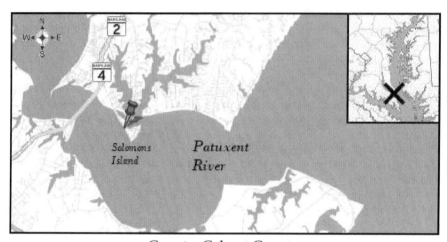

County: Calvert County
Open: Year Round ⚓ Dockage: No
Latitude: N 38° 19' 15" ➤ Longitude: W 76° 27' 32"
Body of Water: Patuxent River
Driving Distance: Baltimore 80 miles,
Washington, DC 63 miles, Easton 95 miles

Atmosphere Meter

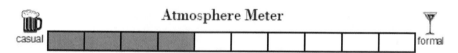

casual — formal

As you stroll along the river walk, you can't miss Solomons Pier jutting out into the water. Whether you grab a bite at the bar, out on the pier, or inside the dining room, you experience southern Maryland's version of dinner and a show. The panoramic views of the Patuxent River are fun to watch any time of day or night. Patuxent Naval Air Station lies to the south, Gov. Thomas Johnson Bridge is to the north, and all types of boats pass before your eyes.

Snacks, appetizers, and entrees represent the best of local seafood — jumbo lump crab cakes, steamed shrimp, littleneck clams, and crusted rockfish — to name a few of the favorites. Special dishes: Crab Monte Carlo and soft-shell sandwiches. There's even a seafood market next door if you haven't consumed enough and want to cook some fish at home later. But you really shouldn't leave here without sampling the oysters. They are local, fresh, and delicious — and these plump bivalves are major players in the town's history.

In the mid-1800s, Solomons was little more than tobacco farms and marshland. Shipbuilding flourished, and by the early 20th century, the fishing industry boomed and seafood processing plants dotted the coastline. Along came J.C. Lore, who opened a processing house down the street and expanded the island's size by building on top of thousands of tons of oyster shells. The oyster house closed in 1978, but at the back of this restaurant, you find a wall dedicated to Lore's oyster shuckers. To learn more, visit Lore Oyster House and Museum, which chronicles the local seafood business.

The Lighthouse Restaurant & Dock Bar

14636 Solomons Island Road South
Solomons, MD 20688
(410) 231-2256
www.lighthouserestaurantanddockbar.com

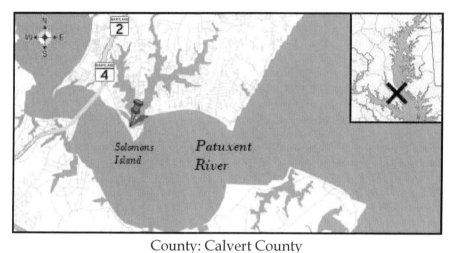

County: Calvert County
Open: Year Round ⚓ Dockage: Yes
Latitude: N 38° 19' 13" ⬌ Longitude: W 76° 27' 26"
Body of Water: Back Creek off the Patuxent River
Driving Distance: Baltimore 80 miles,
Washington, DC 63 miles, Easton 95 miles

Atmosphere Meter

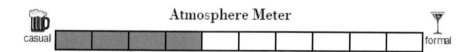

casual ——— formal

When the Lighthouse Inn burned to the ground in 2006, the entire Solomons community shared a great loss of a favorite gathering place. When word spread that a local family planned to build a new restaurant on the same location, everyone rejoiced. The new Lighthouse Restaurant opened in 2014, like a beacon of hope that life on the island had returned to normal. The new owners realized that they had big shoes to fill with their new venture. And it has exceeded expectations.

An eight-foot replica tall trophy fish hangs near the front steps to welcome boaters and fisherman, while the two-tiered back deck lures in visitors for a spectacular view of the marina. The interior is open, breezy and decorated with vintage photos of watermen, mounted rockfish, and other symbols of the Bay.

The menu kicks off with Chesapeake standards: creamy crab dip, steamed mussels, bacon-wrapped scallops, and more. The raw bar is a chilled medley of oysters, crab legs shrimp, and clams. Entrees follow a similar path with rockfish stuffed with crab imperial, fried shrimp, and broiled sea scallops. The Ultimate Seafood Platter brings them all together in one mouthwatering plate. Extra-spicy Angry Crab Cake will light you up, but an Orange Crush or local craft beer can help cool down your palate. Landlubbers aren't ignored, with options such as steaks, burgers, and grilled chicken.

The Tiki Bar
at Solomons Island

85 Charles Street
Solomons, MD 20688
(410) 326-4075
www.tikibarsolomons.com

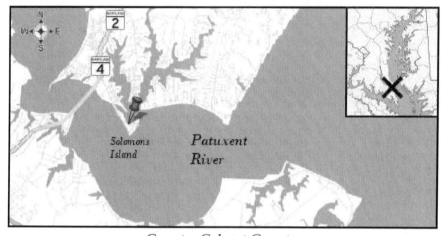

County: Calvert County
Open: Seasonal ⚓ Dockage: Yes
Latitude: N 38° 19' 10" ⚓ Longitude: W 76° 27' 21"
Body of Water: Back Creek off the Patuxent River
Driving Distance: Baltimore 80 miles,
Washington, DC 63 miles, Easton 95 miles

Atmosphere Meter

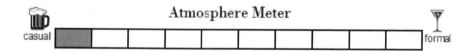

casual ──────────────────────── formal

Brace yourself. When you visit The Tiki Bar at Solomons, you enter the Polynesian epicenter of the Bay. It's the Holy Grail of tropical island fun where people-watching can't be beat. Bikers in black leather buy beers for businessmen who loosen their ties, pleasure boaters and watermen share a smoke over tales of the sea, bikini-clad college girls gracefully skip past tourists in loud Hawaiian shirts — and everyone gets along just fine.

The Tiki Village is comprised of a bar, restaurant, gift shop, tobacco barn, and hotel. Bamboo walls are garnished with wood carvings by California Polynesian pop artist Bosko Hrnjak, and massive Easter Island stone heads keep a steely eye on the crowd. The thatched roof bar is decorated with tiki masks, fish, and erupting volcanoes. Big blue beach umbrellas cover picnic tables, and chairs are painted Key West green, blue, yellow, and orange.

Palm trees and sand are replaced each spring to keep the place looking fresh. Bands play Jimmy Buffett, Bob Marley — anything to top off the island ambiance. Tiki Bar hosts fundraising events for local charities, and parties here are legendary. When the 30th anniversary bash in 2010 attracted 20,000 guests, one had to wonder how they all fit on this tiny island. Opening day at the Tiki Bar in April is like Mardi Gras in Solomons. So, if you're in a tiki state of mind, treat yourself to a mai tai, kokomo, or Cajun margarita and enjoy the untamed tropical breeze blowing across the Bay.

Charles Street Brasserie

120 Charles Street
Solomons, MD 20688
(443) 404-5332
www.charlesstreetbrass.com

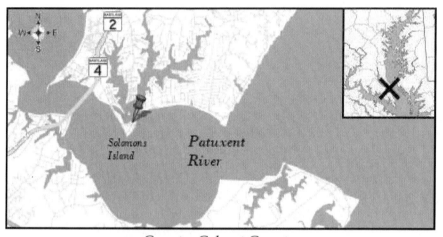

County: Calvert County
Open: Seasonal ⚓ Dockage: Yes
Latitude: N 38° 19' 13" 🐟 Longitude: W 76° 27' 16"
Body of Water: Back Creek off the Patuxent River
Driving Distance: Baltimore 80 miles,
Washington, DC 63 miles, Easton 95 miles

Atmosphere Meter

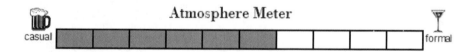

casual   formal

Tapas are an assortment of appetizers, snacks, or petite dishes that originated in Spain but somehow landed on the tip of Solomons Island at Charles Street Brasserie. The chef says his menu creates a fusion of small bites and southern Maryland cuisine that allows you to sample a variety of foods from the kitchen instead of eating just one meal. Does it work? Yes, quite nicely. After a long day on the water, nibble on a couple tapas in the afternoon to hold you over until supper. Or make an entire meal out of a larger sampling to share with friends and enjoy a diverse dining experience.

Traditionalists can order mini crab cakes, fried oysters Rockefeller, cream of crab soup, or steamed shrimp, while the adventurous can select marinated pork kabobs, hummus, bacon-wrapped dates, or peanut chicken skewers. Standard size crab imperial, stuffed salmon, filet mignon, pork chops, burgers, and sandwiches are available if you work up an appetite too big for tapas.

This unique seafood restaurant was launched in 2014 after extensive renovations set a 1930s night club mood. Black walls with burgundy accents are covered with vintage classic movie and French cabaret prints. A fireplace chases away the chill of a wintry night, and live music from the piano elevates the cozy atmosphere. Outside fire pits crackle, and long white swags of sheer fabric hung from poles above the deck create a dreamy romantic ambiance under the stars.

The Back Creek Bistro

14415 Dowell Road
Dowell, MD 20629
(410) 326-9900
www.backcreekbistro.com

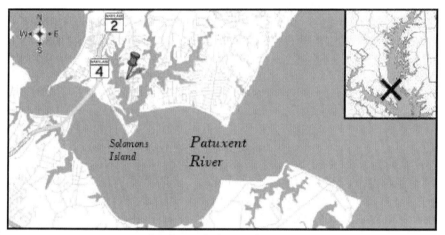

County: Calvert County
Open: Year Round ⚓ Dockage: No
Latitude: N 38° 19' 56" ➤ Longitude: W 76° 27' 22"
Body of Water: Back Creek off the Patuxent River
Driving Distance: Baltimore 78 miles,
Washington, DC 61 miles, Easton 94 miles

Atmosphere Meter

casual 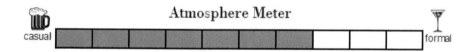 formal

It's hard to imagine that an old power plant could be
converted to an upscale dining establishment, but that's the
case with Back Creek Bistro. In 2010, the restaurant opened
in the spot that used to generate electricity for the U.S.
amphibious training base during World War II. It's located at
Calvert Marina on the second floor of a red brick building

with long green shutters. The Gov. Thomas Johnson Bridge to Solomons Island provides the backdrop to an incredible view of the water and boatyard. Inside, exposed brick walls, oriental rugs, and plush couches create a soothing ambiance, and the staff is eager to please guests with locally grown produce and seafood harvested from regional waters.

The menu presents a lovely array of appetizers, salads, and sandwiches such as crab dip, calamari, lobster bisque, French onion soup, and burgers made of certified Angus beef. The kitchen kicks into high gear when preparing entrees like golden crab cakes, sea scallops, shrimp in a garlic beurre blanc sauce, twin lobster tails, seafood platter, and gnocchi tossed with jumbo crab meat in a silky cream sauce. Only Maryland blue crab from the Bay is allowed in the kitchen. Chicken marsala and prime rib are delightful, and the chocolate-raspberry martini is unforgettable.

The kid's menu offers pasta, chicken nuggets, and burgers served quickly so youngsters can goof around the gazebo outside while parents finish their meals at a more leisurely pace. Evening music features live jazz and blues artists, and the artwork is provided by a local painter.

Hidden Harbor Restaurant

14755 Dowell Road
Dowell, MD 20629
(410) 326-1100

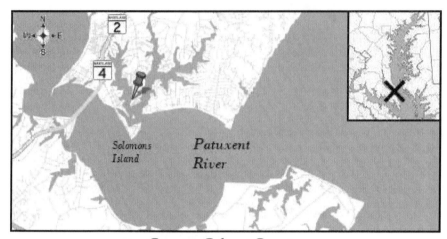

County: Calvert County
Open: Seasonal ⚓ Dockage: Yes
Latitude: N 38° 19' 42" ⤞ Longitude: W 76° 27' 19"
Body of Water: Back Creek off the Patuxent River
Driving Distance: Baltimore 78 miles,
Washington, DC 61 miles, Easton 94 miles

Atmosphere Meter

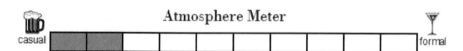

casual | | | | | | | | | | formal

If you want to escape the crowds of downtown Solomons Island, head to the Calvert Marina in Dowell and take a seat at the new Hidden Harbor Restaurant. Even if you don't own a boat, it gives you the feeling of being on the water. This cheerful little place rests on pylons and juts out into Back Creek with Solomons Bridge in the background. Boaters like this location, because docking is a breeze and the atmosphere is casual and friendly. Plus, the charter boat captain next door will take you out for a day of fishing on the Bay if you like.

Blue herons and sea gulls hover around looking for minnows, baby crabs, or french fries that topple overboard from the deck. A smattering of tropical plants and colorful patio furniture on the deck give an island vibe. The skull and crossbones on the restaurant's sign suggest that well-behaved pirates are welcome inside.

It opened in spring 2015, and they're ready for business. With such a small kitchen, it's understandable that the cook keeps the menu simple. Everything is made from scratch, and dining options feature traditional Bay cuisine with a pinch of Caribbean flavors. Seafood selections include creamy Maryland crab soup, conch fritters, jerk shrimp, and Crab Solomons, which is a crab cake turned crispy in a fried wonton. The kale salad with jerk chicken and pumpkin seeds is a plate of healthy freshness. Meat lovers get their fill with dishes such as the Cuban Reuben, steak and cheese sandwich, Old Bay wings, pizza, and veal parmesan subs. Hefty portions mean you get yummy leftovers for lunch.

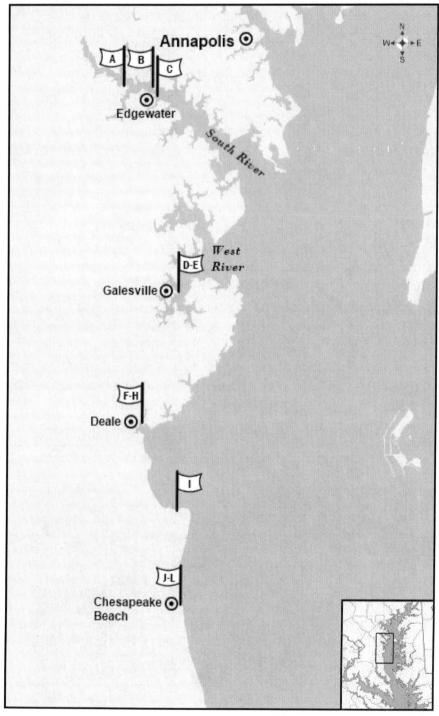

South River to Chesapeake Beach

Mike's Restaurant & Crab House

3030 Riva Road
Riva, MD 21140
(410) 956-2784
www.mikescrabhouse.com

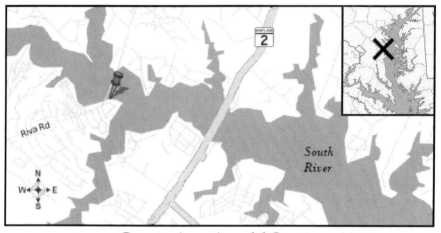

County: Anne Arundel County
Open: Year Round ⚓ Dockage: Yes
Latitude: N 38° 57' 15" Longitude: W 76° 34' 26"
Body of Water: South River
Driving Distance: Baltimore 29 miles,
Washington, DC 33 miles, Easton 46 miles

Atmosphere Meter

casual 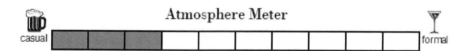 formal

If you want to know what "peelers, keepers, and doublers" are, then you should go to Mike's web site for a tutorial on Maryland blue crabs. But if you want to know what they taste like, you have to visit the restaurant. Mike's has been around since 1958, and it's such a classic that it regularly wins awards for best crab house, crab cakes, and crab soup. You envy locals who can eat there any time they want. The big outdoor deck sits on top of the water giving diners a panoramic view of boaters navigating and having fun on the South River. The two-lane bridge in the background catches the amber light of sunset just right.

Inside the restaurant, casual dining is the lay of the land with tables covered by brown paper and shakers filled with Old Bay. Your nose might dictate what you order when it gets a whiff of fresh crabs steaming in the kitchen. You can't go wrong if you stick with traditional Bay cuisine: crab cakes, steamed shrimp, fried oysters, broiled rockfish, and Chesapeake fried chicken. Steaks, pork chops, baby back ribs, pizza, and burgers please the carnivores in the crowd. Also on site is a country store that sells bait, beer, ice, and snacks — everything you need for a grand adventure on the Bay.

In case you're still wondering, "peelers" are crabs that are ready to molt their outer shell, "keepers" are crabs that have grown to at least 5 inches from tip-to-tip and are big enough to catch, and "doublers" are two mating crabs swimming together with the male on top gently protecting his female.

Yellowfin Steak & Fish House

2840 Solomons Island Road
Edgewater, MD 21037
(410) 573-1333
www.yellowfinrest.com

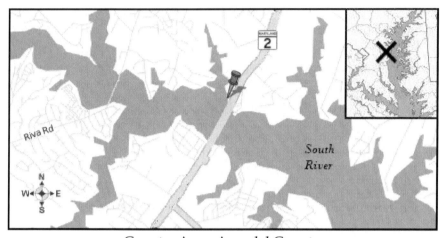

County: Anne Arundel County
Open: Year Round ⚓ Dockage: Yes
Latitude: N 38° 57' 17" 🐟 Longitude: W 76° 33' 13"
Body of Water: South River
Driving Distance: Baltimore 29 miles,
Washington, DC 33 miles, Easton 44 miles

Atmosphere Meter

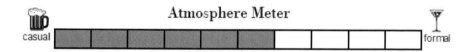

casual ▭▭▭▭▭▭▭▭▭▭▭ formal

If you can cast aside the standard crab house image of
a rickety clapboard building surrounded by a wooden deck,
then you might like Yellowfin. An architectural firm out of
Annapolis did extensive renovations on the 10,000 square foot,
50-year old restaurant using "aquatic metaphors." The result
is Yellowfin's contemporary nautical décor featuring a huge

yellow sail stretched over the entrance, glass mosaic tile work, and giant fish sculptures all over the place. It's owned by Land & Sea Group, who also manages Buddy's Crabs & Ribs, Big Fish Grill, and Fat Boy's Crab Shack.

Yellowfin's dining area and lower deck present a soothing waterfront view. The interior marble and chrome bar wraps around a show kitchen where you can watch cooks prepare your meal. The ambiance fluctuates between casual and fine dining, with patrons wearing everything from T-shirts to ties.

The cuisine is innovative, but not outlandish, and is very seafood-centric. Sushi takes a top spot on the menu, offering rolls, tempura, and tuna tartare. Starters add a creative twist to Bay traditions: seafood tacos, "shrimptini" cocktail, and crab dip with artichokes and garlic. Entrees cover all the bases with a Maryland seafood combo, crab cakes, lobster and shrimp pot pie, steamed mussels, and beer-battered shrimp. The fishy theme continues with paella and clams steamed in garlic sauce. Pasta, poultry, certified Angus steaks, and gourmet sandwiches complete the menu. The new Sunday brunch presents bottomless champagne and mimosas, a breakfast station, and made-to-order omelets.

Coconut Joe's
Hawaiian Bar & Grill

48 South River Road
Edgewater, MD 21037
(443) 837-6057
www.coconutjoesusa.com

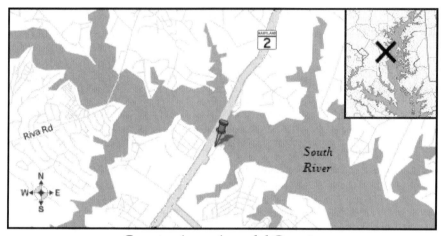

County: Anne Arundel County
Open: Year Round ⚓ Dockage: Yes
Latitude: N 38° 56' 53" ⚓ Longitude: W 76° 33' 21"
Body of Water: South River
Driving Distance: Baltimore 30 miles,
Washington, DC 34 miles, Easton 45 miles

Atmosphere Meter

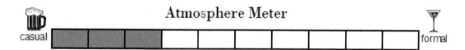

casual   formal

It doesn't matter what time of year you come to Coconut Joe's. It's a great place for every season. This totally tiki spot can melt away the chill of a wintry day. When you walk through the bamboo-and-thatch entrance, past the cage for a bearded dragon lizard, you enter "Hawaiian Paradise." Red and green accent lights and brightly colored surfboards cover the bar's wood and pressed tin walls. Palm trees, coconut candle holders, and Polynesian signs set an aloha tone. The indoor dining area has a vintage 1950s tiki grace. Smooth wooden tables are covered with old photos and postcards from exotic tropical destinations. Fantastic tiki masks are mounted on huge banana leaves and woven palm mats.

In the spring, full tiki regalia unfolds, and it's time to congregate outside. Kids climb around a pirate ship in the white-sand playground area, while adults hit two levels of decks with bars overlooking the South River. Coconut Joe's kicks off warm weather with a blowout Hawaiian luau complete with a pig roast, dancing hula girls in grass skirts, fire eaters, and live bands. This fun is sponsored by a local family that also owns Mango's at North Beach. The deep-water marina and dock welcome boats of all shapes and sizes. The menu highlights coconut shrimp, pan-seared mahi mahi, and Hawaiian seafood scampi that are cooked with an island influence. Traditionalists gobble up steamed crabs, rockfish, oysters, shrimp, and crab cakes. Steaks, BBQ pulled pork sandwiches, Waikiki chicken, and pasta make everyone happy to be hungry. Joe's exotic menu of tropical cocktails offers a gamut of delights from fruit juice crushes to the rum-drenched Big Kahuna and Hawaiian Harvest.

Pirates Cove Restaurant & Oyster Bar

4817 Riverside Drive
Galesville, MD 20765
(410) 867-2300
www.piratescovemd.com

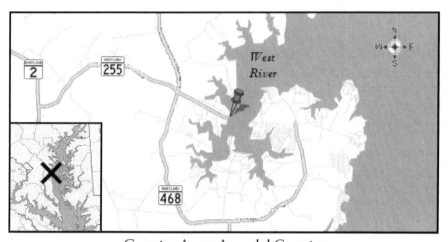

County: Anne Arundel County
Open: Year Round ⚓ Dockage: Yes
Latitude: N 38° 50' 35" ✈ Longitude: W 76° 32' 20"
Body of Water: West River
Driving Distance: Baltimore 39 miles,
Washington, DC 33 miles, Easton 54 miles

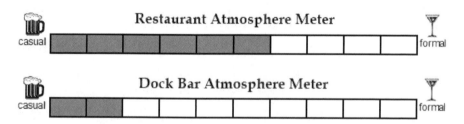

Everybody likes choices, and you've got plenty of good options to match your mood at Pirates Cove. You can enjoy a lovely waterfront meal at the restaurant, which sports a fresh-shirt casual atmosphere. To fit in, just toss a sundress over your bathing suit or swap a clean shirt for one that's stained with suntan oil or bait drippings. The raw bar offers a nice selection of local seafood ranging from oysters Rockefeller to smoked bluefish. Appetizers and entrees focus on the daily catch from the Bay, including crabs, shrimp, mussels, and rockfish. Carnivores indulge in prime rib, steaks, pork chops, and chicken dishes.

You can also hang out at Big Mary's Dock Bar. It's a flip-flop casual place that brings a splash of tropical fun to the Chesapeake. Light fare of crab dip, steamed shrimp, wings, pizza, sandwiches, soups, and salads are served under blue and yellow umbrellas and palm trees. From April to September, you can watch sailboat races every Wednesday and hear live bands on weekends. You can join the VIP Club (Very Important Pirate) to get discounts on return trips.

An added bonus: The Inn at Pirate's Cove offers pleasant rooms for folks who aren't ready to go home. Many of them want more time to walk around Galesville. This charming 350-year old village (one of the oldest in the United States) harkens back to a simpler era when people picked up mail at the local post office or had picnics after church on Sunday.

Thursday's Steak & Crab House

4851 Riverside Drive
Galesville, MD 20765
(410) 867-7200

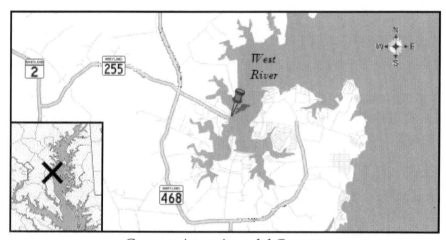

County: Anne Arundel County
Open: Year Round ⚓ Dockage: Yes
Latitude: N 38° 50' 28" ➤ Longitude: W 76° 32' 22"
Body of Water: West River
Driving Distance: Baltimore 39 miles,
Washington, DC 33 miles, Easton 54 miles

Atmosphere Meter

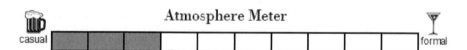

casual   formal

Boaters never have to step on shore and landlubbers get
a 360-degree view of the water when they visit Thursday's.
Located at the end of a pier, this one-story floating crab house
is an island of merriment surrounded by long wooden decks.
Deep blue awnings and brightly colored umbrellas cast
welcome shade upon rows of picnic tables laden with fruits
of the sea. Boats of every size, shape, and pedigree unload

people who come here for fun, good food, and sun. The outside bartenders keep drinks flowing and guests well hydrated in the relentless August heat.

Cooks dish out traditional Bay cuisine at a reasonable price. Steamed crabs, shrimp, and mussels are the menu's centerpiece. Crab soup and south-of-the-border chili team well with salads topped with your choice of grilled chicken, steak, or tuna. Chicken alfredo and shrimp scampi are leaders in the pasta category, while Steak Neptune (covered with shrimp, scallops, and crab meat in a cream sauce) gets high marks among the meat dishes. Ribs are slow-roasted until they practically fall off the bone.

After the last crab is picked and you want to stretch your legs, head up over the hill to historic Galesville. The village was founded in 1652 and is currently home to about 600 residents. It was a hub for Quaker settlement in the 1600s and is named after Richard Gale, a prominent Quaker planter. It grew into a port-of-entry for the shipping trade, and from the 1800s until the early 20th Century, the steamboat *Emma Giles* used to run through Galesville, Baltimore, and Annapolis to shuttle wares.

Dockside Restaurant & Sports Bar

421 Deale Road
Tracys Landing, MD 20779
(410) 867-1138
www.docksiderestaurantmd.com

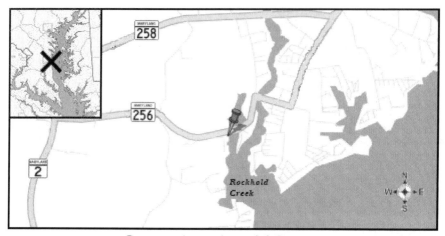

County: Anne Arundel County
Open: Year Round ⚓ Dockage: Yes
Latitude: N 38° 46' 39" Longitude: W 76° 33' 52"
Body of Water: Tracys Creek off Rockhold Creek off Herring Bay
Driving Distance: Baltimore 45 miles,
Washington, DC 30 miles, Easton 60 miles

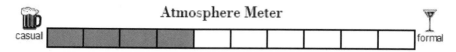

The 20-foot tall tusks still stand guard at the entrance as a memorial to the former Calypso Bay tiki haven that once occupied this property. The thatched roof bar, tiki heads, and palm trees were whisked away to make room for Tracys Landing's latest eatery, Dockside Restaurant. Well-trimmed grass covers the ground where sand had been spread, and murals of Chesapeake aquatic life were covered up with soft gray paint. On the plus side, a formidable deck still offers a lovely view of the bridge spanning the creek, and the entire place was upgraded by the new owners.

Interior walls are now garnished with vintage photos of watermen next to sculptures of fish, and white linens cover the tables. The name implies sports bar, so TVs in the lounge are tuned in to athletic events. It's all about casual dining and a relaxing South Country experience.

Lunch and dinner are served daily and breakfast is served on weekends until 11:00 a.m. Maryland crab soups (tomato and creamy) kick off the menu, while seafood appetizers include crab dip, steamed shrimp, and blackened scallops. The pasta dishes' show-stopper is shrimp Florentine with fresh spinach and your pick of alfredo or marinara sauce. Crab cakes, fried oysters, and grilled salmon are among the seafood entrees. Meat lovers happily push their forks into steaks, pork chops, shepherd's pie, and rack of lamb. Burgers, sandwiches, salads, and the kids menu provide casual fare.

Happy Harbor
Waterfront Restaurant & Bar

533 Deale Road
Deale, MD 20751
(410) 867-0949
www.happyharbordeale.com

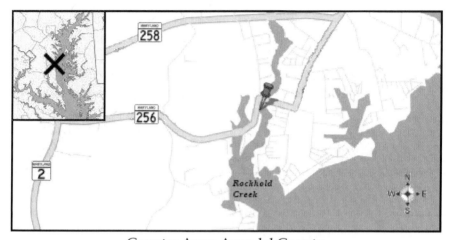

County: Anne Arundel County
Open: Year Round ⚓ Dockage: Yes
Latitude: N 38° 46' 55" ➤ Longitude: W 76° 33' 35"
Body of Water: Rockhold Creek off Herring Bay
Driving Distance: Baltimore 45 miles,
Washington, DC 31 miles, Easton 60 miles

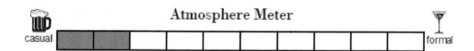

Slow down as you drive east on Route 256 right before you reach the Deale Bridge or you'll miss a slice of classic old Maryland. It doesn't get much more authentic than Happy Harbor Restaurant. This popular spot has served local watermen and landlubbers alike since 1933, and it plans to continue unless "One of them big storms comes up the Bay and blows us into the water," chuckled one of the employees.

On the outdoor wooden deck, charter boats line up along the docks while neighbors and fishermen convene around the bar. Mousetraps are thoughtfully screwed into the unfinished-pine bar top, so you can clamp down your dollar bills and stop the easterly winds from blowing them away. Colorful barstools and umbrellas, and a string of white lights add a festive vibe to the bustling waterfront deck.

Inside is all about casual comfort. At the bar, you'll find a few TVs, dartboards, a decent jukebox, and vintage photos of boaters proudly holding trophy fish. Black chairs around wooden tables are stationed in the dining room. If you're heading out for a day of fishing, you can order hearty breakfasts of crab and cheese omelets, pancakes, sausage gravy with biscuits, or eggs with grits or corned beef hash on the side. Baskets of fried oysters, shrimp, or clam strips come with fresh-cut potatoes. Steamer pots of shrimp, mussels, and crabs are blessed with a dash of Old Bay. Entrees include crab cake dinner, seafood platter, home-style meatloaf, BBQ ribs, and country fried steak. Don't miss Smith Island Cake for dessert. It's made from scratch and is divine chocolate bliss.

Crab Decks & Tiki Bars of the Chesapeake Bay, 2015 Maryland Edition

Skipper's Pier
Restaurant & Dock Bar

6158 Drum Point Road
Deale, MD 20751
(410) 867-7110
www.skipperspier.com

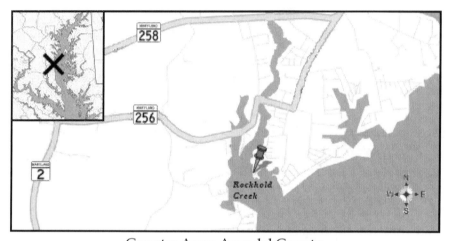

County: Anne Arundel County
Open: Year Round ⚓ Dockage: Yes
Latitude: N 38° 46' 22" ⟼ Longitude: W 76° 33' 38"
Body of Water: Rockhold Creek off Herring Bay
Driving Distance: Baltimore 46 miles,
Washington, DC 32 miles, Easton 62 miles

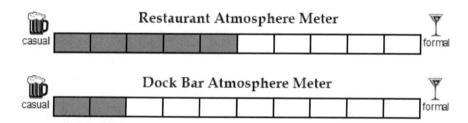

Good times are in store for everyone who visits Skipper's
Pier. About 80 years ago, the building was a clam-shucking

shack. Today it's a casual restaurant with seasoned chefs and a focus on fresh ingredients and local seafood.

Steamer pots are bubbling cauldrons of crab, shrimp, mussels, and clams served with garlic bread to soak up every last drop of broth. Many folks come here for steamed Maryland crabs, but the local rockfish, oysters, and fish tacos are also first rate. Signature dishes include roasted garlic shrimp and scallop scampi, Natty Boh fish and chips, and Cajun striped tuna with coconut slaw. Thick rib eye steaks, whiskey BBQ ribs, and Mason-Dixon buttermilk fried chicken are savory treats.

When the temperatures drop, patrons dine inside next to an old stone fireplace, but summer breezes tempt you to sit at the outside deck where you can watch boats cruise across the creek or toss leftover french fries to ducks paddling below. Children who grow impatient with the slowed-down pace of a waterfront meal can walk the plank in a pirate's play area. As kids crawl around a wooden ship, parents get to finish their meal in peace or tell one last story. The view of the boats, birds, and Bay are captivating.

Mango's Bar & Grill

7153 Lake Shore Drive
Rose Haven, MD 20758
(410) 257-0095
www.mangosonthebay.com

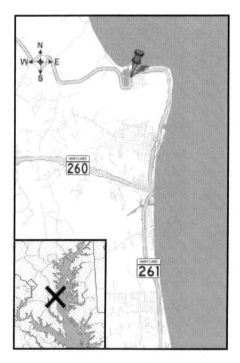

County: Anne Arundel County

Open: Year Round

Dockage: Yes

Latitude: N 38° 43' 36"

Longitude: W 76° 32' 28"

Body of Water: Herrington
  Harbour off Herring Bay

Driving Distance:
  Baltimore 50 miles,
  Washington, DC 34 miles,
  Easton 65 miles

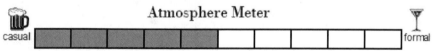

Atmosphere Meter

casual | formal

When you enter Mango's, it feels like a tropical breeze blew up the Bay and left behind a touch of the islands at Herrington Harbor Marina. Built in 2004 with a "tasteful tiki" décor, this place is casual, vibrant, and fun. Vintage photos hang on the walls, including a classic 1950s shot of a group wearing Hawaiian shirts and dancing in a conga line.

Bartenders shake martinis in glistening silver shakers and mix specialty drinks like Mango Mai Tai, Pain Killer, and Herrington Hurricane. A tall stone fireplace is in the corner by a dimly-lit dance floor. A bamboo and etched glass screen marks the entrance to the circular-shaped dining room. Fans with wooden banana leaf blades spin above tropical plants that are strategically placed around the windows so they don't obstruct the view of the water.

The menu creatively combines fresh local ingredients with Caribbean flavors. Traditional dishes like crab cakes and steamed mussels vie for attention with Coco-Bongo shrimp and grilled Caribbean chicken in mango vinaigrette with pineapple and toasted almonds. Show-stopping entrees include Mango Crab Explosion (12-ounce crab cake stuffed with crab imperial) and filet mignon topped with lump crab. Sandwiches, salads, and pasta round out the light fare.

The Cabana Bar out back provides an ideal spot to enjoy a nightcap and gorgeous view of the harbor. Orange umbrellas open next to palm trees and tiny black tiki heads. The poolside menu features lighter fare of snacks, salads, and sandwiches, as well as special cocktails such as the Tropical Punch Bucket, Cherry Popsicle, and Bikini-Tini.

Traders Seafood Steak & Ale

8132 Bayside Road
Chesapeake Beach, MD 20732
(301) 855-0766
www.traders-eagle.com

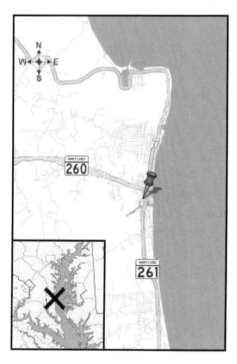

County: Calvert County

Open: Year Round

Dockage: No

Latitude: N 38° 41' 35"

Longitude: W 76° 32' 5"

Body of Water: a block away
from the Chesapeake Bay

Driving Distance:
Baltimore 52 miles,
Washington, DC 35 miles,
Easton 67 miles

Atmosphere Meter

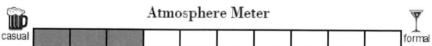

casual   formal

In 2008 when a tornado hit Traders and caused serious damage to the 60-year old building, locals worried that they'd lost a favorite watering hole. With a lot of hard work and community support, renovations were completed within three months and Trader's was back in business. A few years later, a big outdoor deck was added to the structure. Even though it's not located directly on the water, the restaurant is revered as a classic Chesapeake seafood house.

It's also the kind of place where there's always something happening: live bands, karaoke nights, comedy evenings, corn hole tournaments, chili cook-offs, and fundraising events for local youth and sports groups. Inside the boisterous game room, lights flash from gambling machines for playing Keno, electronic bingo, Maryland lottery, and more.

The dining room offers a quieter environment, with subtle hues and dimly lit tables and booths. On the menu, traditional fresh catch from the Bay takes the lead. For starters, you'll enjoy hot crab dip, just-shucked oysters, and steamed shrimp, as well as boardwalk fries and potato skins stuffed with crab, shrimp, and cheese. Specialties include Maryland crab cakes, fried seafood platter, steamed mussels, and scallops sautéed in butter and wine. Want meat instead? Then be sure to sample the country fried steak, hot turkey dinner, or Southern fried chicken. Burgers, salads, wraps, sandwiches, and steaks are also available.

Abner's Crab House

3748 Harbor Road
Chesapeake Beach, MD 20732
(410) 257-3689
www.abnerscrabhouse.net

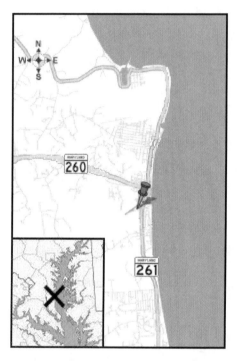

County: Calvert County

Open: Year Round

Dockage: Yes

Latitude: N 38° 41' 23"

Longitude: W 76° 32' 17"

Body of Water: Fishing Creek
off the Chesapeake Bay

Driving Distance:
Baltimore 52 miles,
Washington, DC 35 miles,
Easton 68 miles

Atmosphere Meter

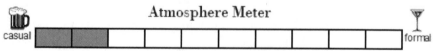

casual   formal

Since the 1950s, the Abner family has hauled crabs from the Bay. The crab house owner, Bobby Abner, owns 10 acres of land at Fishing Creek Marina and 600 crab pots that add to local fishermen's catch for his restaurant. Generations of the Abner family continue to work at this seafood house. The restaurant opened in 1966, and it's witnessed commercial and residential growth around Chesapeake Beach. Back in the mid-1800s, developers dreamed of turning this into a resort town, calling it the "Monte Carlo of Southern Maryland." Slot machines were legalized here in 2008, so you can test your luck at the one-arm bandits, poker and off-track horse racing.

To accommodate the rising popularity of gaming, Abner's renovated the building, reduced the dining area, and added space for gambling machines and a lounge. Poker leagues meet on weeknights, and the game room is filled with players who dream of winning a fortune.

On the dining room's orange and tan walls are murals of watermen working crab pots and fishing boats along the Bay. The outside deck displays a waterfront view of fishermen delivering fresh seafood for the platters inside. Soups include both tomato and cream of crab, as well as oyster stew. Crab cake and fried oyster sandwiches come with cole slaw and fries. Steamer pots are packed with crabs, mussels, clams, shrimp, and oysters and are blanketed with a splash of Old Bay. Burgers, pork BBQ, and chicken are in the house for meat eaters who take a break from the casino machines.

Rod 'N' Reel Restaurant

4165 Mears Avenue
Chesapeake Beach, MD 20732
(410) 286-2106
www.chesapeakebeachresortspa.com/rodnreel.htm

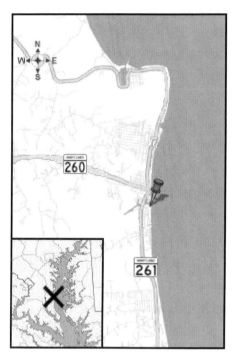

County: Calvert County

Open: Year Round

Dockage: Yes

Latitude: N 38° 41' 26"

Longitude: W 76° 31' 59"

Body of Water: directly on
the Chesapeake Bay at
Fishing Creek

Driving Distance:
Baltimore 52 miles,
Washington, DC 35 miles,
Easton 68 miles

 Atmosphere Meter

casual   formal

The Rod 'N' Reel has been around since 1946. Over
the years, it evolved from a simple crab house to its new
incarnation as the centerpiece of fine dining at Chesapeake
Beach Resort & Spa. This upscale, yet comfortable, facility has
banquet rooms that are ideal for weddings and corporate
retreats. You can pamper yourself with a massage at the spa

or take a dip in the heated indoor pool. All the rooms overlook the Bay and Calvert Cliffs. The tavern and gaming machines are separated from the dining area by etched glass panels with scenes of Chesapeake aquatic life and habitat. At happy hour, you can grab a stool at the bar and snack on rockfish bites, Buffalo chicken sliders, or popcorn shrimp.

In the dining room, you can gaze out the wall of windows at the endless waterfront view. Appetizers present variations on fried, steamed, or raw oysters, clams, shrimp, and crabs. Entrees focus on seafood (local and imported) with dishes such as baked crab imperial, seared scallops, Maine lobsters, grilled salmon, and crab-stuffed rockfish. Crab cakes are ranked among the best along the Bay. New York strip, filet mignon, and chicken breast are on call for meat lovers. Sandwiches, wraps, burgers, and pizza cover light fare choices. Sunday brunch buffets are legendary for opulent displays of eggs, sausages, seafood, pastries, and fresh fruit.

After your meal, check out the Railway Museum on the grounds nearby or take a leisurely stroll along the boardwalk to admire the beauty of the Bay.

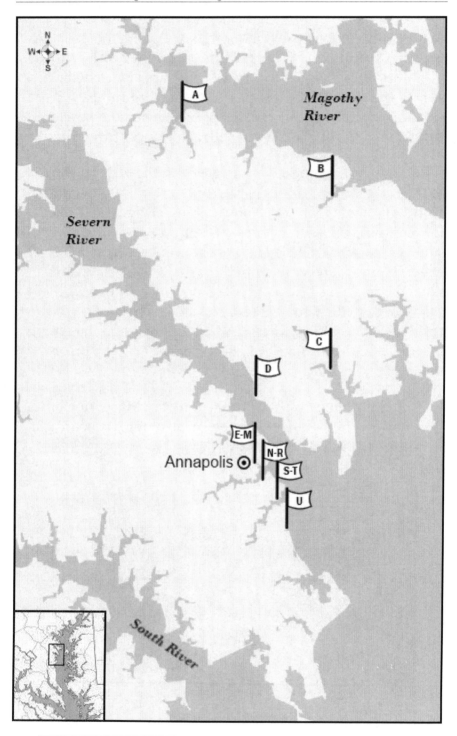

Annapolis & Eastport

The Point Crab House & Grill

700 Mill Creek Road
Arnold, MD 21012
(410) 544-5448
www.thepointcrabhouse.com

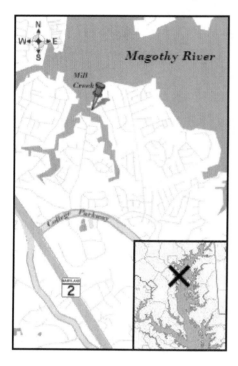

County: Anne Arundel County

Open: Year Round

Dockage: Yes

Latitude: N 39° 4' 4"

Longitude: W 76° 30' 42"

Body of Water: Mill Creek
off the Magothy River

Driving Distance:
Baltimore 25 miles
Washington, DC 40 miles
Easton 42 miles

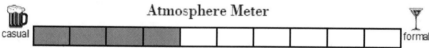

Atmosphere Meter

casual ▮▮▮▮▮▮□□□□□ formal

Labor Day 2012 marked the beginning of a new era in Arnold, MD. The Point opened its doors at the location where Magothy Crab Deck had held court for decades. Filling the shoes of a beloved local restaurant isn't easy, but this newcomer exceeded expectations of seafood fans in the area. The setting certainly helps. The Point is tucked away at Ferry

Point Marina where waters from Dividing Creek, Mill Creek, Cyprus Creek, and the Bay come together. Families sit at picnic tables under the shade of ancient oak trees watching boats cruise to and from the docks. Sunsets are heavenly.

The building's understated design of wood and steel is accented with a red roof and matching crimson benches. Vintage photos of Chesapeake watermen and fishing boats garnish the walls. Floor-to-ceiling retractable windows open wide to welcome a warm summer breeze and close quickly when storms pass through. The cheerful, laid-back atmosphere makes you want to linger as long as you can.

Traditional Maryland cuisine with a contemporary twist steals the show. Seafood and fresh ingredients are brought in from the Bay, Ocean City, Virginia, and Delaware. Hot steamed crabs, oysters, shrimp, and other local delicacies cover the tables. A visit would not be complete without tasting the velvety deviled eggs, oysters baked with Smithfield ham, grilled fish tacos, or the Southern Maryland chicken and crab melt. Slow-cooked pulled pork, burgers, and chicken pot pie provide delicious options for meat eaters. Favorite dessert: the addictive Homemade Chipwich.

Deep Creek Restaurant

1050 Deep Creek Avenue
Arnold, MD 21012
(410) 974-1408 or (410) 757-4045
www.thedeepcreekrestaurant.com

County: Anne Arundel County

Open: Year Round

Dockage: Yes

Latitude: N 39° 2' 56"

Longitude: W 76° 27' 38"

Body of Water: Deep Creek
 off the Magothy River

Driving Distance:
 Baltimore 27 miles
 Washington, DC 40 miles
 Easton 41 miles

Atmosphere Meter

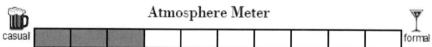

casual   formal

From the first bite of crab bruschetta, you'll know that you stumbled upon a special Chesapeake gem at Deep Creek Restaurant. On a bed of greens, toasted Italian bread slices cradle garden-fresh diced tomatoes and basil with chunks of delicate crab meat mounted on top. The bruschetta — like every other dish cooked in this kitchen — shows Deep Creek cares about details and high-quality ingredients.

The menu features award-winning seafood such as the famous crab cakes, oyster stew, and steamed sampler of local shrimp, clams, and mussels. Jambalaya, crab pizza, salmon strudel, and fried oysters are simply delicious. The cooks accommodate meaty preferences with pulled pork BBQ, chicken piccata, steaks, classic Cuban sandwiches, and burgers with crispy fried onion strings.

Family-owned since 1999, the cozy restaurant has two levels, and the lower tier offers access to an outdoor deck. The place is tucked away in a small marina just off the Magothy River where time seems to stand still on lazy summer afternoons. The waterfront view shows boats sailing by and children at the dock using chicken necks on a string to pull indignant crabs from the water.

Sunsets are superb. When the day is over, tiki torches are lit, a band begins to play, and cold beer is served on the festive deck by the water. It doesn't get much better than this.

Jimmy Cantler's Riverside Inn

458 Forest Beach Road
Annapolis, MD 21409
(410) 757-1311
www.cantlers.com

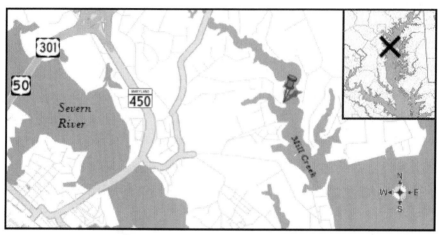

County: Anne Arundel County
Open: Year Round ⚓ Dockage: Yes
Latitude: N 39° 0' 11" ><>< Longitude: W 76° 27' 29"
Body of Water: Mill Creek off Whitehall Bay
Driving Distance: Baltimore 33 miles
Washington, DC 37 miles, Easton 40 miles

Atmosphere Meter

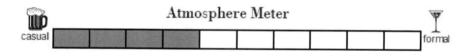

casual   formal

When you drive into Cantler's parking lot and come
face-to-face with a giant Maryland blue crab painted on the
side of a propane tank, think of it as a charming welcome
committee of one. Then take a deep breath and let your
nostrils fill with that unmistakable crab deck smell — the zing
of Old Bay mixed with briny air and crabs steaming. The

rhythmic sound of wooden hammers crushing crabs makes your stomach rumble with anticipation. The deck bustles with a mixed bag of families, watermen, and businessmen savoring the view. With old oak trees holding down the banks and sailboats dutifully pointing their masts toward the sky, the scene is idyllic. Once seated at a picnic table, you see plump crabs piled high on black plastic trays. Cocktail sauce is squeezed out of 12-inch tall plastic bottles to spice up mountains of shrimp. Men push back Ravens caps to get a better view of golf ball-sized steamed clams.

At Cantler's, don't miss a rare Bay treat. Walk down the back steps and peek into the large metal tanks by the docks. These are crab shed tanks. When watermen arrive with crabs ready to molt (shed their shell), they sequester their catch in tanks filled with water. The staff watches for clues that molting is near and transfers those crabs into a shedding tank. They check the tanks several times a day for crabs that have outgrown their shells and place them in yet another tank. Why all the fuss? Hard-shell crabs are aggressive and devour anything in sight, but molting makes soft-shell crabs more docile. Like medieval knights without armor, newly molted crabs hide in the Bay's marshlands, laying low until new shells harden. Tanks lack hiding places, so humans need to protect them — until they're ready to eat them. Not every crab house runs shed tanks, but after five generations in the seafood biz, Cantler's remains committed to the Bay's best traditions.

Severn Inn

1993 Baltimore Annapolis Boulevard
Annapolis, MD 21409
(410) 349-4000
www.severninn.com

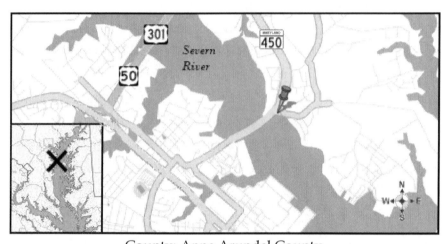

County: Anne Arundel County
Open: Year Round ⚓ Dockage: Yes
Latitude: N 38° 59' 42" ➤ Longitude: W 76° 28' 59"
Body of Water: Severn River
Driving Distance: Baltimore 32 miles
Washington, DC 36 miles, Easton 40 miles

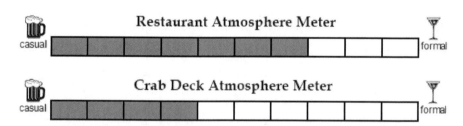

The view is so lovely at Severn Inn that it's tempting to spend all day on its waterfront decks watching boats sail by. Your eyes can't resist following the graceful lines of the bridge spanning the Severn River. Across the water is a panoramic view of historic Annapolis and the U.S. Naval Academy that's been training officers to protect our shores since 1845. Inside the restaurant, the atmosphere is a bit upscale, yet still warm and inviting. Cherry wood chairs surround tables covered with white linens, and floor-to-ceiling windows ensure everyone gets a stellar view of the water. Vintage oyster cans are piled high on top of the bar to salute the history of the Bay. It's got two decks: One hugs the building and the other juts out into the water among the boats.

The menu is seafood-centric, fresh, and takes Chesapeake cuisine up a notch with innovative twists from around the region. The lunch and pub menus offer soups, salads, sandwiches, crab cakes, local oysters, fish tacos, and shrimp. The kitchen pulls out all the stops at dinner with daily specials such as seafood paella, tender scallops, aged steaks, sesame seared Hawaiian yellowfin tuna, Virginia littleneck clams, crab tempura rolls, and grilled mahi mahi.

If you want one last glance at the river before you head home, walk next door to Jonas Green Park (named after a printer who was Ben Franklin's cousin) to check out its beach for boat launching and wooden pier for fishing.

Armadillo's Bar & Grill

132 Dock Street
Annapolis, MD 21401
(410) 280-0028
www.armadillosannapolis.com

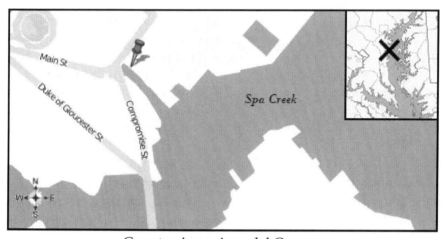

County: Anne Arundel County
Open: Year Round ⚓ Dockage: No
Latitude: N 38° 58' 40" Longitude: W 76° 29' 11"
Body of Water: Annapolis Harbor off Spa Creek off the Severn River
Driving Distance: Baltimore 31 miles
Washington, DC 35 miles, Easton 42 miles

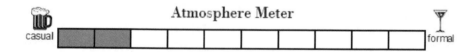

With all the fantastic restaurants in downtown Annapolis dishing out food that can pack on the pounds, it's good to find a place where you can dance off calories. The go-to spot for music at the City Dock is Armadillo's. Through the doors of this two-story brick building you can hear rock, jazz, blues, funk, and more. Bands generally play on the second floor, which also offers a tremendous view of the water.

For 30 years, Armadillo's has entertained locals, tourists, watermen, and sailors. Its low-key atmosphere creates an easy-going venue for unwinding. Photos honoring Navy ships and seamen hang on the old brick walls. Black wooden booths are brightened by purple seat cushions. A few tables are placed outdoors during warm weather.

Full service bars on both floors accommodate thirsty patrons with specialty drinks such as fresh mojitos and orange crushes. The beer selection is extensive, but you won't be surprised to see folks knocking back a few Natty Bohs with chilled Jell-O shooters.

The kitchen is open every night until 11:00 churning out plates of classic American fare. It's decent pub food at reasonable prices. Standouts: Blue Crab Nachos with waffle-cut potatoes, Old Bay, and cheese sauce, and baked flatbreads with your choice of crab, ham, BBQ chicken, salami, or mozzarella toppings. The Midshipmen Bites are a tasty snack with beef tips, garlic toast, and horseradish dipping sauce. Salads, burgers, and sandwiches are filling and fresh.

Dock Street Bar & Grill

136 Dock Street
Annapolis, MD 21401
(410) 268-7278
www.dockstreetbar.net

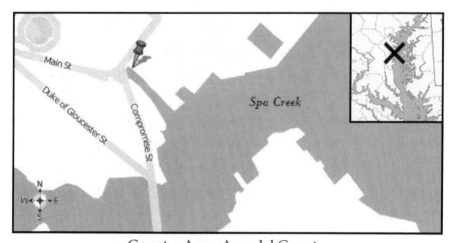

County: Anne Arundel County
Open: Year Round ⚓ Dockage: No
Latitude: N 38° 58' 40" 🐟 Longitude: W 76° 29' 11"
Body of Water: Annapolis Harbor off Spa Creek off the Severn River
Driving Distance: Baltimore 31 miles
Washington, DC 35 miles, Easton 42 miles

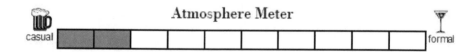

Atmosphere Meter

casual | | | | | | | | | | formal

Sometimes big things come in small packages. That's the case with Dock Street Bar. Its home is one of the many narrow row houses that have survived here for centuries. Once you step inside this historic red brick building, you almost want to duck your head to avoid hitting its low ceiling. But as you look around and take note of details such as the lovely old stonework and curved wooden bar, you realize that you have discovered a tiny treasure along the Bay.

The menu covers all the Bay basics with crab dip, wings, salads, pizzas, sandwiches, quesadillas, burgers, and steaks. But what's big about this place is the flavor of its crab cakes. Some claim they're the best in town. They do taste exceptionally fresh, are made of jumbo lump crab with only a pinch of filler. Shrimp are steamed with sweet onions and Old Bay seasoning, and the grilled tuna sandwich with wasabi aioli is delightful. Crab chowder is laced with corn and clams. All this well-prepared food at reasonable prices won't put a huge dent in your wallet.

Another huge draw at Dock Street is the service. Whether you're just grabbing a quick beer at the bar or bringing a large party for dinner, the staff is eager to please.

If you need a little more elbow room, you can try to snag one of the few tables outdoors when the weather cooperates. And once you've had your fill, go two doors down to the old-fashioned ice cream store. A cone in hand on a summer day is a lovely way to stroll around and explore the quaint cobblestone streets of Annapolis.

Middleton Tavern

2 Market Space
Annapolis, MD 21401
(410) 263-3323
www.middletontavern.com

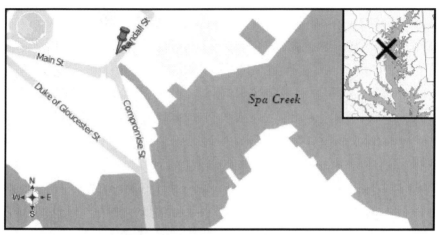

County: Anne Arundel County
Open: Year Round ⚓ Dockage: No
Latitude: N 38° 58' 41" ⟶ Longitude: W 76° 29' 12"
Body of Water: Annapolis Harbor off Spa Creek off the Severn River
Driving Distance: Baltimore 31 miles
Washington, DC 35 miles, Easton 42 miles

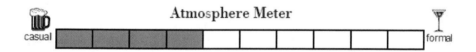

If you want to eat authentic Bay cuisine in a 250-year old
building, Middleton Tavern is the place for you. Established
in 1750, this red Georgian-style building is located at the
City Dock among a row of historic watering holes once
frequented by the likes of George Washington, Thomas
Jefferson, and Ben Franklin. In the mid-1700s, the owner ran

a ferry to the Eastern Shore and managed his shipbuilding business from inside the tavern. In tribute, early American artifacts adorn the restaurant walls, where you see portraits of Revolutionary War heroes, Civil War muskets, and antique Naval Academy uniforms. Seats near an old wood and brick fireplace warm up winter visitors.

At the recently remodeled bar, you can order an array of light fare such as oyster or shrimp shooters, smoked bluefish, or a bucket of mussels. Traditional Chesapeake cooking dominates the dinner menu with seafood steam pots, oyster loaf po' boys, stuffed filet of sole, crab cakes, and "naked" fish prepared just the way you like it. Seafood Tower for Two erects layers of calamari, oysters, clams, shrimp, and scallops. Meat lovers can choose pork tenderloin, steaks, or burgers.

During balmy weather, the best seats in the house are outside on the covered deck, where you can gaze at the water and imagine how much Annapolis has changed since this tavern was built. Hotels, shops and upscale restaurants have replaced the oyster-packing plants and shipbuilding companies, but this vibrant town along the Bay has retained its historic charm.

McGarvey's Saloon & Oyster Bar

8 Market Space
Annapolis, MD 21401
(410) 263-5700
www.mcgarveys.net

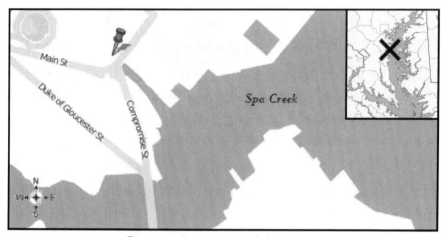

County: Anne Arundel County
Open: Year Round ⚓ Dockage: No
Latitude: N 38° 58' 42" ⊸ Longitude: W 76° 29' 13"
Body of Water: Annapolis Harbor off Spa Creek off the Severn River
Driving Distance: Baltimore 31 miles
Washington, DC 35 miles, Easton 42 miles

Atmosphere Meter

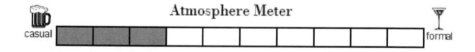

casual | formal

A turn-of-the-century saloon in Annapolis can conjure up images of rugged sea captains, industrious shipbuilders, and lusty businessmen puffing on cigars and clinking frothy mugs of beer. Built in 1871, McGarvey's pays tribute to the city's past with vintage lamps above the tables, stained glass behind the liquor bottles, and nautical artwork on dark brick walls.

A column of the bar posts plaques engraved with names of couples who met here and eventually got married. In 1975, a pilot and sailor named Mike Ashford took over the place, adding his love for flying to the décor. In the dining area, a large model airplane soars through a massive 75-year old ficus tree, and aviator helmets line up above the bar. The place is named for Anna McGarvey, his grandmother.

At the raw bar near the back stand shuckers, who are dedicated to opening up the region's best bivalves by the order. While you watch them work, you can sip on the house brew, Aviator Lager, or sample one of the 50+ American craft beers available on tap.

At this Annapolis institution, you'll find a cheerful crowd eating good food at reasonable prices. One of the most popular choices is the Waterman's Seafood Sampler, an overflowing platter of clams, shrimp, mussels, and oysters.

For light fare, the crab dip is outstanding, as are the crab balls, fried calamari, and Oysters Rockefeller. Shrimp salad and grilled bratwurst are standouts among the sandwiches. McGarvey's also accommodates patrons who want more than seafood. Tender roast beef is piled high in the French Dip Au Jus, filet mignon is grilled just the way you like, and burgers are made with fresh ground sirloin.

The Federal House Bar & Grille

22 Market Space
Annapolis, MD 21401
(410) 268-2576
www.federalhouserestaurant.com

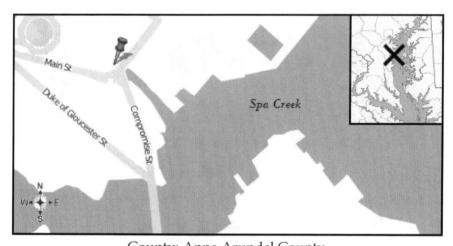

County: Anne Arundel County
Open: Year Round ⚓ Dockage: No
Latitude: N 38° 58' 41" ✈ Longitude: W 76° 29' 15"
Body of Water: Annapolis Harbor off Spa Creek off the Severn River
Driving Distance: Baltimore 31 miles
Washington, DC 35 miles, Easton 42 miles

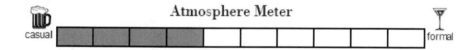

Atmosphere Meter

casual   formal

    Federal House's building has had almost as many lives as
a cat. Dating back to the 1700s, this historic site was a brothel,
a general store, and three separate row houses until the
dividing walls came down to make one lovely space. Two
bare-chested statues that are part eagle and part lion remain
from when it was home to a popular watering hole called

Griffins. Architectural souvenirs from past lives add to the restaurant's charm: gorgeous wooden pillars behind the bar, rich red brick walls, vintage stained glass, black-and-white checkerboard marble floors, and a pressed-tin ceiling.

A treasure trove of antique fixtures under one roof could create a stuffy environment — but that's not the case with Federal House. Instead it's got a good neighborhood bar feeling led by a warm and welcoming staff. Music on weekends attracts a lively crowd.

The beer menu starts with the usual suspects: Bud, Heineken, Coors. Then it takes you on a brewer's journey around the country with "Crafty Characters" such as 400 Pound Monkey from Colorado, Sweet Baby Jesus from Maryland, and Angry Orchard from Boston. Maryland brews are well represented on the list.

American cuisine drives the dining selections with a heavy hand for fresh seafood. The raw bar showcases local oysters, mussels, and shrimp. Cream of crab soup, smoked candy salmon salad, and coconut shrimp are enjoyable starters. House specialties: crab cakes, Sea Bass Annapolitan topped with crab imperial and asparagus, fish tacos, and Seafood Symphony that creates harmony among scallops, shrimp, lump crab, and Old Bay.

Factors Row

26 Market Space
Annapolis, MD 21401
(410) 280-8686
www.factorsrowannapolis.com

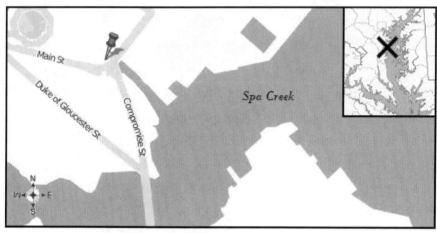

County: Anne Arundel County
Open: Year Round ⚓ Dockage: No
Latitude: N 38° 58' 41" Longitude: W 76° 29' 15"
Body of Water: Annapolis Harbor off Spa Creek off the Severn River
Driving Distance: Baltimore 31 miles
Washington, DC 35 miles, Easton 42 miles

Atmosphere Meter

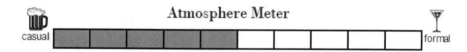

casual   formal

When Factors Row opened in 2013, it had the distinction of being the newest restaurant in the oldest building on the City Dock. After the former occupant (Riordan's) closed in 2007, the space sat vacant, quietly holding on to history that dates back centuries. Built in 1771 by the architect who designed the Maryland State House and St. Anne's Church, it was part of a large mercantile trading warehouse complex. "Factors" were agents of shipping companies that arranged for Colonial tobacco, timber, cotton, and other products to be sent to England in exchange for British goods. In 1883, a fire destroyed most of the buildings, but this site was rebuilt using bricks salvaged from the blaze.

The newly renovated restaurant gracefully integrates antique features into its design. Two hand-hewn wooden beams and exposed brick from the original structure are part of the décor. And they uncovered a wall of ballast stones that were used at the bottom of ships to keep them balanced while they were empty and waiting at port to get filled.

Once you're done absorbing the building's history and restoration, it's time to sit down for a good meal. The menu is fresh and creative, blending new with familiar ingredients of regional Bay cuisine. For starters, you can a sample long list of local oysters, as well as crab and potato soup, duck fat popcorn, steamed mussels, and grilled lamb sliders. Dinner highlights: double crab cakes, shrimp and grits, BBQ pork mac and cheese, and pan-seared rockfish. The crispy oyster sandwich with citrus caper aioli is outstanding.

Buddy's Crabs & Ribs

100 Main Street
Annapolis, MD 21401
(410) 626-1100
www.buddysonline.com

County: Anne Arundel County
Open: Year Round ⚓ Dockage: No
Latitude: N 38° 58' 39" ➤ Longitude: W 76° 29' 16"
Body of Water: Annapolis Harbor off Spa Creek off the Severn River
Driving Distance: Baltimore 31 miles
Washington, DC 35 miles, Easton 42 miles

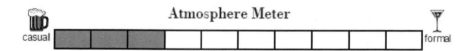

Atmosphere Meter

casual | | | | | | | | | | formal

Of all the restaurants along the City Dock, Buddy's is by far the crabbiest. And in this neck of the Bay, that's a real compliment. Family-owned since 1988, it's a landmark in town with just a few tables and a street sign out front. But once you climb the stairs to the second floor, you reach the Mount Olympus of crab-eaters' heaven.

The restaurant is the largest eatery in Annapolis. Rows of wooden tables are piled high with steamed crabs and baby back ribs. Tall windows offer a bird's eye view of the harbor. Thirsty boaters, locals, and tourists mingle at the bar. Chrome buffet tables give a steamy preview of the all-you-can-eat seafood experience.

The raw bar offers oysters harvested from the Chesapeake Bay and other East Coast hot spots. Buddy's starters include cheesy crab dip, king crab legs, clam strips, steamed shrimp, Cajun crawfish, and fried green tomatoes. Salads blend mixed greens with crab or shrimp sprinkled on top. The sandwiches and baskets feature ahi tuna steaks, rockfish, fish and chips, crab cakes, burgers, and chicken.

Some entrees are only meant for those with a Titan's appetite, namely the steamed blue crab feast or the "Big Big Buddy," a one-pound monster-sized crab cake. Regular mortals can have their fill of local seafood or combo platters with BBQ ribs. Children under 10 eat for free if adults order an entree, and a neon sign promises ice cream and crabs for dessert. It's the perfect combo from a place that aims to please crab eaters of every shape and size.

Pusser's Caribbean Grille

80 Compromise Street
Annapolis, MD 21401
(410) 626-0004
www.pussersusa.com

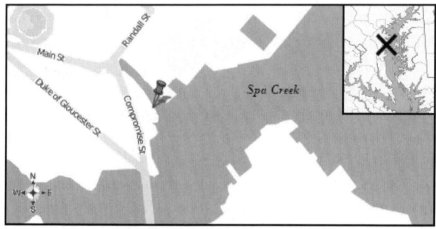

County: Anne Arundel County
Open: Year Round ⚓ Dockage: No
Latitude: N 38° 58' 34" ⚓ Longitude: W 76° 29' 7"
Body of Water: Annapolis Harbor off Spa Creek off the Severn River
Driving Distance: Baltimore 31 miles
Washington, DC 35 miles, Easton 42 miles

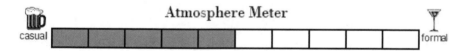

Even though America booted England from our shores
during the War of 1812, a taste of the Colonial Era remains
at Pusser's Caribbean Grille. This expansive British pub is
named after the 350-year old premium rum that fueled the
British Royal Navy. From 1655 until 1970, every British sailor
was allotted a daily ration of rum. Pusser is the corrupted

version of the word "purser," who was the navy officer in charge of doling out that precious amber liquid to the men. This maritime tradition continues at Pusser's with signature cocktails like the infamous Painkiller, Dark & Stormy, Annapolis Sunset, and Jamaican Me Crazy.

The long dockside restaurant belongs to the Marriott Hotel and claims to occupy the most waterfront real estate in downtown Annapolis. Inside you encounter a wooden lady figurehead in 18th century attire who silently ignores advances from sailors at the bar. Nautical artwork hangs on the walls, and white lights twinkle near the ceiling. A retail store on site sells apparel, spices, and seaside souvenirs.

Pusser's music combines acoustic with calypso, while the cuisine marries the Chesapeake with the Caribbean. Crab dip, coconut rum shrimp, fried calamari, and jerk chicken pineapple quesadillas are served as appetizers. Special entrees include crab cakes based on an 1890s recipe, Olde English fish and chips, bacon-wrapped shrimp skewers, and Jamaican jerk tuna. Pasta, chicken, and steaks accommodate meat lovers. On weekends and summer evenings, the outdoor deck can get crowded and parking can be tricky, but it's still a great place to soak up some island fun.

Blackwall Hitch

400 Sixth Street
Annapolis, MD 21403
(410) 263-3454
www.theblackwallhitch.com

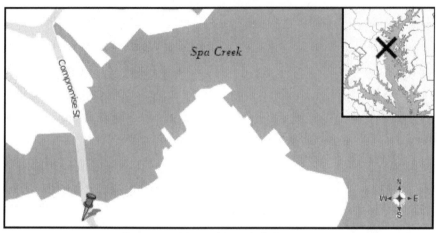

County: Anne Arundel County
Open: Year Round ⚓ Dockage: No
Latitude: N 38° 58' 13" ➤ Longitude: W 76° 29' 5"
Body of Water: Spa Creek off the Severn River
Driving Distance: Baltimore 31 miles
Washington, DC 35 miles, Easton 43 miles

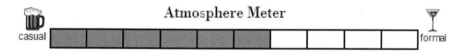

Atmosphere Meter

casual / formal

Blackwall Hitch might not roll off the tongue easily, and it might sound more like a law firm than a fine dining establishment. But the owners picked this name, because it captures the essence of the new restaurant's theme. In the 1800s, London's Blackwall Port was a springboard for immigrants and wares heading to the Chesapeake area.

Docking ships wasn't easy in the Bay's turbulent waters, so shipmates devised the unique "Blackwall hitch knot" to make ropes draw tighter as vessels rose and fell with the tide.

The connection to Bay maritime history plays out in this spacious and beautiful restaurant. The contemporary décor highlights details such as a captain's steering wheel, vintage suitcases, wooden sailboat replicas, paintings of ship knots, and other nautical items throughout the bar and dining rooms. On the roof deck, you're treated to a view of masts bobbing in the harbor, with the capital dome, Naval Academy, and St. Anne's Church steeple in the background.

The food is as exceptional as the surroundings: fresh and innovative, elevating Bay seafood above standard fare. The first attraction is an enticing oyster bar that features local bivalves and shrimp and crab ceviche. Main courses follow suit with specialties such as rockfish topped with jumbo lump crab, mahi mahi tacos, and crab cakes with roasted corn salsa and remoulade. Steaks, prime rib, herbed chicken, and pork chops are char-grilled heaven. Pizzas, pasta, and salads complete the extensive menu selections.

Boatyard Bar & Grill

400 Fourth Street
Annapolis, MD 21403
(410) 216-6206
www.boatyardbarandgrill.com

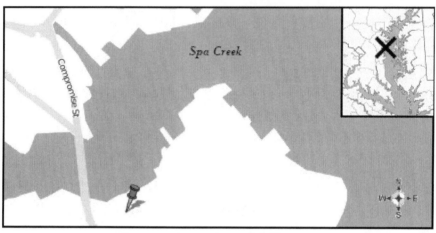

County: Anne Arundel County
Open: Year Round ⚓ Dockage: No
Latitude: N 38° 58' 17" ⤜ Longitude: W 76° 28' 57"
Body of Water: Spa Creek off the Severn River
Driving Distance: Baltimore 31 miles
Washington, DC 35 miles, Easton 43 miles

Atmosphere Meter

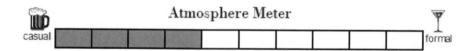

casual | formal

Boatyard isn't directly on the water, but it's all about the water, so we bent the rules to include it in this book. Besides, it's just a block away from Spa Creek and Annapolis City Marina. Once you come inside, you see this restaurant is a happy home for sailors, watermen, and fans of the

Chesapeake. The atmosphere is festive, alive with stories about the fish that got away or the boat that outraced the rest.

Founded in 2001, Boatyard's walls are covered with mounted trophy fish, framed pictures of sailboats, and nautical posters that celebrate life on the Bay. Skates and fish hang from the dining room ceiling. The bar is shaped like a ship's hull with curved lines and a polished wood trim.

Boatyard is open for breakfast, lunch, dinner, and brunch on weekends. The open kitchen is in a state of constant motion, and signs above the raw bar's ice-packed cases announce the daily catch. Expect only the freshest local seafood to appear on your plate. The raw bar offers oysters, clams, shrimp, and mussels. The menu favors local seafood with a nod to the Seven Seas. Specialties include Key West steamed shrimp, crab cakes, conch fritters, fried oysters, and jerk chicken. The Titanic Salad is a wedge of iceberg lettuce drizzled with bleu cheese dressing. Coconut shrimp and oyster fritters are crispy bites of pleasure. Burgers, chicken, steaks, and Cuban roast pork sandwiches are delish. The kid's menu with paper and crayons welcomes everyone aboard.

Carrol's Creek
Waterfront Restaurant

410 Severn Avenue
Annapolis, MD 21403
(410) 263-8102
www.carrolscreek.com

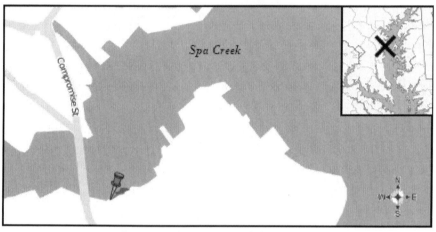

County: Anne Arundel County
Open: Year Round ⚓ Dockage: No
Latitude: N 38° 58' 19" ⤜ Longitude: W 76° 29' 2"
Body of Water: Spa Creek off the Severn River
Driving Distance: Baltimore 31 miles
Washington, DC 35 miles, Easton 43 miles

Atmosphere Meter

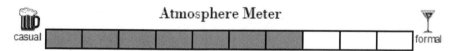

casual ─────────────────────────── formal

You're in for a triple-crown experience when you visit
Carrol's Creek in Eastport — terrific food, an amazing view,
and history dating back to the 1700s. Built in 1983, the dining
area is casual-nice with an open airy feel. Nautical artwork
brings a splash of color to tables covered with white linens.

The menu features fresh seafood with innovative twists. House specialty Oysters Carrol's Creek are pulled from the Bay and then baked with horseradish, bacon, and cheddar. Fresh tuna tartare and pepper-crusted beef carpaccio whet your appetite for the main dishes. Must-try entrees include jumbo lump crab cakes, herbed rockfish, almond-crusted mahi mahi, and pan-seared scallops. Grilled steaks and sautéed chicken breasts are meaty delights. Sandwiches, salads, and burgers provide casual fare.

On the deck, the view keeps everyone busy while waiting for their meal. An armada of boats drifts along Spa Creek, almost close enough to touch. The Eastport neighborhood has played key roles in American history. Spa Creek was originally called Carrol's Creek, named after Charles Carroll — one of Maryland's sons who signed the Declaration of Independence. During the Revolutionary War, Lafayette's troops camped nearby while en route to defeat the British in Yorktown. Decades later, this was the site of Fort Horn, which protected Annapolis during the War of 1812. From around 1913 to 1974, Eastport hummed with the sounds of wooden boatbuilding. Companies like John Trumpy & Sons crafted high-end yachts with the famous "Golden T" on the bow, and Chance Marine Construction build sub-chasers and PT boats for the U.S. Navy during World War II.

O'Learys Seafood Restaurant

310 Third Street
Annapolis, MD 21403
(410) 263-0884
www.olearysseafood.com

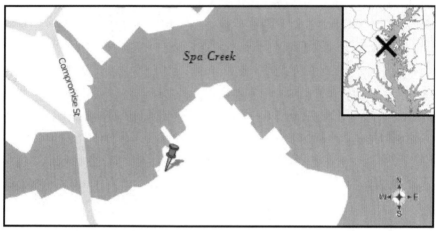

County: Anne Arundel County
Open: Year Round ⚓ Dockage: No
Latitude: N 38° 58' 21" ⟫ Longitude: W 76° 28' 55"
Body of Water: Spa Creek off the Severn River
Driving Distance: Baltimore 31 miles
Washington, DC 35 miles, Easton 43 miles

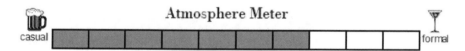

Atmosphere Meter
casual · formal

O'Learys might a little outside of the City Dock buzz, but it's big in commitment to fresh seafood — today and for future generations. Protecting the marine environment is paramount for the chef, who evaluates species, fisheries, and methods of harvest before ingredients appear on his plates. As a result, your conscience is clear to enjoy a fine-dining experience with robust dishes that are prepared in a creative and responsible fashion. O'Learys opened in 1998.

Just for fun, kick off the evening with craft cocktails: hibiscus pomegranate martini, The Bee's Knees, or The Bronx will do nicely. Then move to starters such as sea scallops encased in phyllo pastry, freshly shucked oysters from Virginia, grilled shrimp, or squid stuffed with Italian sausage. Entrees run the gamut from classic Chesapeake crab cakes to whole rockfish provincial and a zarzuela fish stew laden with lobster, shrimp, and other fruits of the sea. Seafood alfredo is a plate of creamy happiness with crab, shrimp, and scallops. Filet mignon, pork tenderloin gorgonzola, and pan-seared duck breast are available for carnivores at the table.

The waterfront view is limited but O'Learys atmosphere reflects the spirit of Annapolis — warm, sophisticated, and welcoming. Soft, mustard-colored walls are covered with vibrant abstract artwork painted by the owner himself. Behind the wooden bar is an exhaustive collection of fine wines from California, France, and around the globe. Put it all together, and you get a special hidden gem at the Bay.

Chart House Restaurant

300 Second Street
Annapolis, MD 21403
(410) 268-7166
www.chart-house.com

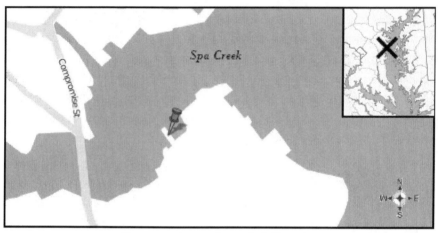

County: Anne Arundel County
Open: Year Round ⚓ Dockage: No
Latitude: N 38° 58' 26" ⋈ Longitude: W 76° 28' 54"
Body of Water: Spa Creek off the Severn River
Driving Distance: Baltimore 31 miles
Washington, DC 35 miles, Easton 43 miles

Atmosphere Meter

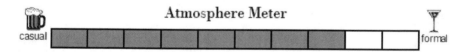

casual — formal

It's only fair to warn you right away that Chart House is part of a chain owned by Landry's Restaurants, with locations from Malibu to Miami specializing in seafood. The paradox is it doesn't feel like a chain. In fact, it is lovely and recently underwent major renovations. Dining rooms now sport a contemporary look with chic blue tones and black highlights in the dining rooms. Two new fireplaces warm guests in the winter, and the view of Spa Creek with the capital dome in the distance remains spectacular. They even restored their collection of framed boat hulls, skipjack paintings, and nautical artwork to underscore the area's maritime traditions.

Chart House is located in an historic boathouse, which was the main shipyard for John Trumpy & Sons. In the early 1900s, Trumpy designed deluxe yachts for clients such as the Du Pont, Gugenheim, and Chrysler families. The famous presidential yacht, *Sequoia,* was also his creation.

The menu's daily catch masters all the Bay standards of crab, shrimp, oysters, and rockfish. Noteworthy appetizers include hot crab dip, sautéed PEI mussels, and lobster and shrimp eggrolls in delicate rice paper. Signature fish dishes: Snapper Hemingway with parmesan crust, flounder stuffed with crab meat, and crab cakes served with avocado corn relish and silky orzo.

They also added turf to the surf with prime rib, steaks, and chicken. Decadent desserts, such as Hot Chocolate Lava Cake with a molten center made of Godiva chocolate liqueur, are big enough to share. And they add a sweet final touch to a pleasant meal along the water.

Wild Country Seafood

124 Bay Shore Avenue
Annapolis, MD 21403
(410) 267-6711
www.wildcountryseafood.com

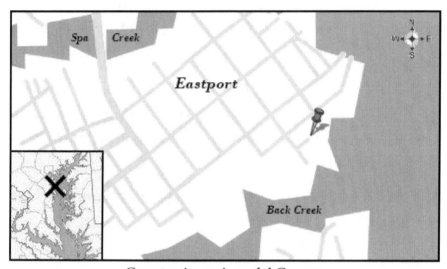

County: Anne Arundel County
Open: Seasonal ⚓ Dockage: No
Latitude: N 38° 58' 11" ➤ Longitude: W 76° 28' 35"
Body of Water: Back Creek off the Severn River
Driving Distance: Baltimore 31 miles
Washington, DC 35 miles, Easton 43 miles

Atmosphere Meter

casual | | | | | | | | | formal

Pat Mahoney owns Wild Country Seafood, and he's been trot-lining for crabs since he was 14. His father was a waterman for 40 years, and Pat wants to preserve this tradition for future generations. His boats, *The Baby Boy* and *Wild Country*, are the last commercial ships to work out of

Eastport. Every morning they hit the Bay and bring the catch to the eatery, which has a classic crab shack feel. It's an old-school fish market, so you can get orders to go or eat outside at umbrella-covered picnic tables and enjoy the view. Fresh seafood party platters will be a big hit at your next event.

The menu is a tally sheet of the best seasonal seafood: steamed crabs, crab cakes, soft-shells, rockfish bites, oysters, jumbo shrimp, clam strips, and calamari. Chicken tenders please the kids. Platters are fried and come with cole slaw and fries. Even though meals are served in Styrofoam containers, it's hard to find fresher seafood anywhere.

After you've tasted the Bay's bounty, you can walk next door and learn more about it at the Annapolis Maritime Museum. Its exhibits showcase the local oyster industry, boats, and maritime heritage. On site is McNasby's Oyster Company, the last packing plant in the area. Hands-on learning happens on the land and sea at this interactive center for Bay traditions. The museum plays an important role in the community with a winter lecture series and summer concerts. Best of all: Don't miss the annual Oyster Roast and Sock Burning to celebrate the beginning of spring and prepare everyone for flip-flop season.

Davis' Pub

400 Chester Avenue
Annapolis, MD 21403
(410) 268-7432
www.davispub.com

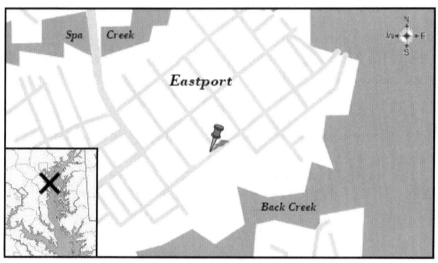

County: Anne Arundel County
Open: Year Round ⚓ Dockage: Yes
Latitude: N 38° 58' 9" 🛥 Longitude: W 76° 28' 49"
Body of Water: Back Creek
Driving Distance: Baltimore 31 miles
Washington, DC 35 miles, Easton 43 miles

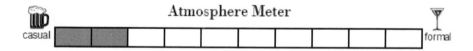

Atmosphere Meter
casual   formal

The sign in the front window says, "Davis' Pub — Where there are no strangers, only friends you haven't met." It's the perfect greeting for a place that makes you feel at home the moment you walk through the door. This local watering hole has been an essential part of the Eastport neighborhood for decades. In the 1920s, it served as a general store, and by the 1940s, watermen chose it as their hangout. Today it's a favorite corner bar for families, friends, and newcomers.

Inside the cozy one-story building, chalkboards announce the daily specials, waitresses wear T-shirts and jeans, and a few flat-screen TVs play Orioles and Nationals games in separate corners of the bar. The atmosphere is friendly and laid back. The covered patio affords the simple pleasure of watching life unfold in this historic waterfront community. The food is standard pub fare — cooked well and served with a smile. Crabs dominate the menu with crab dip, pretzels, soup, and sandwiches. Baltimore-style steamed shrimp are smothered in onions and served with Old Bay and butter. Meat lovers dive into steaks, burgers, and pulled pork.

Once you've had your fill, take a stroll around the quaint streets of Eastport. It used to be an independent town but was annexed by Annapolis in 1951. Residents in the two towns peacefully co-existed until the 1990s when Annapolis officials closed Spa Creek Bridge for repairs and cut off Eastport from the rest of the city. The slighted citizens declared war against Annapolis and created the Maritime Republic of Eastport. The issue was amicable resolved by a tug of war between the towns and is celebrated annually with a festival.

Sam's on the Waterfront

2020 Chesapeake Harbour Drive East
Annapolis, MD 21403
(410) 263-3600
www.samsonthewaterfront.com

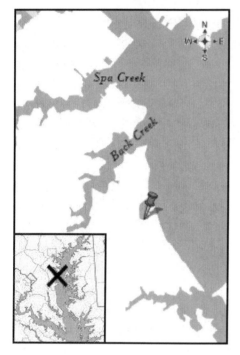

County: Anne Arundel County

Open: Year Round

Dockage: Yes

Latitude: N 38° 57' 27"

Longitude: W 76° 28' 27"

Body of Water: Chesapeake
Harbour

Driving Distance:
Baltimore 33 miles
Washington, DC 36 miles
Easton 47 miles

 Atmosphere Meter

casual ▢▢▢▢▢▢▢▢▢▢ formal

Back in the mid-1800s, screw-pile lighthouses dotted the coastline of the Chesapeake. Their spider-leg design with iron pikes drilled into the soft sand or muddy sea bottoms were ideal for the region. Cottages within the structures housed lighthouse keepers who lived in isolation through scorching summer heat and harsh winter winds.

Only a few of these lighthouses survived the past century, so in 1986 the owners of Sam's on the Waterfront built their restaurant to look like a screw-pile lighthouse as a tribute to Chesapeake maritime history. It's nestled along the waterfront of a new residential development. Cobalt blue wine glasses and white linen tablecloths create an elegant romantic setting. Live music on weekends elevates the atmosphere, and Sunday brunch is memorable.

The chef uses fresh seafood and ingredients bought from local Maryland farmers to create a modern American cuisine with regional influence. For starters, the menu presents a classic cream of crab soup, as well as Cajun BBQ shrimp, Oysters Rockefeller, mussels sautéed in a white wine sauce, and crab and artichoke fondue. Traditional entrees like rockfish and jumbo lump crab cakes share the spotlight with fried oysters and grits, rosemary chicken, Maine lobster roll, pesto seafood fettuccini, and espresso-rubbed rib eye steak.

If you're in the mood for an after-dinner cocktail or a cool chardonnay, stop at Proud Mary's Dock Bar near the water and watch boats parade upon the waves.

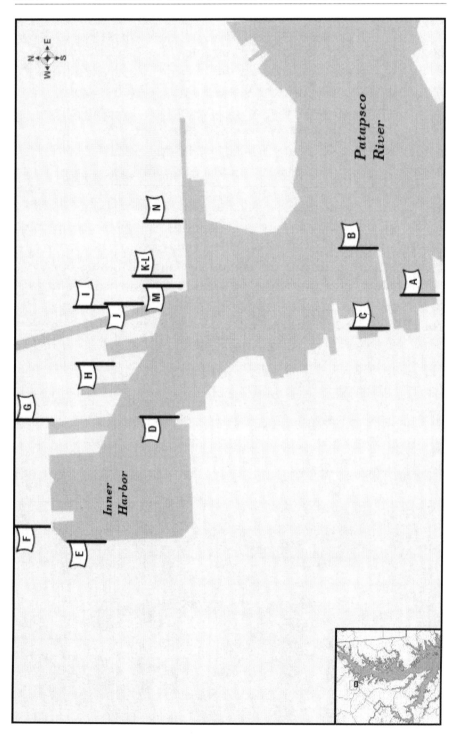

Baltimore Inner Harbor & Harbor East

Little Havana
Restaurante y Cantina Cubana

1325 Key Highway
Baltimore, MD 21230
(410) 837-9903
www.littlehavanas.com

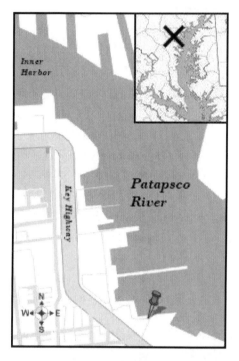

Location: Baltimore City

Open: Year Round

Dockage: No

Latitude: N 39° 16' 29"

Longitude: W 76° 36' 11"

Body of Water: Inner Harbor
off the Patapsco River

Driving Distance:
Annapolis 31 miles,
Washington, DC 42 miles,
Easton 61 miles

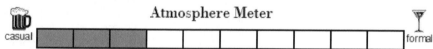

Atmosphere Meter

casual | | | | | | | | | | formal

Around the Bay, people plant palm trees and hang tiki masks to give their restaurants a general tropical feel, but for 15 years, Little Havana has tried to transport you to the island of Cuba. The rustic building looks like the type of cantina where rebels would have plotted to topple the dictator Batista.

The tall chain link fence around the deck almost makes the Baltimore Inner Harbor look like Miami in the distance. A huge picture of Fidel Castro smoking a fat cigar hangs above the hostess station.

Inside, the bar is covered with a pressed tin roof, and exposed brick walls are painted with murals depicting Cuba's history and culture. Hand-drawn wooden signs and vintage metal furniture give the place a unique retro feel, and the pool table and shuffleboard add to the energetic vibe.

The fusion of Spanish, African, and Caribbean flavors that influence Cuban cuisine blend well with seafood from the Bay. Crab cakes with remoulade sauce come on a Cuban roll, and blackened fish sliders arrive with sweet potato fries. Shrimp quesadillas have salsa on the side, and Key West fish tacos take your taste buds on an island vacation. Mariscada simmers shrimp, fish, calamari, clams, and mussels in saffron sauce. The famous Cuban sandwich takes center stage with ham, pulled pork, swiss cheese, and a tart pickle. Meat lovers can also indulge in savory dishes such as marinated pork bites with cilantro lime sauce, Jamaican jerk wings, and grilled rib eye steaks with black beans. Specialty drinks with a tropical flare include mojitos, sangria and rum runners.

Tiki Barge

500 Harborview Drive
Baltimore, MD 21230
(410) 246-6501
www.tikibargebmore.com

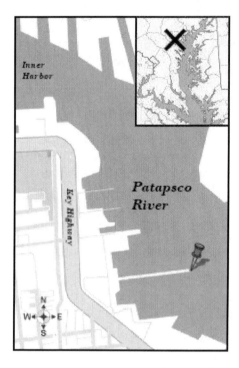

Location: Baltimore City

Open: Seasonal

Dockage: Yes

Latitude: N 39° 16' 34"

Longitude: W 76° 36' 4"

Body of Water: Inner Harbor
off the Patapsco River

Driving Distance:
Annapolis 31 miles,
Washington, DC 42 miles,
Easton 61 miles

Atmosphere Meter

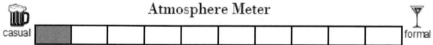

casual ▢▢▢▢▢▢▢▢▢▢ formal

Whoever came up with the idea of plopping a tiki bar on the end of a pier in the middle of Baltimore's Inner Harbor was a genius. Tiki Barge is Charm City's idea of an adult pool party, and it's become the epicenter for fun on the water. It looks like a happy misfit with bright orange and turquoise walls contrasting with the grays of old industrial plants and corporate skyscrapers standing nearby. On top of the two-story vessel rests a thatched roof with a wooden deck and colorful lights strung from pole to pole. Pirate signs and ship flags hang above the bamboo bar. Down below on the well deck, another thatched-roof bar serves up cool beverages next to a swimming pool that's surrounded by beach chairs facing the sun. Swaying palm trees encircle the deck.

Food isn't really essential to life on the Tiki Barge. D'Grill cranks out extremely casual fare of hot dogs, burgers, and fries. But specialty rum drinks with fruit juices provide enough vitamin C to ward off scurvy. The best part about the Tiki Barge is its 360-degree view of the water. The Domino Sugar factory and Inner Harbor skyline shape the background, while sailboats, power boats, cruise ships, and barges glide past before your eyes.

Docked beside the Tiki Barge is a relic of local history — the *Maryland Independence*. Originally built as a submarine chaser in 1944, it was converted to a luxury yacht in the 1970s. Gov. Hughes bought it in the 1980s to court dignitaries and business executives. In a grand gesture of fiscal responsibility, Gov. Ehrlich auctioned it on eBay in 2003. Now in private hands and newly restored, *Maryland Independence* is available for parties or inspection of the curious passing by.

Tabrizi's Restaurant

500 Harborview Drive
Baltimore, MD 21230
(410) 727-3663
www.tabrizis.com

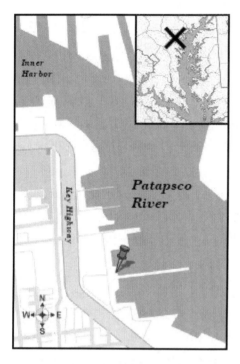

Location: Baltimore City

Open: Seasonal

Dockage: Yes

Latitude: N 39° 16' 34"

Longitude: W 76° 36' 16"

Body of Water: Inner Harbor
off the Patapsco River

Driving Distance:
Annapolis 31 miles,
Washington, DC 42 miles,
Easton 61 miles

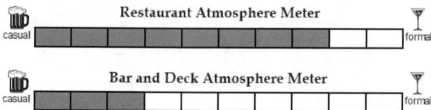

Restaurant Atmosphere Meter
casual ▮▮▮▮▮▮▮▮□□ formal

Bar and Deck Atmosphere Meter
casual ▮▮▮□□□□□□□ formal

At Tabrizi's, the Mediterranean meets the Bay in a culinary marriage that presents the best of both worlds. It's located at the Harborview Marina on the "secret" side of Baltimore's Inner Harbor where locals come to escape the mayhem of the crowds and tourists. The ambiance is casually sophisticated with a soothing Tuscan feel. The L-shaped dining room glows in soft gold and brown colors, with an open kitchen for observing the chef at work. A long blond wood bar beckons you to take a seat and sip chilled cocktails. A baby grand piano in the middle sets a relaxing yet lively tone. The upstairs banquet room's graceful décor makes it a popular venue for weddings and special gatherings.

On the outside deck, live music plays on weekend nights in the summer, while diners relish an unforgettable waterfront view of the stars coming out above the scenic city skyline in a more casual setting.

The menu dresses up Chesapeake seafood with fresh Italian and Greek ingredients. For starters, crab meat with creamy aioli is nestled in avocados, and the Greek salad pops with feta cheese and Kalamata olives. Stuffed grape leaves, hummus, and baba ghanoush are reminders of the cook's Mediterranean roots. Entree standouts: Chilean sea bass encrusted with sesame seeds, grilled lamb kabob over rice, rock shrimp on angel hair pasta, and sushi-grade tuna tartare. For dessert, cool down with crème brulee custard or warm up with pistachio baklava drizzled with honey.

Rusty Scupper Restaurant

402 Key Highway
Baltimore, MD 21230
(410) 727-3678
www.rusty-scupper.com

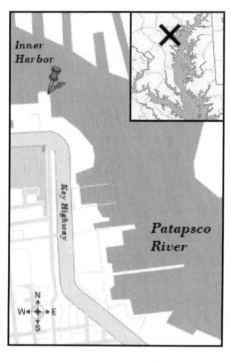

Location: Baltimore City

Open: Year Round

Dockage: Yes

Latitude: N 39° 16' 55"

Longitude: W 76° 36' 26"

Body of Water: Inner Harbor
off the Patapsco River

Driving Distance:
Annapolis 31 miles,
Washington, DC 42 miles,
Easton 61 miles

Atmosphere Meter

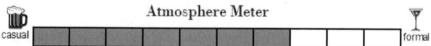

casual | | | | | | | | | | formal

Rusty Scupper would be a handsome restaurant no matter where it stood, but the panoramic view of Baltimore's Inner Harbor raises the dining experience to a whole new level. On the roof deck, debates rage on about the best time of day to be there. Sunsets often garner the most votes with the heavens streaked in rose and salmon. Evenings get their share of approving nods when lights in the office buildings are in sync with a starry night. During the day, the skyline feels like it's closer, revealing details on every structure from Legg Mason to the Royal Sonesta Harbor Court.

Inside the restaurant, the ambiance is contemporary and urban, but nautical artwork and exposed-wood rafters soften the décor. Cobalt blue wine glasses echo the waters of the Bay. It's a large place — 270 seats in the dining room and 75 stools at the bar. The famous Sunday brunch is so popular that you should call ahead for reservations. The menu is inspired by the Chesapeake region: local oysters, lump crab cakes, grilled rockfish, and Kent Island crab-stuffed shrimp. Dishes that aren't pulled from the sea include New York strip steak, pasta, and lemon garlic chicken.

Rusty Scupper has been a local seafood icon for years, but it's now owned by Select Restaurants out of Cleveland. Bay purists shouldn't turn up their noses at a chain restaurant, because Rusty Scupper buys from local fishermen. As a good neighbor, it joined the Chesapeake Bay Oyster Recovery Partnership (ORP), an alliance of Maryland, D.C., and Virginia eateries that recycle used oyster shells. As a result, ORP collected thousands of bushels of used shells last year and planted millions of baby oysters around the Bay.

Bubba Gump Shrimp Company

301 Light Street
Baltimore, MD 21202
(410) 244-0838
www.bubbagump.com/locations/baltimore

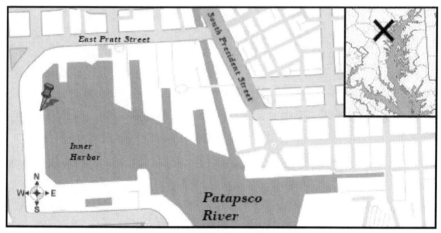

Location: Baltimore City
Open: Year Round ⚓ Dockage: No
Latitude: N 39° 17' 5" ><> Longitude: W 76° 36' 43"
Body of Water: Inner Harbor off the Patapsco River
Driving Distance: Annapolis 32 miles,
Washington, DC 41 miles, Easton 61 miles

Atmosphere Meter

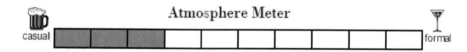

casual ——————————————————————— formal

Only in America can the theme for a successful chain restaurant come from an Oscar-winning movie and a character who talks a lot about shrimp. That's how Bubba Gump Shrimp Company was born. This expansive Inner Harbor eatery pays tribute to the story of Forrest Gump stumbling through the turbulent Vietnam War era. Pictures of Tom Hanks, Gary Sinise, and other actors from the film hang on the walls. Even the carry-out section shows Forrest taking his cross-country run, and TVs play the flick while you wait for your meal.

Established in 1996, it's located in the spot previously held by Phillips Seafood, so it's got big shoes to fill when serving fish. A spacious outdoor deck wraps around the building and offers a terrific waterfront view. The centrally located bar is a popular hangout, and the dining rooms are large enough to feed up to 400 locals and hungry tourists. A gift shop sells T-shirts, coffee mugs, posters, and mementos from the film and your Baltimore visit.

Variations on shrimp seem endless: Peel-and-eat shrimp, popcorn shrimp, shrimp cocktail, shrimp mac and cheese, Cajun shrimp, shrimp po' boys, coconut shrimp, and even shrimp stuffed in hush puppies. Crab meat comes in cakes or is stuffed in mushrooms. Other seafood dishes include grilled salmon, fried Dixie fishwich, pan-seared tilapia, and Bubba's Bucket of Boat Trash with fried shrimp, fish with Cajun spices, and snow crab legs. Salads, chicken, steaks, ribs, jambalaya, and burgers are also available.

M&S Grill

201 East Pratt Street
Baltimore, MD 21202
(410) 547-9333
www.mccormickandschmicks.com/mandsgrill.aspx

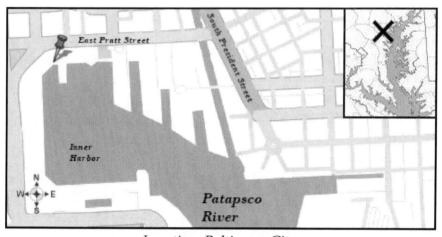

Location: Baltimore City
Open: Year Round ⚓ Dockage: No
Latitude: N 39° 17' 10" ⚓ Longitude: W 76° 36' 42"
Body of Water: Inner Harbor off the Patapsco River
Driving Distance: Annapolis 32 miles,
Washington, DC 41 miles, Easton 61 miles

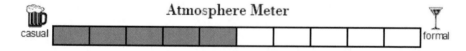

M&S Grill is like the cute little sister of its big brother restaurant, McCormick & Schmick's. It's not as large or expensive, and you can't beat the location. M&S Grill sits at the crown of Baltimore's Inner Harbor just blocks away from Camden Yards and M&T Bank Stadium. In front of the patio floats the *U.S.S. Constellation*, which was built in 1854 as the last all-sail warship. It's the final Civil War vessel still afloat, and you can climb aboard to imagine life as a 19th century sailor. Or you could walk over to the Baltimore World Trade Center. Its floor-to-ceiling windows present a glorious 360-degree view of downtown and the waterfront.

With all this to see outside, why go inside M&S Grill? The décor is cozy and casual with lots of warm cherry wood and vintage stained glass. Colorful pennants of baseball teams are draped around the oval-shaped bar. Wooden booths with soft green cushions encircle the dining room, while contemporary nautical artwork hangs on the walls.

The chef concentrates on delivering fresh ingredients at the peak of their season, and a "Fresh List" highlights the daily catch. There's seafood aplenty with Maryland crab cakes, shrimp scampi, and mussels steamed in garlic, herbs, and white wine. Signature fish dishes: flounder stuffed with crab and shrimp, almond-crusted rainbow trout, and seared ahi tuna. Custom-aged steaks and blue crab chicken cordon bleu with Old Bay cream sauce are crowd pleasers. Sunday brunch, featuring regional fare, is simply Delmarvelous. The kitchen offers wallet-friendly specials, and happy hour pleases budget-conscious patrons with half-price cheeseburgers.

Phillips Seafood

601 East Pratt Street
Baltimore, MD 21202
(410) 685-6600
www.phillipsseafood.com

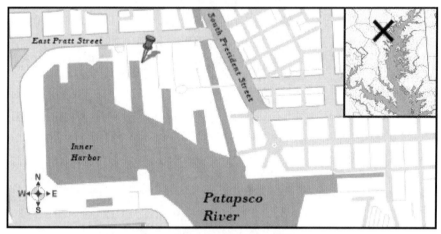

Location: Baltimore City
Open: Year Round ⚓ Dockage: No
Latitude: N 39° 17' 12" ➤ Longitude: W 76° 36' 26"
Body of Water: Inner Harbor off the Patapsco River
Driving Distance: Annapolis 32 miles,
Washington, DC 41 miles, Easton 61 miles

Atmosphere Meter

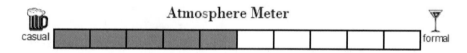

In the 1960s, Inner Harbor looked much different than it does today. Run-down warehouses and dilapidated buildings stood along murky waters. But Mayor William Donald Shaefer and some local developers envisioned a rebirth of the harbor with skyscrapers, tourists, a convention center, and a world-class aquarium. All they needed was a few businesses to take a risk and join the urban renewal. Shaefer wanted an anchor restaurant to attract visitors, so he approached the Phillips family who had supplied Baltimore with seafood since 1914 and ran a bustling restaurant in Ocean City. Brice and Shirley Phillips shared the vision of a resurrected waterfront and opened Phillips Harborplace in 1980. For 30 years, the restaurant steamed crabs, other businesses joined the bandwagon, and Shaefer's dream became a reality.

In 2011, Phillips packed up its mallets and moved the landmark restaurant around the corner to a more prominent location in the Power Plant building. The new spot is lovely. Renovations to the space in 2015 moved the front bar to add more seating. Vintage photos of the original Phillips give the space a warm charm. The outdoor floating deck recreates lazy summers on Maryland's Eastern Shore.

The raw bar of fresh local oysters, clams, and shrimp is an ideal start to a Chesapeake feast. Signature cream of crab soup and Hoopers Island crab cakes regularly win blue ribbon awards. Rockfish stuffed with crab and shrimp is heavenly. Fried seafood platter of crab, shrimp, clams, and fish is a crunchy Phillips classic. Steaks, pork chops and fried chicken elbow their way on the menu to keep meat eaters happy.

McCormick & Schmick's Seafood & Steaks

711 Eastern Avenue
Baltimore, MD 21202
(410) 234-1300
www.mccormickandschmicks.com

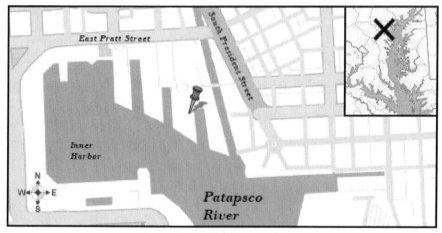

Location: Baltimore City
Open: Year Round ⚓ Dockage: No
Latitude: N 39° 17' 3" ⚓ Longitude: W 76° 36' 20"
Body of Water: Inner Harbor off the Patapsco River
Driving Distance: Annapolis 32 miles,
Washington, DC 41 miles, Easton 61 miles

Atmosphere Meter

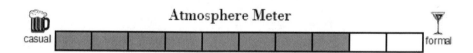

casual   formal

McCormick & Schmick's menu offers 30 types of seafood daily. That's a boatload of fish, but with 70+ locations around the country and a headquarters in Portland, OR, the company has developed effective systems for bringing great ingredients to its restaurants. And the chef manages to retain quality and freshness. Standing near the open galley kitchen with its shiny chrome pick-up station, you can watch how smoothly dishes move from range to tabletop. Oysters, catfish, shrimp, crabs, salmon, and scallops are pulled from Atlantic waters and prepared with a contemporary twist. Aged steaks, chicken, savory soups, and crisp salads complete the culinary options. McCormick & Schmick's calls itself "affordable upscale, with a warm, sophisticated atmosphere."

The waterfront building has stood across from Pier 5 since 1998. Stools with black leather seats are stationed along the wooden bar and stained glass lights overhead create an old, established feeling. Sailboats, ocean fish, and pictures of oysters garnish dark wood paneling. The dining room's floor-to-ceiling windows give everyone a lovely view. Blue and green umbrellas on the brick patio tempt you to take a seat outdoors and watch the bustling harbor.

Nearby stands the red and black Seven Foot Knoll Lighthouse. Built in 1855, it's the oldest screwpile lighthouse in Maryland. The lighthouse used to warn ships of danger at the mouth of the Patapsco River but was moved to Pier 5 in 1988 as part of the Baltimore Maritime Museum. Climb inside to get a unique glimpse of the Bay's nautical past.

Mo's Fisherman's Wharf

219 South President Street
Baltimore, MD 21202
(410) 837-8600
www.mosseafood.com/fishermanswharf

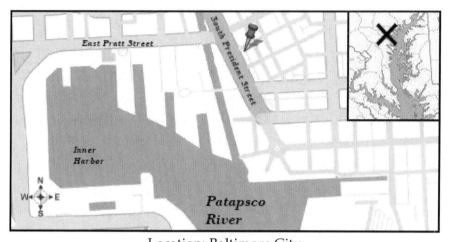

Location: Baltimore City
Open: Year Round ⚓ Dockage: No
Latitude: N 39° 17' 11" 🐟 Longitude: W 76° 36' 12"
Body of Water: Patapsco River
Driving Distance: Annapolis 31 miles
Washington, DC 42 miles, Easton 69 miles

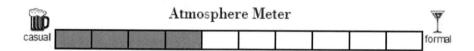

Atmosphere Meter
casual   formal

If you could look up the phrase "classic Baltimore seafood house" in the dictionary, a picture of Mo's might be next to the definition. Since 1986, the family-owned place has upheld local traditions of serving Maryland crabs, fish, and other Chesapeake delicacies amidst the influx of trendy eateries and corporate food chains. It's hard to miss Mo's. If its big blue neon sign doesn't catch your eye, you're sure to see the mural of tropical fish and aquatic creatures swimming around the azure waters of a coral reef. Trucks unloading fresh catch at Mo's seafood market might also draw your attention.

A pair of neon blue marlins flanks the restaurant's front entrance. The dining room has a cozy vintage feel, accentuated by an easy understated décor and a scattering of mounted trophy fish on the walls. Service is warm and friendly.

Even though you can order steak, chicken, and pasta, seafood undoubtedly steals the show. The menu offers a gamut of irresistible options with local crabs as the centerpiece in creamy soup, cakes, and imperial. The Crab Fluff is battered and fried to a puffy golden brown. Clams casino, steamed mussels, and oysters Rockefeller are wonderful starters. Shrimp and lobsters are brought to new heights when stuffed with jumbo lump crab meat. Daily fish specials let you experience bites of freshness from the Bay.

Apropoe's

700 Aliceanna Street
Baltimore, MD 21202
(410) 895-1879
www.apropoesharboreast.com

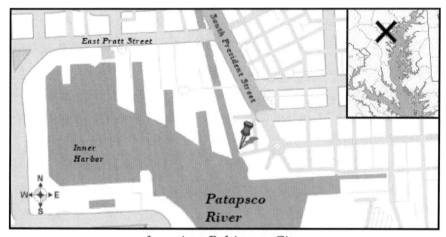

Location: Baltimore City
Open: Year Round ⚓ Dockage: No
Latitude: N 39° 17' 0" ⟐ Longitude: W 76° 36' 12"
Body of Water: Patapsco River
Driving Distance: Annapolis 31 miles
Washington, DC 42 miles, Easton 69 miles

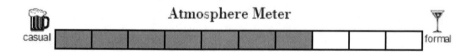

Apropoe's location in the Baltimore Marriott Waterfront
marks the border of Harbor East, which spreads from the
Inner Harbor to Fells Point. Plans for this area began back
in the 1980s when city officials wanted to convert decaying
industrial buildings and warehouses into a new urban
destination with a waterfront promenade. Now this thriving

neighborhood hums with luxury hotels, restaurants, shops, office buildings, movie theaters, and high-ticket condos.

The restaurant's large space has a sophisticated contemporary design and is divided into smaller sections with sheer black screens creating privacy areas. On either side of the long dark bar are lounges with comfy couches and exposed brick walls. Tall windows overlook the Pier 6 Pavilion music venue.

The menu pays homage to Baltimore favorites: crab cakes, fried oysters, soft-shell crab BLT, steamed PEI mussels, and grilled shrimp. Maryland crab also appears in unexpected places such as Crab Louis deviled eggs and white pizza with pesto and crab. Also available: burgers, chicken, steaks, and pork chops.

Specialty cocktails follow the Charm City theme with the Baltimore Blossom and The Raven. Apropoe's also carries an impressive array of local beers from Heavy Seas Peg Leg to Natty Boh. During a recent visit, a bartender explained why Mr. Boh only has one eye. When he was drawn in 1936, National Bohemian's main competition was Gunter Beer, and its slogan was "Gunter's got it." Natty Boh played off this line and produced ads with a child asking what happened to Mr. Boh's other eye? The mother would shake her head and sadly answer, "Gunther's got it." What a clever way to drive public sympathy toward your brand of beer!

Roy's Hawaiian Fusion

720-B Aliceanna Street
Baltimore, MD 21202
(410) 659-0099
www.roysrestaurant.com/locations/md/baltimore

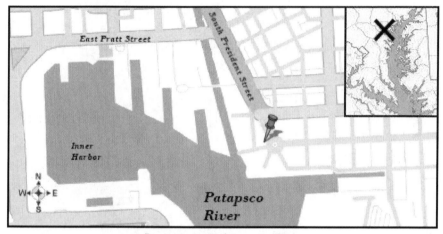

Location: Baltimore City
Open: Year Round ⚓ Dockage: No
Latitude: N 39° 17' 0" ⤖ Longitude: W 76° 36' 7"
Body of Water: Patapsco River
Driving Distance: Annapolis 31 miles
Washington, DC 42 miles, Easton 69 miles

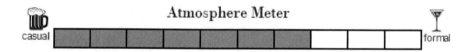

Atmosphere Meter
casual ▯▯▯▯▯▯▯▯ formal

When you enter Roy's Hawaiian, you are transported back
to the Golden Age of Tiki. It all started in 1934 during the
Depression when a traveler named Don Beach opened a
Polynesian restaurant in Hollywood, CA. Flaming torches,
bamboo furniture, and carved masks from his island journeys
caught people's attention. Soon 12 more locations were

spawned, and other restaurateurs like Trader Vic spread an island theme across the country. This set the stage for American soldiers returning home from the Pacific Corridor in World War II with stories of exotic lands. Housewives held luaus instead of backyard barbeques and dressed their men in tropical-print shirts instead of white button-downs. Tiki's boom-time hit when Hollywood got on board. Movies like *Jaguar God* and *South Pacific* gave America a glimpse of island life, and girls went wild over Elvis during his Blue Hawaii Period. By the time *Gilligan's Island* aired, tiki-mania had shifted into high gear.

Roy's Hawaiian celebrates hip tiki. Its elegant décor glows with island hues. Golden yellow walls are decorated with pictures of hula girls, palm trees, and hibiscus blossoms. Tables are set with purple cloth napkins, and bamboo stools surround the bar.

Classic cocktails at Aloha Hour set the mood for an evening of Polynesian pleasure. The Hawaiian Martini is shaken with pineapple-infused vodka and coconut rum, and Roy's Island Mai Tai is a 1940s classic. Canoe Appetizer for Two with Thai peanut chicken satay, vegetable spring rolls, and Szechuan ribs initiate your island feast. Bold Pacific Rim flavors create standout seafood dishes such as mahi mahi with macadamia nut crust, Red Dragon shrimp, and blackened ahi tuna. Braised beef short ribs, and Thai style lemongrass chicken with jasmine rice present exotic spices to meat lovers.

The Oceanaire Seafood Room

801 Aliceanna Street
Baltimore, MD 21202
(443) 872-0000
www.theoceanaire.com/locations/baltimore

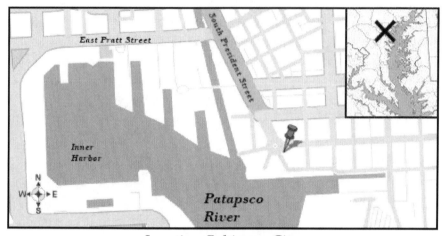

Location: Baltimore City
Open: Year Round ⚓ Dockage: No
Latitude: N 39° 16' 59" ⋙ Longitude: W 76° 36' 5"
Body of Water: Patapsco River
Driving Distance: Annapolis 31 miles
Washington, DC 42 miles, Easton 69 miles

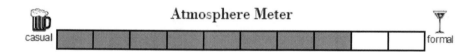

The famous quote "To eat an oyster is to kiss the sea on its lips" is engraved on the dining room wall. Mounted marlins, sea bass, and other trophy fish are artfully displayed. A large circular oyster bar is positioned at center stage with 10 to 12 different types of bivalves waiting to be shucked. The décor is modeled after a 1930s cruise liner with plush red leather booths, round porthole windows, and circular art deco light fixtures above the tables. Put this all together and you know you found a place that cherishes seafood.

For nearly a decade, Oceanaire has been a dining staple in Baltimore's Harbor East, answering the call for an upscale setting to dine on seafood. It's got other locations in 12 major U.S. cities and is staffed with chefs who scour local fish markets to find fresh, seasonal ingredients.

The price tag for eating here is high, but a quality dining experience is guaranteed with seafood leading the charge. Oysters on the half shell are pulled from the shores of Virginia, Maryland, and Massachusetts. The Grand Shellfish Platter is a towering sampler of chilled shrimp, crab, lobster, and oysters. Chesapeake crab cakes are bound with creamy mustard mayonnaise, and Fin and Shell Fish Stew is a bubbling pot of seafood swimming in a Pernod and garlic sauce. A few land dishes are available — steaks, pork chops, and pan-roasted chicken — with savory sides such as cheesy bacon au gratin potatoes and asparagus with hollandaise. Chef Select Four Course Pre-Fixe Dinner is available if you want the kitchen to choose from its daily specialties.

Splash Pool Bar & Grill

200 International Drive
Baltimore, MD 21202
(410) 576-5800
www.fourseasons.com/baltimore

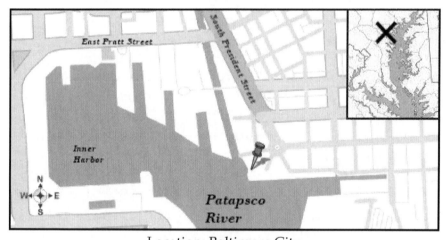

Location: Baltimore City
Open: Seasonal ⚓ Dockage: No
Latitude: N 39° 16' 57" ⮞ Longitude: W 76° 36' 9"
Body of Water: Patapsco River
Driving Distance: Annapolis 31 miles
Washington, DC 42 miles, Easton 69 miles

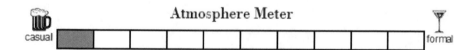

Atmosphere Meter

casual | formal

A pool with a view — that's what you find when you take the elevator to the fourth floor of the Four Seasons Hotel on Baltimore's Pier 7. On a clear day, this high-end observation deck offers a panoramic vantage point for seeing the entire Inner Harbor from the Domino Sugar plant to the National

Aquarium and beyond. Starlit evenings are magical when you're surrounded by the lights of the city skyline.

This five-star snack bar is open to the public, not just reserved for hotel guests. Its clean contemporary design arranges tables and lounge chairs around a swimming pool, creating an ideal space for sitting under large patio umbrellas and sipping cocktails. The menu is more about snacking than dining. You can start with Old Bay chips, crisp fried calamari, spicy tuna tempura roll, or a Mezze sampler of hummus, baba ghanoush, and olives. If the fresh air bolsters your appetite, go for a large plate with a burger, fish taco, grilled chicken sandwich, or an entree salad.

Across the harbor rises Federal Hill, named in 1789 for being the end of a parade celebrating the ratification of the new U.S. Federal Constitution. That hill also played a key role in the Civil War. After the Baltimore Riots in 1861, Northern officials worried about Confederate sympathizers taking control of the city. So, late one night Union troops erected a fort on top of the hill. Citizens awoke to cannons pointed at the waterfront threatening to let loose their fury if Baltimore joined the secessionists to break apart the Union. The forced allegiance worked, and Maryland remained with the North.

Ouzo Bay Greek Kouzina

1000 Lancaster Street
Baltimore, MD 21224
(443) 708-5818
www.ouzobay.com

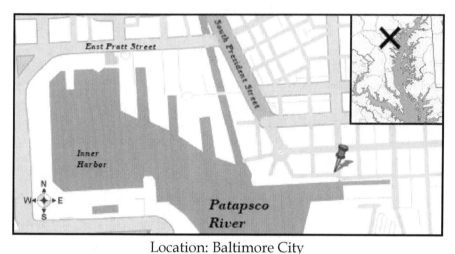

Location: Baltimore City
Open: Year Round ⚓ Dockage: No
Latitude: N 39° 16' 57" ⇥ Longitude: W 76° 35' 57"
Body of Water: Patapsco River
Driving Distance: Annapolis 31 miles
Washington, DC 42 miles, Easton 69 miles

Atmosphere Meter

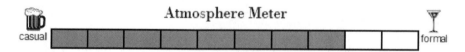

casual — formal

Ouzo Bay is an exceptionally attractive restaurant. Vibrant blue colors that match its waterfront location and clean contemporary design ideas strike a perfect balance for fine dining in a casual-nice setting. The building looks like a cruise ship with a flag was placed on top, and a two-tiered outdoor deck wraps around the ground level. Strings of blue and white blown-glass balls dangle above tables to create an illusion of bubbles floating upward in the sea. Next to a tall display of wines, windows along the front open up to let Bay breezes meander through the dining rooms.

At the stylish bar, cigars are stored in a discrete wooden humidor. Liquor bottles are stacked up to the ceiling on shelves that are home to one of the best ouzo collections in the area. It's the house specialty drink for a kitchen that marries Chesapeake with Greek cuisine. The combination succeeds, because seafood is the driving force in both styles of cooking.

Dinner starts with a medley of seafood appetizers such as crab cakes, mussels steamed in tomato sauce with feta cheese, cheese-stuffed or grilled calamari with capers, and head-on grilled shrimp. Fresh whole fish selections include red snapper, Dover sole, yellow tail tuna, and black sea bass. Crab cakes and seared scallops retain a connection to the Bay. Land-based entrees include a savory slow-braised lamb shank with toasted orzo, juicy pork chops, steak with roasted lemon potatoes, and feta-brined chicken.

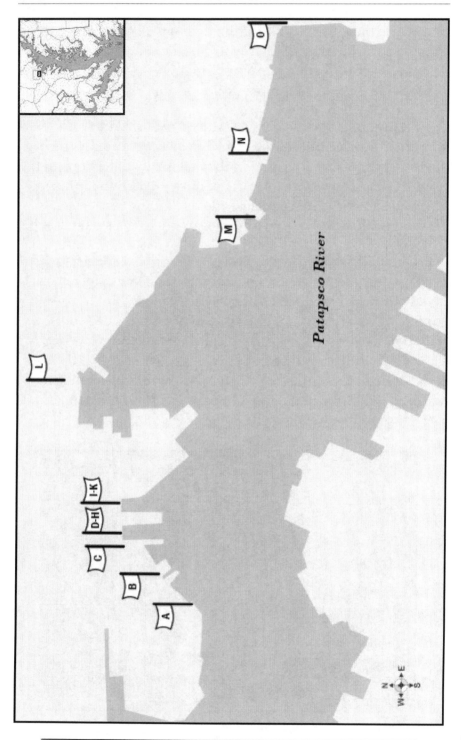

Patapsco River

Baltimore Fells Point & Canton

Waterfront Kitchen

1417 Thames Street
Baltimore, MD 21231
(443) 681-5310
www.waterfrontkitchen.com

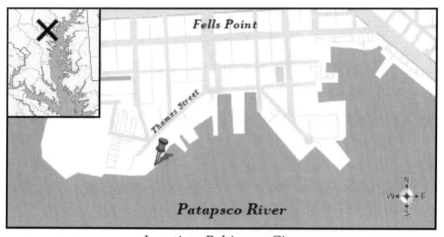

Location: Baltimore City
Open: Year Round ⚓ Dockage: No
Latitude: N 39° 16' 46" ➤ Longitude: W 76° 35' 45"
Body of Water: Patapsco River
Driving Distance: Annapolis 31 miles
Washington, DC 42 miles, Easton 64 miles

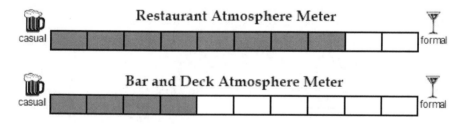

Don't judge a book by its cover. That's a good adage to keep in mind when you arrive at Waterfront Kitchen. The nondescript brick building that houses this restaurant acts as camouflage for one of the loveliest dining rooms on the Bay.

The décor is contemporary yet warm and inviting. High ceilings with thick wooden beams are softened with elegant swags of creamy fabric and a stellar view of the water.

Being beautiful isn't enough for Waterfront Kitchen; it also does good deeds and serves outstanding food. They partner with Baltimore Urban Gardening with Students (BUGS), a nonprofit that teaches inner-city youth about plants and nutrition. BUGS kids grow produce for the restaurant in tidy gardens down the street. The result is seasonal, seed-to-table dishes. Menu standouts: crab cakes, seared scallops, catfish, pan-roasted rockfish, and oyster stew with bacon and tarragon. Grass-fed beef, roasted organic chicken, duck breast, grilled pork chops, and braised short ribs are waiting for meat lovers.

In 2006, the Frederick Douglass & Isaac Myers Museum opened next door to the restaurant. Douglass came to Fells Point as a slave in 1826 and ran away to claim his freedom when he was 20. Myers was born free, and with 14 other men, he founded the first African American-owned shipyard in the United States. Interactive exhibits bring to life stories of this significant time in Baltimore history.

Kali's Court Restaurant

1606 Thames Street
Baltimore, MD 21231
(410) 276-4700
www.kaliscourt.com

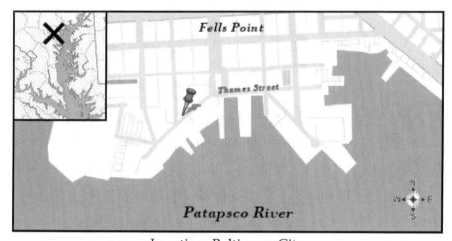

Location: Baltimore City
Open: Year Round ⚓ Dockage: No
Latitude: N 39° 16' 53" ⭢ Longitude: W 76° 35' 41"
Body of Water: Patapsco River
Driving Distance: Annapolis 31 miles,
Washington, DC 42 miles, Easton 64 miles

Atmosphere Meter

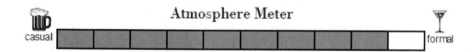

casual ──────────────────────────────── formal

When you walk onto Kali's red brick patio, you feel like you've entered a secret garden, plush with miniature roses, cheerful impatiens, and ferns that push their way through the wrought iron fence. White umbrellas block the afternoon sun, and the buzz of the city streets seem to fade away. Long strands of ivy cascade from the second story balcony where patrons enjoy an exquisite view of the water.

Inside the restaurant, you're greeted with Old World elegance. The dining room glows in warm gold and burgundy, accented by dark woods, Persian rugs, and crimson velvet curtains. Red leather seats line up along the brass rail at the bar. White linens cover the tabletops, and candlelight creates an intimate, romantic ambiance.

The fresh fish display on a bed of ice tells you that seafood takes center stage here, and rich Mediterranean flavors are carefully blended with the Chesapeake's bounty. The menu changes with the seasons. First course and small plate choices include roasted salmon with sesame BBQ sauce, shark fritters, and fried calamari. Tuna carpaccio on a bed of arugula is silky and delicious. Crab and artichoke crisps are served with red pepper and cream sauce.

For the main course, you can't go wrong with classics such as jumbo lump crab cakes, shrimp with pasta, or grilled whole fish of the day. Meat options include beef and lamb meatballs topped with feta, duck confit, New York strip tips, and chicken breast sautéed in olive oil, lemon and spinach.

The Admiral's Cup Restaurant & Bar

1647 Thames Street
Baltimore, MD 21231
(410) 534-5555
www.theadmiralscup.com

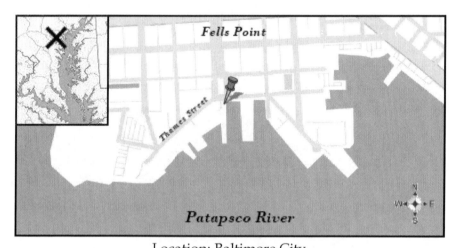

Location: Baltimore City
Open: Year Round ⚓ Dockage: No
Latitude: N 39° 16' 54" ⬌ Longitude: W 76° 35' 36"
Body of Water: Patapsco River
Driving Distance: Annapolis 31 miles,
Washington, DC 42 miles, Easton 64 miles

Atmosphere Meter

casual 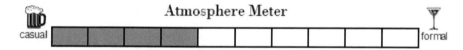 formal

The Admiral's Cup is the type of place where you go after work, loosen your tie, and relax with friends over a couple of beers. The list of Maryland brews is impressive, featuring such colorful names as Heavy Seas Loose Cannon, Brewer's Art Ozzy, and Flying Dog Pearl Necklace. After tasting specialty drinks, sipping local craft beers, and listening to tunes from a live local band, your worries quickly become a distant memory.

The location closed for renovations, but the bar reopened in October 2012 and the kitchen was ready to roll by February 2013. Fortunately the new décor preserved the historic building's features with golden stained glass windows, exposed brick, and pressed tin ceiling. But they added a few modern touches such as flat-screen TVs. Royal blue walls are peppered with nautical items such as propellers, oars, ship gauges, and steering wheels. And you can't beat the waterfront location, right in the heart of Fells Point.

The menu is divided into two sections: "Starters" and "Hand Held & Big Plates." Tasty beginnings include crabby mac and cheese, smoked salmon with dill cream spread, steamed mussels with toast points, grilled tuna cob salad, and smooth crab dip. Heartier plates of local seafood: crab cake sandwich, shrimp salad on brioche roll, salmon wrap with bacon and cheddar, and seafood quesadilla with shrimp, crab, peppers, and jack cheese. Beef sliders, jumbo wings, and chicken nachos are steps above standard pub fare.

Woody's Rum Bar
& Island Grill

1700 Thames Street
Baltimore, MD 21231
(410) 563-6800
www.woodysrumbar.com

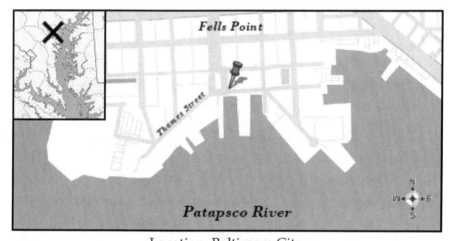

Location: Baltimore City
Open: Seasonal ⚓ Dockage: No
Latitude: N 39° 16' 55" ⚓ Longitude: W 76° 35' 34"
Body of Water: Patapsco River
Driving Distance: Annapolis 31 miles,
Washington, DC 42 miles, Easton 64 miles

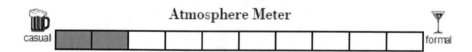

Atmosphere Meter

casual · · · · · · · · · · · formal

When someone says Fells Point, tiki and Caribbean music don't usually come to mind. Most people think of old taverns and cobblestone streets that date back to the early 1700s. But as palm trees and thatched roofs are popping up all around the Bay, another tiki stronghold has taken root in Fells Point.

Woody's Rum Bar, a sister restaurant of Sláinte Irish Pub, is located above an ice cream parlor. It's easy to miss the side entrance even though the door is painted with tropical flowers and a parrot. So, keep an eye out for the pirate flags with black-and-white skulls and crossbones waving from the third floor deck. Once you climb the stairs, you're rewarded with island-inspired murals, bamboo, and tables made of hand-painted steel drums.

It recently won awards for Best View Overlooking the Harbor and Best Bar to Get Day Drunk, and offers an extensive rum collection. But there's more to Woody's than just pretty scenery and potent cocktails. Its Caribbean-style food mixes fresh seafood with island flavors, creating standouts like coconut shrimp bathed in sweet chili sauce, jerk chicken wraps, mahi mahi fish tacos, and BBQ pork taquitos. The menu accommodates traditional palates with burgers, crab cakes, salads, and tangy wings.

The thatched-roof bar serves specialty drinks, including the Rum Runner, Dark & Stormy, Hurricane, and Mai Tai. After the first sip, you'll feel the breeze, relax, and make a toast to celebrate island influences on the Bay.

Sláinte Irish Pub & Restaurant

1700 Thames Street
Baltimore, MD 21231
(410) 563-6600
www.slaintepub.com

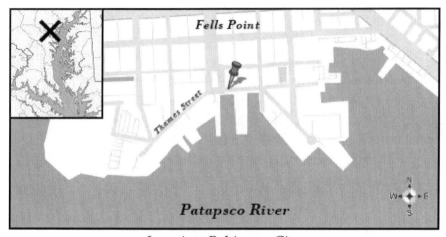

Location: Baltimore City
Open: Year Round ⚓ Dockage: No
Latitude: N 39° 16' 55" ⟶ Longitude: W 76° 35' 33"
Body of Water: Patapsco River
Driving Distance: Annapolis 31 miles,
Washington, DC 42 miles, Easton 64 miles

Atmosphere Meter

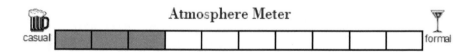

casual ··· formal

   In 1816, America welcomed 6,000 Irish immigrants. By
the end of 1854, nearly 2 million of them had come to our
shores, which was a quarter of Ireland's population. After
New York and Boston, Baltimore was the third largest point of
entry for Irish who had been driven from their homeland by
the Potato Famine. Many took jobs on the Baltimore & Ohio

Railroad, at the shipyards, or as domestics, and they became an integral part of Chesapeake life and heritage.

At Sláinte's you get to experience how perfectly Irish culture blends with the Bay. The bartender speaks in a gentle brogue while handing you a cool pint of Guinness. The walls downstairs are covered with soccer and rugby team banners, and vintage photos of Irish ancestors hang in the upstairs dining room. You can attend whiskey tastings or pint pouring contests, and eat fish and chips while listening to Gaelic tunes.

Local workers arrive for morning happy hour with bottomless Bloody Marys at one of Baltimore's Best Breakfasts. Those with vigorous appetites order Waterman's Breakfast of fried eggs, sausage and shrimp gravy, and fried oysters on white toast. Omelets and pancakes are paired with bangers and rashers. At lunch and dinner, the kitchen orchestrates a flawless balance of Chesapeake and Irish cuisines. Crab cakes, pan-seared cod, steamed shrimp, and mussels sautéed in Harp lager attract Bay seafood fans. If you're feeling a wee bit Irish, go for the shepherd's pie, lamb stew, or corned beef and cabbage. And if for no other reason than the name, ask for a side of crispy O'Nion Rings.

Kooper's Tavern

1702 Thames Street
Baltimore, MD 21231
(410) 563-5423
www.kooperstavern.com

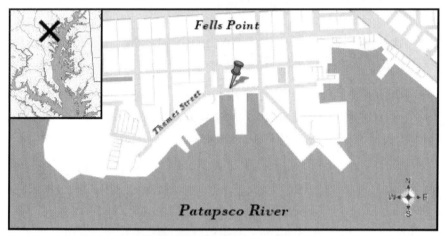

Location: Baltimore City
Open: Year Round ⚓ Dockage: No
Latitude: N 39° 16' 55" ⊶ Longitude: W 76° 35' 33"
Body of Water: Patapsco River
Driving Distance: Annapolis 31 miles,
Washington, DC 42 miles, Easton 64 miles

Atmosphere Meter

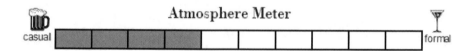

casual ░░░░░░░░░░░ formal

Kooper's calls itself a "classic American tavern," but as you look around this place, you see that it's a whole lot more. Above the doorway to this beautiful row house is a stained glass window that immortalizes the owners' yellow Labrador retriever called Kooper. When the pup passed away in 2007, they named the restaurant after him. Same case with Woody's

Rum Bar just two doors down. Woody was the owners' black Lab. Sláinte's is the third member of this family of popular Fells Point watering holes.

Framed portraits of family pets hang on the restaurant walls near pictures of 19th century Chesapeake steamboats and fishing ships. Antique wooden booths on aged hardwood floors encircle a crackling fireplace. The atmosphere is cozy, and the staff welcomes guests warmly.

Legendary brunch dishes include blue crab omelets and Bananas Foster flapjacks. At dinner, seafood lovers are drawn to shrimp steamed in Old Bay and Natty Boh or crispy calamari with marinara sauce. Jumbo lump crab cakes and blackened ahi tuna are tucked inside kaiser rolls. You can build your own burger out of beef, lamb, or bison, or wrestle with a pulled pork BBQ sandwich. Meatloaf and mashed potatoes taste like the kind your mom used to make. Don't miss daily specials such as Crab Cake Wednesdays and Dollar Oyster Happy Hour Fridays. For dessert, find a friend to split the Irish Cream Sunday with Oreo cookies, brownies, ice cream, and Irish cream.

What else makes Kooper's unique? Charity. The restaurant is involved with several community causes such as Maryland's Society to Prevent Cruelty to Animals and the Krieger Institute for brain and spinal cord disorders.

The Waterfront Hotel

1710 Thames Street
Baltimore, MD 21231
(410) 537-5055
www.waterfronthotel.us

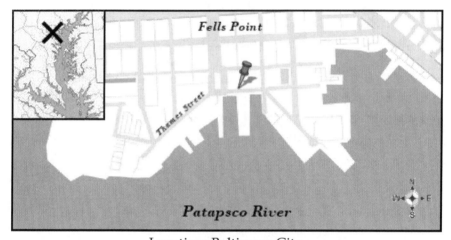

Location: Baltimore City
Open: Year Round ⚓ Dockage: No
Latitude: N 39° 16' 55" 🐟 Longitude: W 76° 35' 32"
Body of Water: Patapsco River
Driving Distance: Annapolis 31 miles,
Washington, DC 42 miles, Easton 64 miles

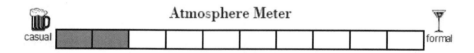

Atmosphere Meter
casual / formal

Remember that gritty TV series, *Homicide: Life on the Street*, that ran from 1992-1999? It was filmed across from the Waterfront Hotel and used the restaurant for its bar scenes. But this location's history goes back even farther. The building, established in 1771 as a private residence, is the second oldest remaining structure in Baltimore. In 1861, it was converted into a hotel and tavern, which catered to soldiers in the Civil War. In 1955, it became a restaurant.

The current décor retains an old-fashioned saloon look with vintage light fixtures, dark wood furniture, original brick walls, and exposed I-beams supporting the ceiling. A steer's horned skull hangs on the bar wall above the shelf for vodka and whiskey bottles. The two-story building has a full bar on both levels, and the upper floor's lounge reveals a fabulous view of the harbor from its cushy leather sofas. Bands play most evenings without a cover charge, and the atmosphere is upbeat, casual, and fun.

The food is quite good, enhancing Chesapeake and standard pub fare with southern flavors. Everything tastes fresh and well-prepared. Standout starters include fried green tomatoes, steamed shrimp, oyster stew, and crab dip with soft pretzels that's got more jumbo lumps than cream. Gourmet tacos bring a dash of spice to your palate, especially the blackened catfish, pork belly, and buffalo shrimp and chorizo. Skillet mac and cheese is a delightfully gooey house specialty.

Riptide by the Bay
Restaurant & Bar

1718 Thames Street
Baltimore, MD 21231
(410) 732-3474
www.riptidebythebay.net

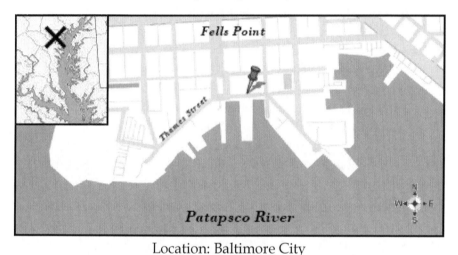

Location: Baltimore City
Open: Year Round ⚓ Dockage: No
Latitude: N 39° 16' 55" ➤ Longitude: W 76° 35' 31"
Body of Water: Patapsco River
Driving Distance: Annapolis 31 miles,
Washington, DC 42 miles, Easton 64 miles

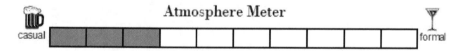

Atmosphere Meter

casual | | | | | | | | | | | formal

Riptide's is located inside a charming red-brick row house that harkens back to Fells Point in the early 18th century. A few patio tables out front provide a nice view of water taxis and boats pulling into the harbor. To the right of the front doors is the Riptide Crab Room. Its rustic wooden doors lead into an open-air covered seating area with murals depicting Chesapeake sailboats, lighthouses, and wildlife. Inside the dining area, wooden booths and sea foam-green walls showcase pictures of schooners and nautical artifacts.

The menu kicks off with Bay classics such as steamed crabs, oysters on the half shell, and peel-and-eat shrimp. Salads are fresh with locally grown ingredients. Must-try dishes include crab cakes, pan-seared scallops, blackened cod filet, and lobster ravioli. Baby back ribs fall off the bone, and steaks are topped with thyme-shallot butter. Burgers, chicken tacos, and crab mac and cheese rule the light fare.

During a recent visit, a local told tales about taverns like this during the oyster bonanza of the 1800s. Wealth was created through shipbuilding and seafood processing, which attracted men from around the globe. A Wild West boom-time ensued with saloons and brothels crowding the docks. Gunfights erupted between Maryland and Virginia crews competing for oyster beds. Dredging oysters was rough work, and many men didn't want to do it. But sea captains needed able hands on the ships, so they'd scour local taverns for recruits. Often targeting new immigrants, captains would get men drunk, drag them to the docks, and shanghai them to work on their ships. Some workers got paid, but many were tossed overboard without a receiving a penny. So, when you belly up to a Fells Point bar, keep an eye out for unscrupulous captains lurking in the shadows waiting to take you aboard.

Thames Street Oyster House

1728 Thames Street
Baltimore, MD 21231
(443) 449-7726
www.thamesstreetoysterhouse.com

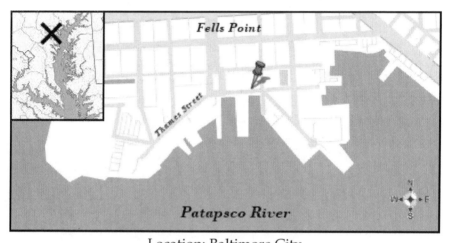

Location: Baltimore City
Open: Year Round ⚓ Dockage: No
Latitude: N 39° 16' 55" 🐟 Longitude: W 76° 35' 30"
Body of Water: Patapsco River
Driving Distance: Annapolis 31 miles,
Washington, DC 42 miles, Easton 64 miles

🍺 **Restaurant Atmosphere Meter** 🍸
casual ▓▓▓▓▓▓□□□□ formal

🍺 **Bar Atmosphere Meter** 🍸
casual ▓▓▓□□□□□ formal

An oyster lover's paradise is the best way to describe
Thames Street Oyster House. It's a beautiful restaurant with a
gorgeous view of the water, but it's the way they treat oysters
that makes you dream about when you can come back here

again. They carry oysters from Maryland and Virginia — Choptanks, Barren Islands, and Rappahannocks — but they also scour the East and West Coasts to find the best bivalves in each region. Similar to a sushi card, you get a raw bar sheet with a tally of the daily oysters, listing them from briny to buttery. You choose the ones that fit your taste.

How can Thames Street offer so many types year-round? They've joined the bandwagon of restaurants that embrace the new method of cultivating oysters in aquafarms. Rather than growing on the river bottom in shoals, these new-age oysters are raised in cages the size of tabletops near the surface where water is cleaner and predators can't reach them. The result is healthier oysters that are available in every season.

Once you've had your fill of oysters (if that is possible), you can sample more raw bar delicacies: clams, shrimp, and crab claws. The rest of the menu offers a range of seafood dishes that are fresh and well prepared. Sure-bet appetizers: grilled rock octopus and crispy calamari. Sandwich favorites include creamy lobster rolls, Old Bay shrimp salad, and Atlantic mahi mahi. Cast iron crab cakes, seared scallops, fish and chips, and New England clam and lobster boils are popular main courses. Burgers and rib eye steaks are available for carnivores in the crowd.

The Cat's Eye Pub

1730 Thames Street
Baltimore, MD 21231
(410) 276-9866
www.catseyepub.com

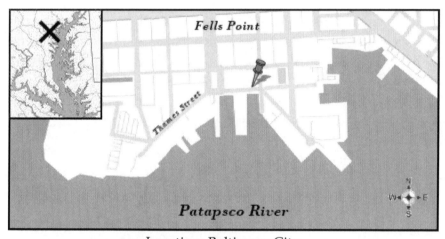

Location: Baltimore City
Open: Year Round ⚓ Dockage: No
Latitude: N 39° 16' 55" ⤇ Longitude: W 76° 35' 30"
Body of Water: Patapsco River
Driving Distance: Annapolis 31 miles,
Washington, DC 42 miles, Easton 64 miles

Atmosphere Meter

casual | | | | | | | | | | | formal

Plenty of Fells Point places offer live music, but Cat's Eye Pub is legendary for its unique array of bands. For decades, it's been the hot spot to hear authentic Celtic, jazz, rock, blues, and zydeco music, and the location is easy to find. Look for the building painted bright turquoise that bears a sign with a pirate cat tilting his head back in raucous laughter. The space isn't large, but it's divided into three sections: the front room for the main bar and bands, the middle area where the volume is a tad lower and conversation is possible, and the back patio that has heaters in the winter, fans in the summer, and ashtrays on every table.

With 40 beers on tap served at a perfect 34 degrees and one of the best Bloody Marys in town, Cat's Eye is determined to quench any thirst. Food is not available, but there's plenty of eye candy. Packed into this rustic bar is a cornucopia of mismatched but intriguing items: hand-carved wooden pirate cats, flags, fish, ships, a stuffed bear's head wearing a captain's hat, and a Christmas tree hung upside down from the ceiling. The focal point is a series of murals by local artist C.T. Newton that depicts the history of Ireland through colorful maps and drawings of heroes, priests, immigrants, and bar regulars.

Dating back to the early 1700s, this waterfront saloon has seen its share of dubious characters and barroom antics. During a recent visit, the bartender pointed out a spot where the wood didn't match the rest of the floor. Allegedly in the early 1900s during a brawl, a bar patron was shot in the chest. His blood didn't wash out, so they had to replace the boards with a different type of wood. Ghost stories are also a vital part of the building's folklore. A punching bag upstairs swings as if taking blows even when the windows are shut, and pictures mysteriously fall off the walls at night. Ah, if only those walls could talk.

The Point in Fells

1738 Thames Street
Baltimore, MD 21231
(410) 327-7264
www.thepointinfells.com

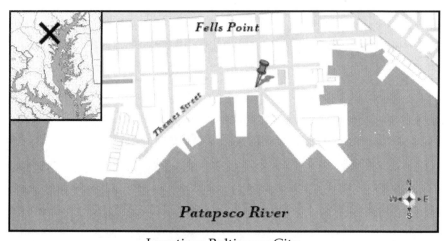

Location: Baltimore City
Open: Year Round ⚓ Dockage: No
Latitude: N 39° 16' 55" 🐟 Longitude: W 76° 35' 29"
Body of Water: Patapsco River
Driving Distance: Annapolis 31 miles,
Washington, DC 42 miles, Easton 64 miles

Restaurant Atmosphere Meter
casual | formal

Bar Atmosphere Meter
casual | formal

When you're navigating the crowds in Fells Point's busy bar scene, do you ever wish for a mellow spot to enjoy a good meal? Then head down to the corner of Thames and South Ann, and enter The Point in Fells. This family-owned gem is a one-stop shop where you can dine on well-prepared dishes and have a little fun, too.

On the street level, you find a comfortable, laid-back bar where chalkboards display the daily specials and TVs hum with news or sports events. If you're in the mood for light fare, grab some Pub Grub or indulge in a specialty cocktail. Orange Crushes are recommended. In the back is a lounge with an old brick floor that suggests it might have served as a patio in a past life. Now it's fully enclosed by white walls decorated with black-framed vintage pictures of Baltimore landmarks. Locals leisurely converse around the pool table and shuffleboard while keeping an eye on the Orioles game.

A calm ambiance awaits you upstairs in the dining room with mahogany floors, white linen tablecloths, beveled ceilings, and understated artwork. The subtle décor reflects the kitchen's desire to craft fine food in a casual-upscale climate. Small Plates encourage you to sample a variety of treats, especially the chef's selection of local oysters, trio of sliders (Angus, venison, and crab cakes), and shrimp scampi bruschetta. Large Plate highlights include seafood risotto, herb-crusted salmon, and Argentine buffalo skirt steak.

Captain James Seafood Palace

2127 Boston Street
Baltimore, MD 21231
Restaurant: (410) 327-8600
Crab House & Carry Out: (410) 675-1819
www.captainjameslanding.com

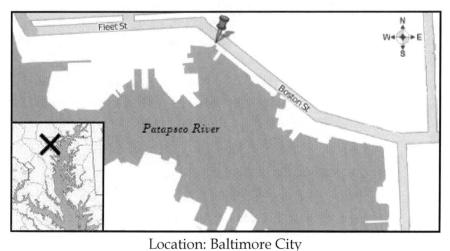

Location: Baltimore City
Open: Year Round ⚓ Dockage: Yes
Latitude: N 39° 17' 2" 🐟 Longitude: W 76° 35' 10"
Body of Water: Patapsco River
Driving Distance: Annapolis 33 miles,
Washington, DC 42 miles, Easton 66 miles

🍺 **Restaurant Atmosphere Meter** 🍸
casual | | | | | | | | | | formal

🍺 **Crab Deck Atmosphere Meter** 🍸
casual | | | | | | | | | | formal

As you cruise down Boston Street, don't be surprised
to see a building that looks like a huge ship anchored at the
curb. It's Captain James Seafood Palace — Baltimore's only

dining establishment shaped like a merchant vessel. Five brothers built the restaurant in 1978, and it's been a unique local landmark ever since.

The dining room's circular wooden bar with a crow's nest light fixture and O-shaped windows create the illusion of eating on board a cruise ship. Recent renovations to the interior resulted in a sleek nautical décor and set the tone for fine dining. The menu's classic Chesapeake cuisine showcases seafood specialties such as crab cakes, shrimp stuffed with crab imperial, sea scallops, lobster tail, flounder filet, roasted garlic mussels, and oysters Rockefeller. Want them all in one plate? Then go for the seafood steamer pot bubbling with shrimp, mussels, clams, crab, sausage, corn, and Old Bay.

If you're in the mood for casual fare, walk across the street to the crab house, where crabs and cold beer take center stage. Located right on the water overlooking Baltimore Harbor, the blue and white roof atop a wooden deck draws boaters and seafood lovers from miles around. All-you-can-eat steamed crabs head the menu's lineup, followed by littleneck clams, mussels, snow crab, and shrimp. Hush puppies, corn-on-the-cob, and boardwalk fries are served on the side. To help everyone partake in crab picking, a tutorial on the menu offers an 8-step program for releasing tender meat from the shell.

Bo Brooks Restaurant

2780 Lighthouse Point
Baltimore, MD 21224
(410) 558-0202
www.bobrooks.com

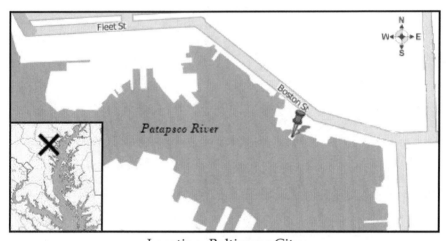

Location: Baltimore City
Open: Year Round ⚓ Dockage: Yes
Latitude: N 39° 16' 38" ➤ Longitude: W 76° 34' 44"
Body of Water: Patapsco River
Driving Distance: Annapolis 32 miles,
Washington, DC 45 miles, Easton 65 miles

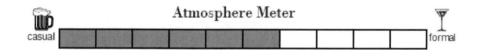

Atmosphere Meter

casual ▢ formal

Bo Brooks opened its doors in 1964 in the Gardenville section of East Baltimore. When it moved to the Canton Waterfront in 2000, owners refused to change their traditional Maryland style of cooking. Rather than boiler-steaming mass amounts of crabs and letting them sit around for hours, each meal is made to order to maximize flavor and texture. The secret spice blend has been delighting Baltimore taste buds for decades. Plus the atmosphere is hard to beat. Strolling past a gorgeous antique oak bar leads you to the dining area, where you can slide into a high-backed booth for privacy when picking crabs or spread out at a wooden table for more elbow room. The understated contemporary décor presents wall-to-wall windows and an occasional nautical item or map of the Chesapeake Bay.

When waiters deliver plastic trays piled high with hot steamed crabs, you see patrons' faces light up, anticipating these award-winning treats. The menu offers plenty of Bay classics: crab cakes, fried shrimp, and chicken Chesapeake. The kitchen shows a whimsical spirit with crab deviled eggs, crab pretzels, Crab Fluff (a beer-battered, deep-fried backfin cake) and the Balmer Steam Pot (crab claws, lobster tail, corn, and potatoes). The Half-and-Half irreverently swirls together tomato-based and cream crab soups.

Outside next to a black-and-white striped lighthouse, you can toss back rum drinks at the thatched-roof tiki hut while listening to bands. Who can resist specialty drinks named The Crab Knife (sweet tea vodka with pink lemonade) or Ocean City Crush (orange, grapefruit, lime, or strawberry)? If you have time, check out the *Black Eyed Susan* next door. This 19th century paddlewheel boat touts Victorian craftsmanship with nine-foot ceilings, brass sconces, and Tiffany lighting.

The BoatHouse Canton

2809 Boston Street
Baltimore, MD 21224
(410) 773-9795
www.boathousecanton.com

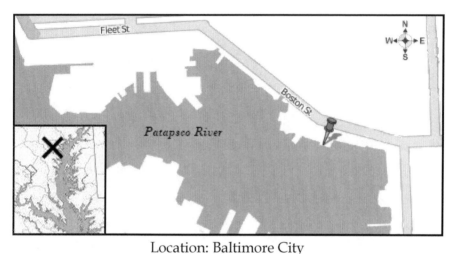

Location: Baltimore City
Open: Year Round ⚓ Dockage: Yes
Latitude: N 39° 16' 37" 〰 Longitude: W 76° 34' 35"
Body of Water: Patapsco River
Driving Distance: Annapolis 32 miles,
Washington, DC 45 miles, Easton 65 miles

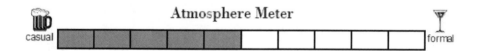

Gone are palm trees and sand of the former tiki-themed Bay Café. In its place is the new BoatHouse Canton, which artfully combines good food with an exceptional waterfront view. In the early 20th century, the building was part of the Tin Decorating Co., or Tindeco, that manufactured colorful decorative tin containers for cigarettes, cookies, candies, medicine, beer, and talcum powder. At peak production, Tindeco cranked out 4 million tins a day.

The factory's old smokestack towers above the newly renovated restaurant that sports a lovely contemporary décor with exposed brick walls, vaulted ceilings, arched windows, and wood tables with black metal legs. Outside, you can dine on the front patio or side deck with white lights stretched across the top. A covered space keeps rain away from the bar and band area. A row of white lifeguard chairs faces the water. The atmosphere is casual and fun, and it's even dog friendly, if your pup behaves.

Raw bar selections change daily. You can slurp down dozens of the Bay's best oysters from Maryland and Virginia, or nibble on fresh steamed clams, shrimp, or mussels. Fries dusted with Old Bay and topped with lump crab meat are irresistible, and the crab cakes are cooked to perfection. More seafood favorites: blackened tuna, fish and chips, and grilled salmon. Other options include salads, sandwiches, chicken, flatbreads, and burgers.

Hamilton's Canton Dockside

3301 Boston Street
Baltimore, MD 21224
(410) 276-8900
www.cantondockside.com

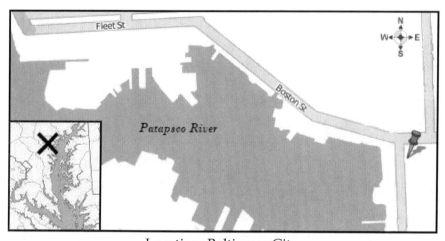

Location: Baltimore City
Open: Year Round ⚓ Dockage: No
Latitude: N 39° 16' 35" ➤ Longitude: W 76° 34' 8"
Body of Water: Patapsco River
Driving Distance: Annapolis 32 miles,
Washington, DC 45 miles, Easton 65 miles

Atmosphere Meter

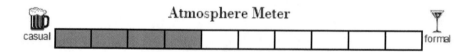

casual   formal

When you come to Canton Dockside, you better be serious about Maryland seafood. They are. Sure, you can order chicken, steak, or burgers, and you won't leave disappointed. But sticking to what they do best almost guarantees a terrific evening. The family deals directly with local watermen to ensure the best of the daily catch is served.

Everything is cooked to order — authentic Bay style and homemade. The menu offers a cornucopia of seafood options. And at the risk of sounding like Forrest Gump with his shrimp litany, Canton seems to have unlimited imagination for crab dishes: crab balls, crab pretzel, crab dip, crab cakes, crab soup, crab imperial, crab fluffs, crab alfredo, and crab marinara. Also on the menu: mussels, oysters, shrimp, sandwiches, burgers, salads, chicken, steak, and BBQ ribs.

Eating outside on the expansive wooden deck beneath a row of palm trees lets you feel warm breezes from the Bay. Dining inside offers a visual tribute to Maryland history and nautical tradition where murals depicting oystermen and crab pots, Baltimore and Annapolis landmark buildings, and local sports legends brighten the walls. Wherever you sit, the energy and personable staff make you want to return soon.

You're in for a treat if you head inland toward Canton Square, Baltimore's newest hot spot. The area was settled in the late 1800s by Polish, Irish, German, and other European immigrants who toiled in local factories and canneries. Twenty years of recent development have resulted in new condos, restaurants, and shops around a quaint grassy square.

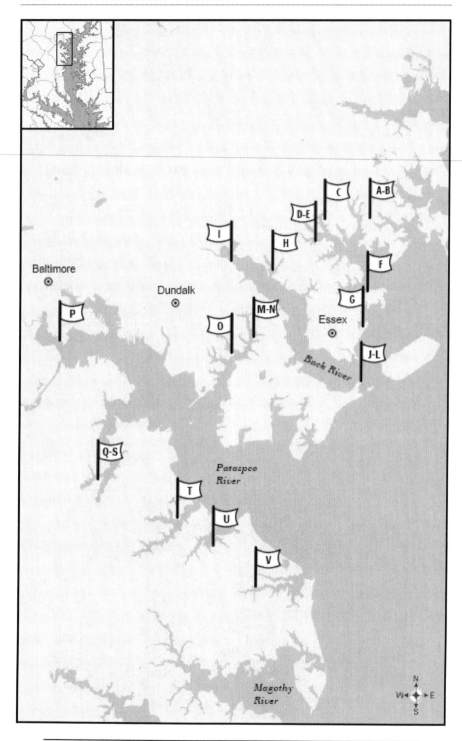

Baltimore Outskirts

Long Beach
Restaurant & Tavern

818 Bowleys Quarters Road
Middle River, MD 21220
(410) 335-9444
www.longbeachrestaurant.net

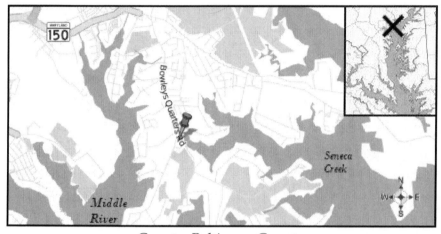

County: Baltimore County
Open: Year Round ⚓ Dockage: Yes
Latitude: N 39° 19' 16" 🛥 Longitude: W 76° 23' 33"
Body of Water: Seneca Creek
Driving Distance: Baltimore 15 miles,
Washington, DC 55 miles, Easton, 76 miles

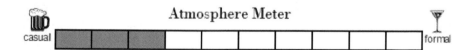

🍺 **Atmosphere Meter** 🍸
casual ░░░░   formal

When new owners renovated Long Beach Restaurant in
2012, they wisely preserved its down-home feel in the dining
room. Families and friends gather in a casual setting for
hearty meals at reasonable prices. Top Side Bar on the second
floor pours a nice sampling of local beers and hosts bands on

weekends. The tiki bar up on the roof combines tropical fun with a stellar view of the marina.

The "Steamed Crabs" sign holds a prominent place outside, showing the kitchen's knack for preparing traditional Chesapeake seafood. Local crabs are steamed fresh to order. Maryland crab soup or homemade chili can take the sting out of a wintry day. Crab cakes weigh in at 7 ounces, and 12 ounces of rib eye are grilled to your liking. Local rockfish and shrimp are doused with Old Bay, and Chincoteague oysters are fried to a golden crisp. Salads, wraps, pasta, ribs, and burgers complete the extensive menu.

Bowleys Quarters is named after Daniel Bowley, a sea captain who owned 2,000 acres of land here in the mid-1700s and housed his slaves in these "quarters." Decades later, his estate was converted to a game preserve where presidents, politicians, and even Babe Ruth came to hunt ducks. The steel manufacturing heyday of the 1900s brought blue-collar families to the area. More recently, floods from Hurricane Isabel wreaked havoc here and destroyed hundreds of buildings. But these hard-working folks have rebuilt their community and welcome visitors to their home on the Bay.

Sunset Cove

3408 Red Rose Farm Road
Middle River, MD 21220
(410) 630-2031
www.sunsetcovemd.com

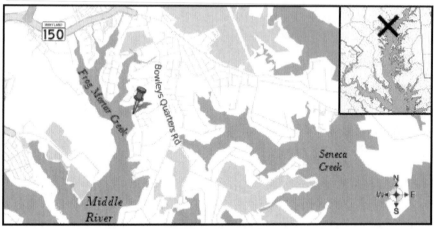

County: Baltimore County
Open: Year Round ⚓ Dockage: Yes
Latitude: N 39° 19' 26" ➤ Longitude: W 76° 23' 59"
Body of Water: Frog Mortar Creek off the Middle River
Driving Distance: Baltimore 18 miles,
Washington, DC 55 miles, Easton 76 miles

Atmosphere Meter

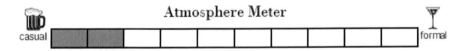

casual | | | | | | | | | | | formal

Sunset Cove is the type of place that makes you want to call in sick on a warm spring day, because it's a tropical island escape right in Baltimore County. You're tempted to sneak out of the office to dig your toes in the sand, listen to a band, or watch boats cruise along Frog Mortar Creek. T-shirts, flip-flops, and baggy shorts work just fine, because people come here to kick back, soak up the sun, and eat good food. The restaurant changed hands in 2012 (formerly Wild Duck Café), bringing a new energy to this fantastic location. Four service bars and a thatched hut shake things up with orange crushes and icy beers. Tiki lanterns on the beach cast a warm light along the water's edge.

The elevated deck is covered with a blue awning that shades folks who want to enjoy the view of a tree-lined marina where boats tie up to a 300-foot pier. The air-conditioned dining room offers relief from the dog days of summer. Live bands elevate the festive atmosphere.

A mixed menu fits the locale perfectly, blending Maryland seafood classics with Caribbean island cuisine. Jumbo lump crab cakes claim to be "all killer and no filler," and steamer pots are packed with shrimp, mussels, and littleneck clams. Jerk chicken, and Key West shrimp strut their tropical roots. Pub fare basics like burgers, wings, salads, and wraps match every whim and wallet. Exceptional entrees include Chesapeake seafood marinara and chicken topped with crab imperial and cheddar cheese. Follow the smoky aroma and you'll find the pit beef stand hard to resist.

Carson's Creekside
Restaurant & Lounge

1110 Beech Drive
Middle River, MD 21220
(410) 238-0080
www.carsonscreekside.com

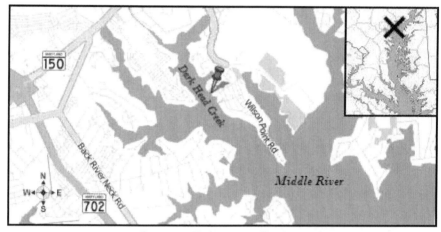

County: Baltimore County
Open: Year Round ⚓ Dockage: Yes
Latitude: N 39° 19' 16" ⚓ Longitude: W 76° 25' 35"
Body of Water: Dark Head Creek off the Middle River
Driving Distance: Baltimore 15 miles,
Washington, DC 56 miles, and Easton 77 miles

Restaurant Atmosphere Meter

casual ▢▢▢▢▢▢▢▢▢▢▢ formal

Bar and Deck Atmosphere Meter

casual ▢▢▢▢▢▢▢▢▢▢▢ formal

You wouldn't expect to find a Chesapeake gem so close to a busy state airport, but that's where you'll discover Carson's

Creekside. An antique wooden fish, old crab pots, and buoys outside reveal a clue that Bay culinary traditions and laid-back lifestyles are cherished inside. Its one-story red brick building is larger than it appears from the parking lot, but once you step inside, the place opens up to reveal a cozy dining room, as well as a casual bar area and waterfront deck with stunning views of Dark Head Creek. Children feed noisy ducks at the dock down by the water.

A long hallway to the restrooms displays nautical items, hand-painted murals of fishing boats, and vintage photos of family members who cooked meals under this roof decades ago. Pickled pigs' feet and fried chicken were crowd pleasers back in 1948 when the restaurant opened. Today's patrons line up to sample a variety of crab dishes: fist-sized crab cakes, crab nachos, crab egg rolls, crab pretzels with melted cheddar, and fries topped with a crab-laced cream sauce.

The menu changes seasonally to ensure the freshest local ingredients. Regional seafood and classic steaks take center stage. Bay-influenced entrees, such as shrimp stuffed with crab imperial and bouillabaisse with crusty bread are matched by meat lovers' prime rib, chicken marsala, and baby back ribs. Pasta with shrimp and mussels is a savory treat. Light fare includes salads and sandwiches such as French dip, seafood wrap, and pulled pork.

Crab Decks & Tiki Bars of the Chesapeake Bay, 2015 Maryland Edition

The River Watch Restaurant

207 Nanticoke Road
Essex, MD 21221
(410) 687-1422
www.riverwatchrestaurant.com

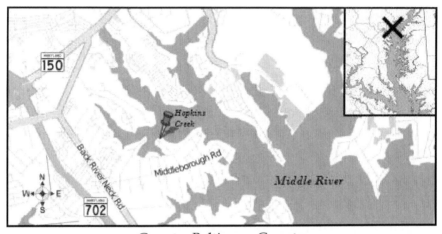

County: Baltimore County
Open: Year Round ⚓ Dockage: Yes
Latitude: N 39° 18' 42" ⟞ Longitude: W 76° 25' 56"
Body of Water: Hopkins Creek off the Middle River
Driving Distance: Baltimore 12 miles,
Washington, DC 54 miles, Easton 74 miles

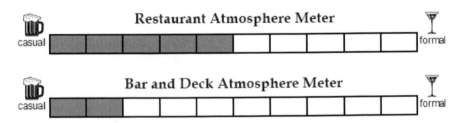

Some people like the calm solitude of the Bay in winter.
They hunker down in places with stone fireplaces and
steaming bowls of crab soup that offer a respite to the bitter
cold. Others prefer the livelier pulse of summer, where

bikinis, boats, and beer rule in the sun. River Watch finds a way to accommodate both seasons and temperaments.

The dining room's cozy atmosphere can melt away the worst case of the dreary February blues. Rows of beautifully etched glass panels depict the region's nautical heritage through schooners and sailboats, and remind you that winter will eventually end and you'll soon be back out on the water.

When the weather breaks, people pack away their bulky sweaters, pull on a T-shirt and shorts, and head for River Watch. The huge outdoor deck is big enough to fit everyone who's emerging from hibernation. A covered deck with a bar runs the entire length of the building. A lower-level patio, with bars on both ends, sparkles from strings of white lights overhead. Boaters tie up at the marina, ready for action. A band starts to play, and the moonlight party begins.

The food is fresh, and the kitchen skillfully blends Chesapeake cuisine with classic American fare. Salads are crisp, and steaks are juicy. Noteworthy entrees include slow-cooked prime rib, creamy crab imperial, and chicken and crab marsala. Sandwiches cover the basics from fried oyster subs to reubens and burgers. You can end the night with a special rum cocktail or a brownie sundae for two.

The Crazy Tuna Bar & Grille

203 Nanticoke Road
Essex, MD 21221
(443) 559-9073
www.thecrazytunabar.com

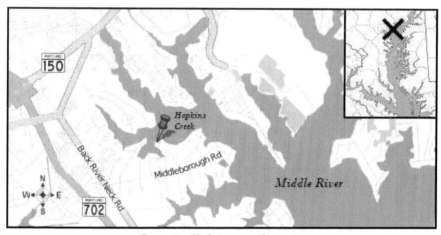

County: Baltimore County
Open: Year Round ⚓ Dockage: Yes
Latitude: N 39° 18' 41" 🐟 Longitude: W 76° 25' 58"
Body of Water: Hopkins Creek off the Middle River
Driving Distance: Baltimore 12 miles,
Washington, DC 54 miles, Easton 74 miles

Restaurant Atmosphere Meter
casual | | | | | | | | | | | formal

Bar and Deck Atmosphere Meter
casual | | | | | | | | | | | formal

They call it Crazy Tuna, but it looks more like crazy tiki
when you pull up to the dock on Hopkins Creek. Palm trees
sprout out of the sand, bright blue and yellow beach
umbrellas cover picnic tables at the waterfront, white lights

are strung from pole to pole, and crowds of merry folks line up at the outdoor bar with cool beverages in their hands. It's the newest addition to this area, launched in 2014.

Things settle down a bit when you go inside the restaurant, where the décor favors a traditional nautical theme. The bar is located in the center of the building with dining areas on either side. Fishnets hold starfish and seashells above tall windows facing the water. Vintage anchors, oars, and fish are hung on the walls. The casual vibe makes it an easy-going neighborhood hangout.

The menu features variations on local seafood, and all the Chesapeake staples are covered with crab cakes, shrimp salad, fried oysters, and rockfish bites. Blackened tuna tacos and salmon BLT are welcome additions. Noteworthy entrees include chicken breast stuffed with crab imperial and 12-ounce rib eye steaks. Sandwiches, wraps, salads, pasta, and a kids menu with cheese pizza and chicken tenders make sure everyone leaves the table happy. Note to boaters: Crazy Tuna offers 45 free transient slips that can hold boats of any size up to 100 feet if you call ahead for reservations.

Sue Island Grill & Crab House

900 Baltimore Yacht Club Road
Essex, MD 21221
(443) 574-0009
www.sueislandgrillandcrabhouse.com

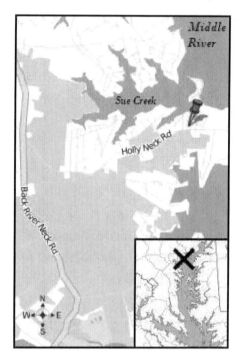

County: Baltimore County

Open: Year Round

Dockage: Yes

Latitude: N 39° 17' 4"

Longitude: W 76° 23' 43"

Body of Water: Sue Creek
off the Middle River

Driving Distance:
Baltimore 15 miles
Washington, DC 57 miles
Easton 76 miles

Atmosphere Meter

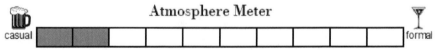

casual / formal

It's perfectly fine to serve crabs and beer at a marina dock bar. But once you add a touch or two of tiki, people start to smile ... and relax ... and have a little more fun. That's what is happening at Sue Island Grill. Nestled among the boats at Sue Creek, this charming little place offers a fabulous view of the water. The rustic tiki bar brings a dash of color with strings of hibiscus flowers, a mermaid piñata, a few plastic sharks, and a palm tree made of lights.

Under the covered pavilion, picnic tables are lined up with families in T-shirts and bathing suits, and tiki torches cast an amber glow along the white picket fence.

A sign above the doorway to the dining room, "Friends Gather Here," simply states that neighbors and guests are always welcome. The walls are covered with hand-painted pictures of power and fishing boats with names of the beloved captains and vessels that cruise the local waters. Friday karaoke nights and bands on weekends energize the crowd.

Hot steamed crabs, shrimp, and corn-on-the-cob are presented on blue plastic trays with wooden hammers for whacking shells. Oysters in season are sumptuous. If you're not in a seafood mood, check the daily specials board for hearty home-style dishes such as a rack of ribs, New York strip steaks with fries. Spicy wings, burgers, and grilled BBQ chicken breast are cooked just right. At Sue Island, it's all about easy living and Chesapeake summertime.

Crab Decks & Tiki Bars of the Chesapeake Bay, 2015 Maryland Edition

Island View Waterfront Café

2542 Island View Road
Essex, MD 21221
(410) 687-9799
www.islandviewwaterfrontcafe.com

County: Baltimore County

Open: Seasonal

Dockage: Yes

Latitude: N 39° 16' 8"

Longitude: W 76° 23' 46"

Body of Water: directly on
the Chesapeake Bay at
Browns Creek

Driving Distance:
Baltimore 16 miles
Washington, DC 58 miles
Easton 78 miles

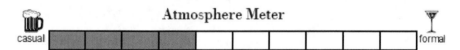

Atmosphere Meter

casual ▮▮▮▮▮▮▯▯▯▯▯▯ formal

When this Chesapeake gem was built in 1928, Island View served as a dance hall, tavern, and picnic grove. Even in the remote necks of the Bay, jazz and blues had permeated the radio waves, and Prohibition rules were beginning to crumble. Imagine women dressed in their Saturday night best testing the latest dance moves with men who took an occasional sip from a flask tucked inside their jackets. In 1968, the Laing family bought the restaurant. They've handed it down for three generations to family members who add upgrades but maintain a welcoming down-home feel.

The calm blue walls are decorated with duck decoys, paintings of waterfowl, and antique memorabilia. On the deck, you're treated to a beautiful waterfront scene of picnic tables on the lawn, families playing horseshoes, and boats tied up to a long wooden pier. The home-style food reminds you of what was served in your grandmother's kitchen. Crab cakes, oyster po' boys, catfish, pot roast, fried chicken, stuffed pork chops, and seafood marinara are dished out in hefty portions. Shrimp salad, pulled pork tacos, and burgers are delicious. Crab omelets and chipped beef with gravy are highlights on the breakfast menu.

Be sure to check out the gun ceremoniously hung on the door frame leading to the bar. It's a replica of a historic Bay punt gun that makes environmentalists cringe. These cannon-like shotguns were used in the 1800s to hunt waterfowl. The gun's recoil was so strong that hunters had to mount them on flat-bottom boats called "punts." After loading these guns with a pound of shot, they'd fire with a deafening roar and kill up to 50 ducks with one blast. Groups of hunters could bag 500 birds in a day. This decimated the waterfowl population, and Federal laws banned punt guns by 1920.

Brewer's Landing Bar & Grill

801 Woodrow Avenue
Essex, MD 21221
(443) 231-5037
www.brewerslanding.net

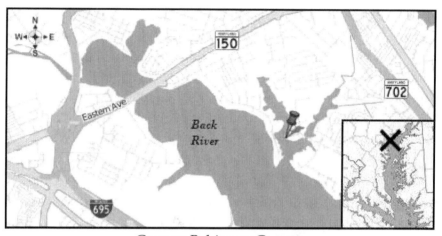

County: Baltimore County
Open: Year Round ⚓ Dockage: Yes
Latitude: N 39° 17' 45" ⤜ Longitude: W 76° 27' 49"
Body of Water: Duck Creek off Back River
Driving Distance: Baltimore 11 miles,
Washington, DC 51 miles, Easton 71 miles

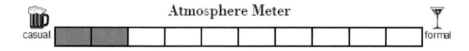

There's always something happening at Brewer's Landing.
Bands get things moving on the dance floor each weekend
and Ravens or Orioles fans are glued to 14 flat-screened TVs.
They've got buckets of beer, pool tables, Texas Hold 'Em
tournaments, darts leagues, and even Keno machines if you're
feeling lucky. Crab shells painted with NFL team logos are

displayed on a wall tracking each team's progress during the football season. It's a home away from home for sports fans.

If you can pull yourself away from this indoor fun, you'll discover plenty to do outside. Under the awning, long lines of wooden tables and chairs offer a view of Duck Creek. Picnic tables scattered about the grassy area bring you closer to the water's edge. Tiki lights mounted on the wooden fence cast a festive light while people take turns tossing horseshoes.

The menu gives early birds the choice of eggs, pancakes, creamed chipped beef with gravy, or buttery french toast for breakfast. You need to use both hands for the Brewer's Special Sandwich of scrapple, bacon, sausage, egg, and cheese.

Daily specials offer good prices for steamed shrimp, meatball subs, or steak and crab cake dinner. The regular menu starts with standard pub favorites of nachos, spicy chicken wings, crab dip, and loaded potato skins. Burgers, wraps, salads, pizza, and quesadillas round out the casual fare, while steamers, crab cakes, and batter-fried fish give a nod to old-school Chesapeake cooking. Steak, chicken breasts, and pork chops encourage carnivores in the crowd to eat, drink, and be merry.

Malibu Beach Bar Restaurant

8247 Eastern Avenue
Baltimore, MD 21224
(410) 282-5050

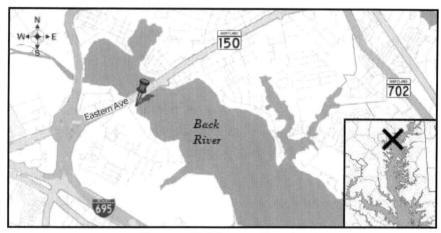

County: Baltimore County
Open: Year Round ⚓ Dockage: No
Latitude: N 39° 18' 1" ➦ Longitude: W 76° 29' 26"
Body of Water: Back River
Driving Distance: Baltimore 7 miles,
Washington, DC 48 miles, Easton 68 miles

Atmosphere Meter

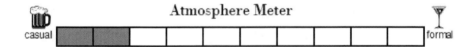

casual ... formal

As you drive west out of Essex on Route 150 and cross the bridge over Back River, it's hard to miss Malibu Beach Bar. Mounted on top of a 20-foot tall pole is a giant blue swordfish sign that serves as a beacon to the restaurant below. The top of the building is trimmed with a row of neon blue waves cresting toward a pair of lighthouses on the front corners.

Formerly named Bluefins until 2012, this place is a secret island getaway. On the beach area, green glowing palms trees line up along a white lattice fence to mark the spot where music and laughter are top priorities. Wooden picnic tables are packed with patrons enjoying the waterfront view or working their way through a dozen steamed crabs.

This place starts hopping on warm summer nights. Between the bands and the DJs, the air is filled with happy noise. At the outside bar, a large blue swordfish trapped in a wooden Tommy Bahama Rum crate holds glasses for the Crush Station, where tropicolada, melonball, and orange crushes are ready to quench your thirst.

The inside dining area's rustic tiki décor reminds you of a dark tropical jungle with touches of bamboo and island artwork leading out to a plant-lined patio. Crabs — all you can eat or by the dozen — are spiced just right. Crab cakes and burgers lead the charge of casual fare. It's a summer celebration destination that serves local seafood, chicken, and assorted munchies at a reasonable price.

Islander Inn

9008 Cuckold Point Road
Sparrows Point, MD 21219
(410) 388-0713
www.islanderinnandcatering.com

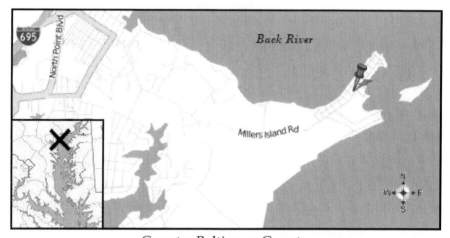

County: Baltimore County
Open: Year Round ⚓ Dockage: No
Latitude: N 39° 14' 0" 🐟 Longitude: W 76° 24' 13"
Body of Water: between the Back River and the Chesapeake Bay
Driving Distance: Baltimore 14 miles,
Washington, DC 51 miles, Easton 66 miles

Atmosphere Meter

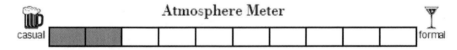

casual   formal

    When Hurricane Isabel came barreling up the East Coast in 2003, her damage to the Bay was catastrophic. She was especially harsh to Millers Island, dumping 3.2 tons of debris on residents' front lawns and destroying more than 300 buildings. But as you look at the neighborhoods near

Islander Inn, you see new homes defiantly built up high and to code to withstand nature's next tempest.

Islander Inn has a stubborn sturdiness that makes you believe it can survive anything — and it has since 1991. The blue dining room walls are trimmed with a border of red and white lighthouses, and a nautical theme plays throughout.

Crabs, fishing poles, blue marlins, pictures of boats, and even a six-pack of Bud caught in a net decorate the dining area. Duck decoys and fishing gear garnish the top of the wood and pressed-tin bar. Ravens fans gather around a dimly lit pool table to discuss strategies for winning another world championship.

The food is traditional Bay cuisine: crabs are blended in a creamy dip, tucked into soft pretzels, pressed into cakes, fried soft, or simply steamed fresh and hot. Jumbo shrimp is lightly breaded and fried until golden brown. Pork is pulled into tender BBQ bites, and prime rib is slow-cooked to mouth-watering perfection. Sour beef comes with potato dumplings, and purple shooters are passed around after Ravens' touchdowns. It's hard to skip a place as authentic as this.

Crab Decks & Tiki Bars of the Chesapeake Bay, 2015 Maryland Edition

Dock of the Bay

9025 Cuckold Point Road
Sparrows Point, MD 21219
(410) 477-8100
www.dockofthebay.net

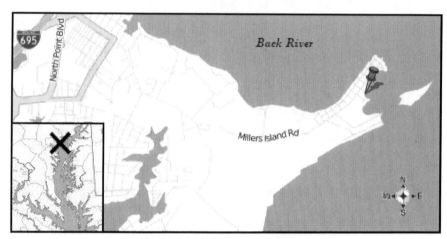

County: Baltimore County
Open: Year Round ⚓ Dockage: Yes
Latitude: N 39° 14' 1" 🐟 Longitude: W 76° 24' 6"
Body of Water: directly on the Chesapeake Bay at the Back River
Driving Distance: Baltimore 14 miles,
Washington, DC 51 miles, Easton 66 miles

Atmosphere Meter

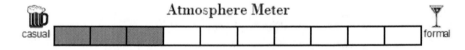

casual   formal

Dock of the Bay is a landmark on this neck of the Bay.
"I've been coming here picking crabs since I was just a little
girl. I can't imagine a time when it wasn't part of our lives,"
says the bartender and smiles. Well, it was shuttered for a
brief period, but reopened in 2014 with an 80-foot long wood
bar and seven wide-screen TVs mounted on the walls.

A big green awning stretches over the patio and matching umbrellas shield patrons from the sun on 6,500 square feet of outdoor seating. Kayla's Cover, a sandy play area, tempts kids to crawl around a wooden pirate ship and imagine a swashbuckler's life on the seas.

Boaters like the free docking on the 105-foot long pier, where sets of Adirondack chairs are placed, encouraging you to enjoy the view. And what a sight you'll see. Surrounded by glistening waters stands the historic Craighill Lighthouse, built in 1875. It's the tallest lighthouse in Maryland. The red and white, four-sided pyramid design was constructed with a granite base and wood and iron structure.

The only thing that could drag you away from this spectacular sight is the smell of crabs steaming and steaks sizzling. The menu runs the gamut of fresh seafood delivered each morning by local watermen: crab cakes, shrimp, rockfish, oysters, fish and chips, and more. Fried, steamed, or broiled — whatever you want; cooked the way you like it. Burgers, chicken, and a little pirates menu ensure everyone gets his fill.

Rowboat Willie's Dock Bar

9033 Cuckold Point Road
Sparrows Point, MD 21219
(410) 477-5137

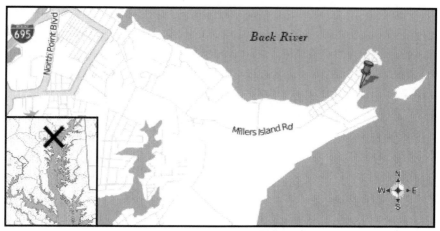

County: Baltimore County
Open: Seasonal ⚓ Dockage: Yes
Latitude: N 39° 14' 2" ⤖ Longitude: W 76° 24' 6"
Body of Water: directly on the Chesapeake Bay at the Back River
Driving Distance: Baltimore 14 miles,
Washington, DC 51 miles, Easton 66 miles

Atmosphere Meter

casual ▮▯▯▯▯▯▯▯▯▯ formal

It's a simple two-story structure — more wooden deck than building — with a few palm trees, colorful umbrellas, and tables scattered around.

But what makes Rowboat Willie's special is the spectacular location. It's smack dab in the middle of a boatyard at the tip of Millers Island where the Back River flows into the Chesapeake, and you'd be hard-pressed to find a more expansive view of the Bay.

With music playing gently in the background, kick back on the upper deck, grab a cold beer or frozen drink, and watch the boats arrive at Bill's Yacht Basin Marina. Owners recently added a new roof to the upper deck and a kitchen to cook basic seafood dishes and hearty pub fare.

Out beyond the shore is Hart-Miller Island State Park, a 244-acre preserve that's only accessible by boat. It used to be three islands — Hart, Miller and Pleasure — but the spaces in between are getting filled in with dredge materials from Baltimore Harbor.

In the 1940s, Pleasure Island was developed as an amusement park, connected to the mainland by a wooden bridge, but storms knocked out the bridge in the 1960s. Today, the island's main visitors are waterfowl, migrating birds, and adventure-seeking boaters who come ashore to wade along its sandy beaches or enjoy a scenic picnic lunch.

The Sea Horse Inn

710 Wise Avenue
Dundalk, MD 21222
(410) 388-1150

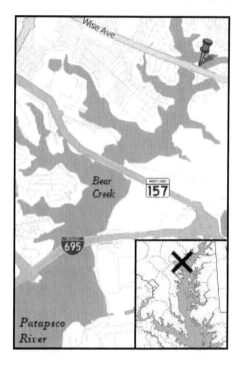

County: Baltimore County

Open: Year Round

Dockage: Yes

Latitude: N 39° 15' 38"

Longitude: W 76° 28' 29"

Body of Water: Oakleigh Cove
off Bear Creek off the
Patapsco River

Driving Distance:
Baltimore 10 miles
Washington, DC 49 miles
Easton 64 miles

Atmosphere Meter

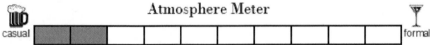

casual ▮▮▮ formal

One should never underestimate the value of a good neighborhood bar. It's the place to go in good times and bad to find a little cheer among friends. Even if you don't live in Dundalk — which has seen its share of life's ups and downs — Sea Horse welcomes you like you're family.

It's located in a neighborhood that makes anyone who grew up in an industrial Northeast town feel a sense of nostalgia, if not a little homesick. Streets are lined with red brick ramblers built for working families who toiled for generations in the steel mills. It harkens back to the day when churches, union halls, and corner bars created a holy trinity of social life in tight-knit, blue-collar communities.

Sea Horse's two-story building was recently renovated, giving the space a brighter, upbeat feel. The walls and ceiling display a unique collection of stuff that blends a nautical theme with an assortment of things left behind. Plastic fish, blue crabs, over-sized fishing lures, and yellow water skis are tacked up next to beer steins — and best of all, a two-foot long baby doll's leg that gets a fresh sock to mark holidays.

On the upper deck, you're treated to wooden patio furniture painted a rainbow of bright Caribbean colors. Down by the water, the tree-lined banks present a lovely view, and boaters come ashore ready for a cold one and a game or two of horseshoes.

Standard American fare claims the menu, with a home-cooked touch and seafood fresh from local waters. Cream of crab soup and crab cakes are exceptional, and the shrimp salad makes a perfect lunch. Seafood steamers give you a tasty sampling of the Bay's best treats. Landlubbers enjoy grilled chicken salad, pizza, juicy burgers, spicy wings, steaks, and hot roast beef sandwiches.

The Seasoned Mariner

601 Wise Avenue
Dundalk, MD 21222
(443) 242-7190
www.seasonedmariner.com

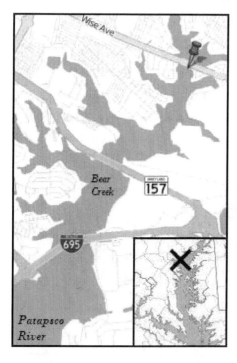

County: Baltimore County

Open: Year Round

Dockage: Yes

Latitude: N 39° 15' 37"

Longitude: W 76° 28' 36"

Body of Water: Bear Creek
off the Patapsco River

Driving Distance:
Baltimore 10 miles
Washington, DC 49 miles
Easton 64 miles

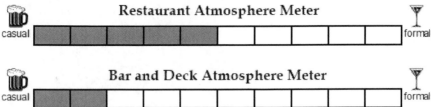

Restaurant Atmosphere Meter

casual — formal

Bar and Deck Atmosphere Meter

casual — formal

Over the years, it's been called Beach House, Bahama Mama's, Dick's on the Dock, and Bear Creek Inn, but for quite some time, the sign out front has read The Seasoned Mariner. Despite all its name changes, the location remains spectacular, and the location joins the club of hidden treasures on the Bay. Views of the bridge over Bear Creek and curving banks form a lovely backdrop for casual waterfront dining and crab deck fun. Palm trees in the sand, children's play area, busy outside bar, and colorful umbrellas create an upbeat island vibe.

Indoors, the owners give diners a cozy ambience and a pleasant setting to enjoy a nice meal. They painted the walls creamy gold and earthy sage and posed tropical plants in the corners. The subtle nautical theme uses hand-painted fish to brighten the décor. A porcelain mermaid wearing a bikini top made of turtle shells keeps an eye on the dining room. The ceiling-to-floor, indoor waterfall behind the bar lulls you into a relaxed state of mind.

The menu focuses on fresh seafood and makes the most of local watermen's daily catch. Special starters include cod fish cakes, crab dip, and clam strips. Cream of crab soup is velvety and laced with jumbo lump chunks. Mountains of steamed crabs are terrific. Irresistible entrees: Piping hot Smith Island stew, crab mushroom casserole in a sherry cream sauce, and horseradish crusted rockfish. Steaks, sandwiches, chicken, sushi, and pasta are also available.

Hard Yacht Café

8500 Cove Road
Dundalk, MD 21222
(443) 407-0038
www.hardyacht.com

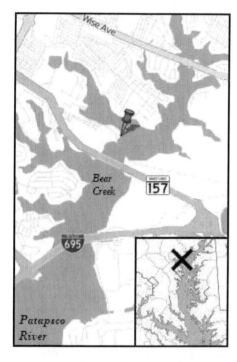

County: Baltimore County

Open: Year Round

Dockage: Yes

Latitude: N 39° 15' 4"

Longitude: W 76° 29' 20"

Body of Water: Bear Creek
off the Patapsco River

Driving Distance:
Baltimore 49 miles
Washington, DC 49 miles
Easton 64 miles

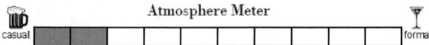

Atmosphere Meter

casual | | | | | | | | | | formal

Some of the best restaurants around the Bay tell stories of humble beginnings — an oyster shucking plant or a spot at the local marina with a few beach chairs and a cooler. The birth of Hard Yacht Café follows this admirable tradition. In the 1980s the property was "nothing more than a trash pile for debris that was pulled from the rest of the dump-like marina."

They laid a deck, added picnic tables, and put up a cover as shelter from bad weather. After walls were built, it became the Crab Shack. Over the years came refrigerators, coffeepots, a stove, and other amenities until it evolved into a beloved local hangout and a testament to what friends and family can accomplish after a few beers and a lot of sweat equity.

Today, Hard Yacht Café is a visual cornucopia of stuff collected and tacked up on the walls. Palm trees sprout from the deck, a ship's bridge serves as the deck cover, and the tiki bar sign is painted on an overturned row boat. Surfboards, rusty crab pots, Ravens banners, nautical flags, electric guitars, and more fill every nook and corner.

Amidst the easy-going Key West atmosphere is a staff that bends over backward to please and food that is creative and casual. Local seafood, appetizers, and sandwiches dominate the menu with signature dishes like crab and shrimp egg rolls, fried haddock with Yuengling beer batter, Big Ass Steak, and mussels steamed with feta and tomatoes. At night, the place rocks with music, cold beer, and merriment. Warning: It's not easy to find, so pay attention to your GPS. If you get lost, you'll wind through rusty buildings that represent Dundalk's proud industrial heritage — when national treasures such as the Golden Gate Bridge, Madison Square Garden, and Metropolitan Opera House were built with Bethlehem steel.

Nick's Fish House

2600 Insulator Drive
Baltimore, MD 21230
(410) 347-4123
www.nicksfishhouse.com

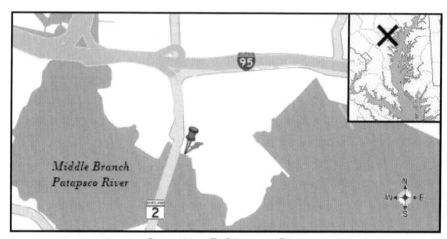

Location: Baltimore City
Open: Year Round ⚓ Dockage: Yes
Latitude: N 39° 15' 38" ➤ Longitude: W 76° 36' 49"
Body of Water: Middle Branch Patapsco River
Driving Distance: Annapolis 30 miles,
Washington, DC 41 miles, Easton 60 miles

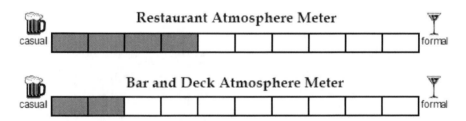

Nick's is a just-right kind of place — not too fancy, not
too rowdy — and the staff pulls out all the stops to ensure
everyone has a good time. It's located in Baltimore's industrial
Locust Point, where brick and steel warehouses provide a

backdrop for boats gliding along the water. The area is poised for development, and new owners of the restaurant made modest upgrades in 2015, but Nick's is still a perfect place to hear a band and take in a fabulous view of the Hanover Street Bridge. Built in 1916, its graceful arches meet in the middle to support a drawbridge that opens for ships traveling to and from Baltimore. Rosy sunsets accentuate the design.

Inside the bustling restaurant, you see a tribute to Chesapeake traditions in both the décor and cuisine. Vintage signs, boats, and crab pots pay homage to the Bay, and the menu focuses on seafood caught nearby. The food is terrific, and the raw bar is packed with fresh local oysters. Hefty signature crab cakes with creamy cole slaw, Natty Boh fish and chips, and New England steamer pots with shrimp, clams, and mussels guarantee you won't leave hungry. Beef tenderloin and Old Bay wings make meat lovers grin.

When you're finished eating, pause for a moment outside and listen for the ghosts of Captain John Smith and his crew. In 1608, he sailed the length of the Patapsco in an unsuccessful attempt to find the Pacific Ocean. Some say late at night you can hear Smith's men shouting and the ship's floorboards creaking on the water. You're more likely to spot a spirit if you take along one of Nick's rum punch cocktails.

Crab Decks & Tiki Bars of the Chesapeake Bay, 2015 Maryland Edition

Reckless Ric's Bar & Grill

1702 Furnace Drive
Glen Burnie, MD 21060
(410) 590-2280
www.recklessrics.com

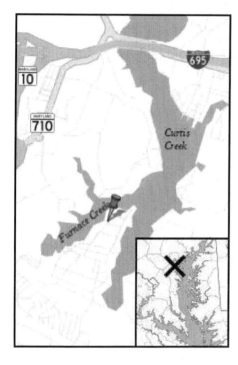

County: Anne Arundel County

Open: Year Round

Dockage: Yes

Latitude: N 39° 11' 1"

Longitude: W 76° 35' 9"

Body of Water: Furnace Creek
off Curtis Creek off the
Patapsco River

Driving Distance:
Baltimore 10 miles
Washington, DC 42 miles
Easton 53 miles

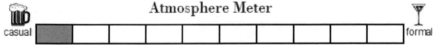

Atmosphere Meter

casual ▮▮▮▮▮▮▮▮▮▮ formal

If you follow the roaring thunder of a Harley passing through Glen Burnie, you might end up at Reckless Ric's. A big red sign out front welcomes bikers, boaters, and locals into this self-described "Redneck Yacht Club."

A mural in blue tones along the side wall depicts the dreamy side of motorcycle living through babes, beaches, and bikes. Patrons are reminded to be on their best behavior with messages stating, "Respect the neighborhood, will ya. Show your class and not your ass."

Not a bad idea, because everyone should get a chance to enjoy this high-energy locale. The centerpiece of the large waterfront beach area is a massive tree trunk detailed with ominous-looking tiki masks. Palm trees in the sand stand out in contrast to maples and oaks that grow in the neighborhood. Bright blue and yellow umbrellas invite you to kick off your boots and push your toes into the sand. Inside is a collage of leather, tattoos, and pool tables. Billiards leagues and bike shows attract a colorful crowd of folks having a good time.

The menu is hearty casual with appetizers like crab dip, steamed shrimp, jerk chicken, and hot wings. Crab soup and chili take the edge off a cold wintry ride. Salads and shrimp wraps help cool you down in the summer. Seafood entrees include crab cake sandwiches and blackened fish tacos. Meat eaters go for hot roast beef platter, Reckless rib eyes, burgers, chicken, and pizza. Specialty drinks include the vodka-rich Reckless on the Beach and Bamboo Bacardi Brew. It's all classic Americana, with an extra dash of freedom.

Point Pleasant Beach Tavern

1750 Marley Avenue
Glen Burnie, MD 21060
(410) 553-0600

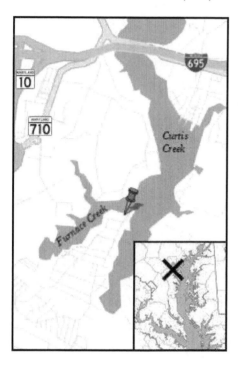

County: Anne Arundel County

Open: Seasonal

Dockage: No

Latitude: N 39° 11' 6"

Longitude: W 76° 34' 56"

Body of Water: Curtis Creek
off the Patapsco River

Driving Distance:
Baltimore 10 miles
Washington, DC 42 miles
Easton 53 miles

Atmosphere Meter

casual 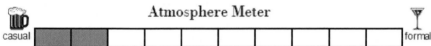 formal

Point Pleasant Beach Tavern's one-story red building has a low-key, unassuming vibe. Even the restaurant's name gets second billing to the Pepsi logo on the sign out front. No matter. Folks around Glen Burnie know it's there. Neighborhood watering holes like this are the backbone of working-class communities, along with churches, schools, union halls, and family-owned shops.

The restaurant doesn't have many windows on the front. Instead, it saves the fabulous view for the tables that face the creek and boats tied up at the dock. It sits right on the water's edge — so close that you might wonder how it has survived the storms and floods that hit these towns far too often.

During summer, the beach area is packed with picnic tables and children who don't dare traipse inside if their bathing suit is dripping wet. You can swim, sunbathe, or take a catnap in the shade — whatever suits your fancy. Inside the rustic tavern you can unwind at the pool tables, dartboards, or pinball machine. Beer posters and neon signs provide the artwork for walls painted with a splash of purple to show Ravens pride.

The down-home food is simple and connected to the seafood of the Bay. Burgers, sandwiches, crabs, and pub fare are tasty and filling. And the staff aims to please everyone who comes to Point Pleasant. Need proof? They lifted up the bottom of a chain-link fence so ducks can take an easier route to the water. Now, that's hometown hospitality.

Mutiny Pirate Bar & Island Grille

1653 Marley Avenue
Glen Burnie, MD 21060
(410) 787-2050
www.mutinypiratebar.com

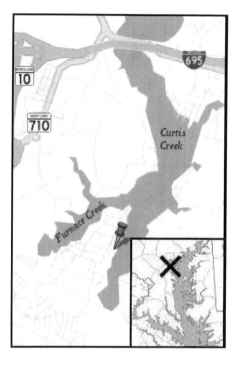

County: Anne Arundel County

Open: Year Round

Dockage: No

Latitude: N 39° 10' 51"

Longitude: W 76° 35' 3"

Body of Water: Marley Creek
off Curtis Creek off the
Patapsco River

Driving Distance:
Baltimore 10 miles
Washington, DC 42 miles
Easton 53 miles

Atmosphere Meter

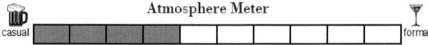

casual ———————————————————— formal

The Golden Age of Pirates ran from about 1690-1730, and during that time the Chesapeake saw its share of infamous swashbucklers. Blackbeard hung out at the mouth of the Bay and sailed to the Eastern Shore when his ships needed repairs or his men wanted a break from pillaging. Stede Bonnet, named "The Gentleman Pirate" because of his aristocratic birth, terrorized ships all around the mid-Atlantic. And according to legend, William Kidd buried treasure in the Bay's sandy coves before his corpse was hung in a gibbet cage above England's Thames River to discourage other privateers.

In November 2011, the buccaneers' way of life was resurrected in Glen Burnie at a place called Mutiny. Even though the restaurant features a pirate motif, it doesn't feel like a theme park. In fact, the décor is lovely with vintage maps of Caribbean trade routes, wooden barrels for tables, bamboo shades casting an amber glow, and lights made out of bloated pufferfish. At the bar, a skeleton dressed as a pirate holds a pewter mug. If he could talk, he'd tell you about the Passport Rum Club that rewards you for yo-ho-hoing his 140 types of rum from around the globe.  Signature cocktails, such as Queen Anne's Revenge, Scurvy Dog, and Dark Storm are certain to make you say "arrrgh."

The galley combines Chesapeake seafood with island flavors. Grilled salmon salad wards off scurvy with mixed greens and honey orange vinaigrette. Delish starters: Kraken Tentacles (fried calamari) and Crispy Cannon Balls (crab). The Shellback (fried oyster sandwich) and Bermuda Triangle Fish Tacos are fresh and filling. Landlubbers can plunder platters of New York strip steak with Old Bay roasted corn potato salad or Shiver Me Tenders chicken breast.

Stoney Creek Inn

8238 Fort Smallwood Road
Greenland Beach, MD 21226
(410) 439-3123
www.stoneycreekinnrestaurant.com

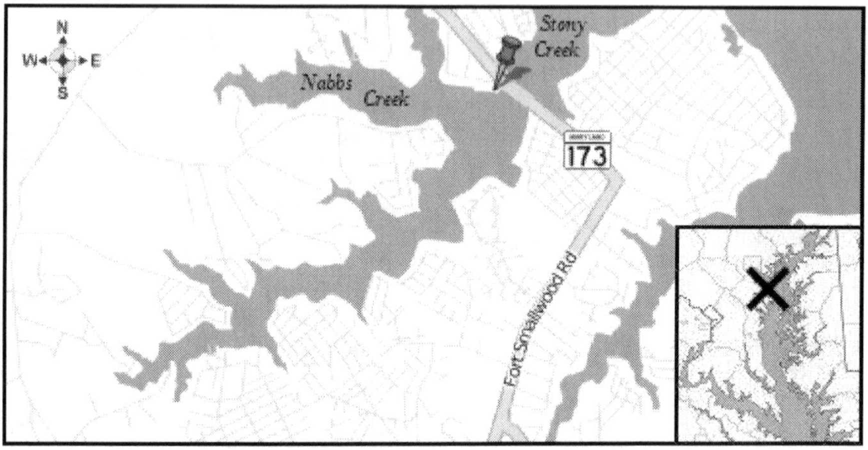

County: Anne Arundel County
Open: Year Round ⚓ Dockage: Yes
Latitude: N 39° 9' 48" Longitude: W 76° 31' 37"
Body of Water: Stony Creek off the Patapsco River
Driving Distance: Baltimore 12 miles,
Washington, DC 44 miles, Easton 51 miles

Atmosphere Meter

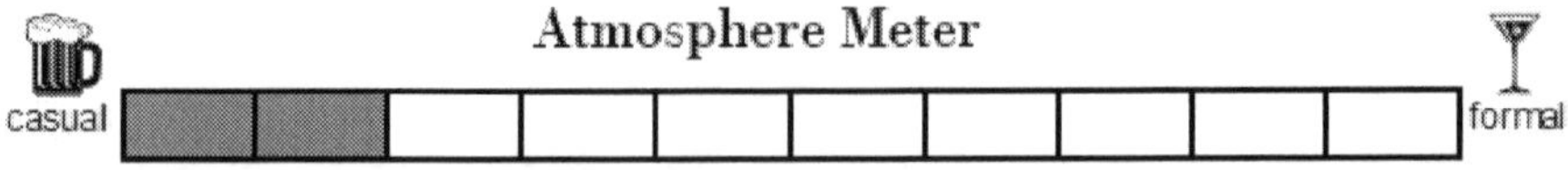

Being at Stoney Creek Inn might remind you of having a home-cooked meal at your favorite aunt's house. It started out as Bill's Seafood Carry-Out & Crabs in 1998 and moved to its current location in 2001, but this classic crab shack feels like it's been around forever. The exterior walls of the one-story building are made of faux-stone cement blocks that prove you're just south of Baltimore. Those walls worked so well on the outside that they used them inside as well, softened with old-fashion white lace curtains, pale blue tablecloths, and honey-brown linoleum floors.

Crabs that are wood-carved, painted red, or glorified in photos show the owners take pride in serving the best fruits of the Bay. A special blend of seasonings and ears of corn cover crabs while they steam for exactly 25 minutes. Shrimp and scallops come wrapped in bacon, and oysters are fried to a crispy golden bliss. The Baltimore Classic deep-fries a large hard crab that's stuffed with a crab cake and coated in batter. Meat eaters are welcome to order chicken or steaks.

All entrees, including chicken and steak, arrive with tasty sides such as creamy cole slaw, hush puppies, and a refreshing cucumber salad pickled with white vinegar, sugar, and sweet white onions. You can order all these treats inside the charming restaurant or on the wooden deck while enjoying views of the marina, Stony Creek Bridge, and fabulous sunsets on the water. Warning: Stoney Creek has limited seating, so you might want to call ahead if you're bringing a large group.

Mike's Crab House North

1402 Colony Road
Pasadena, MD 21122
(410) 255-7946
www.mikesnorth.com

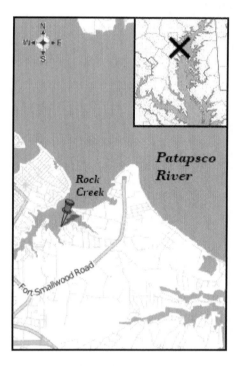

County: Anne Arundel County

Open: Year Round

Dockage: Yes

Latitude: N 39° 8' 59"

Longitude: W 76° 30' 13"

Body of Water: Rock Creek
off the Patapsco River

Driving Distance:
Baltimore 23 miles
Washington, DC 47 miles
Easton 52 miles

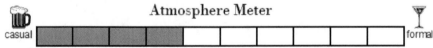

Atmosphere Meter

casual | | | | | | | | | | formal

The original Mike's was established in 1958 in Riva, MD, and this location in Pasadena opened in 2012 at White Rocks Marina. The second generation of Mike's might be new, but it's steeped in old Chesapeake traditions. The enormous deck is a crab lover's heaven with dozens of picnic tables lined up and ready to receive mountains of steamed crabs and shrimp.

Sinks are conveniently located at the back of the deck for rinsing Old Bay and flecks of shells off your hands. Red umbrellas, the color of cooked crabs, provide shade in the summer. A full-service bar on the deck mixes cocktails for patrons who soak up a magnificent waterfront view.

The indoor dining room is spacious and decorated with framed black-and-white photos of the Bay, fishing boats, and watermen. Rows of vintage oyster cans are arranged above the tables, and an impressive collection of classic beer cans are displayed on shelves above the bar. Live bands and karaoke nights enhance the festive atmosphere.

By far, your best bet on the menu is steamed crabs — they're Maryland's finest, fresh and delicious. If you're a crab-picking novice, Mike's web site and in-house placemats offer tutorials on plucking the sweet meat from the shells. Spiced shrimp and a bucket of mussels are also excellent choices, as well as the combo platter with crab cakes, oysters, shrimp, and the fish of the day. The all-you-can-eat salad bar balances your meal. If you're not in a seafood mood, Mike's offers steaks, shish kabobs, broiled chicken breast, burgers, and pizza. But crabs here really steal the show.

Cheshire Crab Restaurant

1701 Poplar Ridge Road
Pasadena, MD 21122
(410) 360-2220
www.pleasurecovemarina.com/cheshire-crab-restaurant

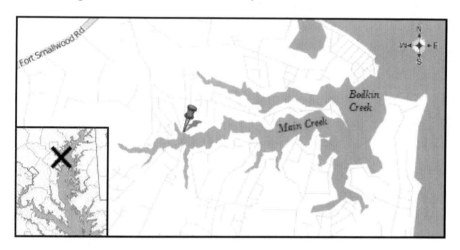

County: Anne Arundel County
Open: Seasonal ⚓ Dockage: Yes
Latitude: N 39° 7' 38" ⤚ Longitude: W 76° 28' 24"
Body of Water: Main Creek off Bodkin Creek off Chesapeake Bay
Driving Distance: Baltimore 23 miles,
Washington, DC 47 miles, Easton 52 miles

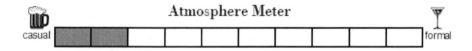

If you haven't been to the Cheshire Crab in a while, you're in for a big surprise. Literally. Right beside the restaurant now stands an astonishingly gigantic structure built by the owners of Pleasure Cove Marina.

This canary yellow and white striped monster of a building offers parking for boats up to 45 feet tall, with enough space for mega-yachts, souped-up pleasure crafts, and maybe even the Queen Mary.

Somehow the Cheshire Crab holds its own next to this behemoth neighbor. The sign's red crab grins its toothy grin and holds a sudsy beer. The waterfront wooden deck creaks under the weight of folks enjoying a meal or singing along with a live band. The tiki bar on the deck sports a colorful Maryland flag and crab design. Thanks to new management, the indoor dining rooms have undergone renovations to accommodate the growing summertime crowds. The décor features vintage oyster signs and watermen photos.

The cook dishes out fresh steamed crabs, beer-battered rockfish, shrimp sprinkled with Old Bay, and other fresh seafood. Crab cakes are plump round orbs of Chesapeake flavor. In addition to Bay standards, dining options have expanded to include salads, wings, jerk chicken sticks, burgers, pulled pork or Cuban sandwiches, pasta, grilled steaks, and BBQ ribs. The bar also presents a nice selection of local brews including Loose Cannon and Flying Dog.

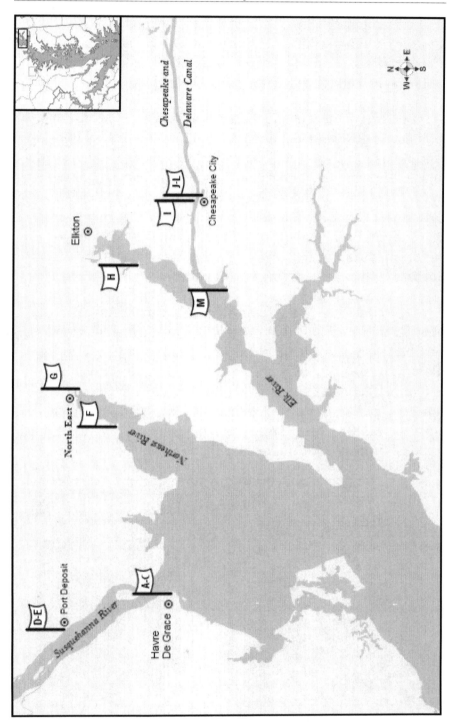

Headwaters of the Bay

Tidewater Grille

300 Franklin Street
Havre de Grace, MD 21078
(410) 939-3313
www.thetidewatergrille.com

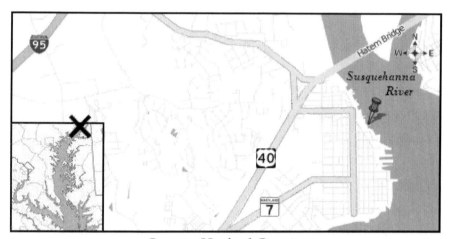

County: Harford County
Open: Year Round ⚓ Dockage: Yes
Latitude: N 39° 33' 2" ⤞ Longitude: W 76° 5' 22"
Body of Water: Susquehanna River
Driving Distance: Baltimore 37 miles,
Washington, DC 78 miles, Easton 83 miles

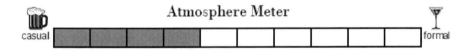

Atmosphere Meter

casual ▒▒▒▒▒▒ formal

Tidewater Grille sits along a picturesque riverbank where the Susquehanna meets the headwaters of the Bay. Out on the pet-friendly deck, cool breezes come off the river. You can watch trains chug across the Amtrak bridge or inspect the boats tied up at the 90-foot dock (free for guests). Listening to bands at sunset is a special summer treat. If stormy weather chases you inside, you won't miss anything. The open design and walls of windows guarantee a good view no matter where you sit. Dark oak floors and creamy white walls are accented with pictures that salute Chesapeake heritage with renderings of sailboats, lighthouses, crabs, and fishermen.

You'll need to take your eyes off the view for a moment to glance at the menu. It's a thoughtful marriage of fine dining and casual fare, and the choices are so extensive that if you can't find something you like, then maybe you're not hungry. They offer everything from seafood to sandwiches, ribs, pasta, chicken, steaks, burgers, and salads — all cooked fresh with local ingredients. Standouts include jumbo crab bruschetta, Tidewater jambalaya, and veal Chesapeake with crab meat, tasso ham, and shallots in a smooth cream sauce.

Another bonus to visiting Tidewater is its location. Stroll around the charming streets of Havre de Grace, and you discover antique stores, gift shops, a duck decoy museum, and buildings that date back to the early 1800s. The town got its name in 1782. In a letter to George Washington, the Marquis de Lafayette noted that this "graceful harbor" reminded him of a lovely French seaport called Le Havre. Centuries later, the town still lives up to its name.

MacGregor's Restaurant & Tavern

331 St. John Street
Havre de Grace, MD 21078
(410) 939-3003
www.macgregorsrestaurant.com

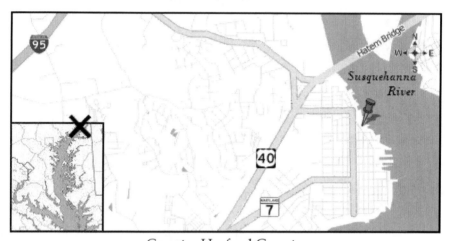

County: Harford County
Open: Year Round ⚓ Dockage: No
Latitude: N 39° 33' 2" 🐟 Longitude: W 76° 5' 25"
Body of Water: Susquehanna River
Driving Distance: Baltimore 37 miles,
Washington, DC 78 miles, Easton 83 miles

Atmosphere Meter

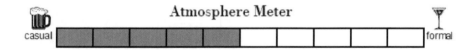

casual | formal

MacGregor's is an excellent choice for people seeking a waterfront experience in a quaint town. Its restaurant spans two tiers of an old bank building with exposed brick, soft lighting, and tall windows creating a lovely ambiance. Menus accommodate appetites for lunch, dinner, and Sunday brunch. Local seafood leads the pack with jumbo lump crab cakes,

Chesapeake stuffed shrimp, and Harbor of Mercy rockfish. Meaty favorites: bacon and bleu New York strip steak and Chicken Baltimore topped with crab imperial. For casual fare, head for the tavern where Scottish pub charm gets a modern upgrade with plasma TVs. Rockfish, crab fluffs, salads, burgers, and sandwiches are served here.

When you're ready to step outside for a gorgeous view of the Susquehanna River, mosey out to the deck bar. The wood floor, black patio furniture, and colorful beer signs set the tone for casual fun. And if you want a space for corporate or family gatherings, the Banquet Room is equipped with multimedia systems and catering facilities.

While admiring the Gaelic influence at MacGregor's, keep in mind that other Emerald Isle natives have left their mark on the town. During the War of 1812, it was attacked by 15 barges of British soldiers. A local militiaman named John O'Neil tried to defend the town but was injured by the recoil of his own cannon. He was captured and sentenced to death by hanging, but his daughter rowed out to the English admiral and pleaded for her father's life. O'Neil was spared, but the torch-happy British burned the city anyway.

Price's Seafood Restaurant

654 Water Street
Havre de Grace, MD 21078
(410) 939-2782

County: Harford County
Open: Year Round ⚓ Dockage: No
Latitude: N 39° 33' 14" ⚓ Longitude: W 76° 5' 33"
Body of Water: Susquehanna River
Driving Distance: Baltimore 37 miles,
Washington, DC 77 miles, Easton 83 miles

Atmosphere Meter

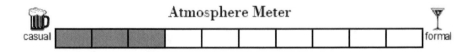

casual   formal

      If the image of old wood paneling decorated with fishnets, crabs, and striped bass doesn't hook you, then the briny aroma of steamed crabs will. At Price's, you experience an authentic Maryland crab house that has upheld Chesapeake traditions since 1944. Located on the shore where the Susquehanna River meets the Upper Bay, it's the kind of place where both adults and children wear protective bibs while wrestling tender chunks of crab meat from the shells.

Boys who grow restless from the slow pace of picking whack each other with crab hammers, and local fishermen toast the day's favorable weather. Silver buckets are placed on tables for discarded shells and empty beer bottles. Price's deck is lit with orange and green paper lanterns and strings of lights that spell out the restaurant's name. Wood picnic tables are painted purple, blue, and green to add cheer.

Inside and out, the food is reasonably priced and well cooked. Price's signature seasoning on crabs and shrimp is heavenly. Also memorable are shrimp po' boys, fish and chips, and drunken mussels tossed in a garlic butter and white wine sauce. Six ounces of ground beef is wedged inside a hamburger bun, while southern chicken sliders come with BBQ sauce and pickles. Pulled pork is slow-roasted for hours and served with cole slaw. Salads, wings, and soups are also available. Whatever you pick for your meal, it's a delightful, homey place to enjoy an old-fashioned summer getaway and watch the sun set over the bridges.

Lee's Landing Dock Bar

600 Rowland Drive
Port Deposit, MD 21904
(410) 747-4006
www.leeslandingdockbar.com

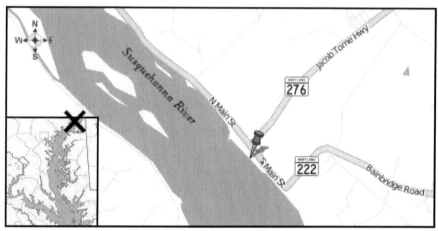

County: Cecil County
Open: Year Round ⚓ Dockage: No
Latitude: N 39° 36' 15" ⦁ Longitude: W 76° 6' 58"
Body of Water: Susquehanna River
Driving Distance: Baltimore 43 miles,
Washington, DC 83 miles, Easton 85 miles

Atmosphere Meter

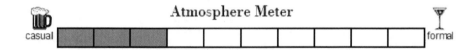

casual — formal

When you arrive at Lee's Landing, you might think that the place is all about location. The new restaurant is just off the main street in an incredibly quaint town and sits on the banks of the Susquehanna River. The waterfront view presents a conga line of bridges leading to the Bay. But the pretty view wasn't enough for new owners who converted a comedy club into a great destination. They built a 3,000 foot wooden deck that wraps around the restaurant and put a tiki bar on the side that faces the water. Add in a pirate ship playground, palm trees, rows of picnic tables, and 1,100 feet of free dockage for boaters, and you've got a spot that aims to please everyone. Even pets are welcome if they behave.

The building's interior also benefitted from a major face-lift. Walls of knotty reclaimed wood are accented with colorful vintage signs for oysters, fishing lures, and seafood. Eight flat screen TVs light up the lounge, and an oversized shucking knife and oyster shell hang above the raw bar. The atmosphere is easy-going, and bands play on weekends.

All this attention to the décor did not take away from the quality of the food, which is fresh, local, and well-prepared. The menu kicks off with creative appetizers such as crabby cheese fries, Cajun mahi mahi bites, and Buffalo clam strips. The classic wedge salad gets bumped up a notch with jumbo shrimp and hickory smoked bacon. All-lump crab cakes, oyster po' boys, and rockfish club sandwiches prove the cooks know their way around the Bay. Burgers and chicken are on hand for meat lovers.

Backfin Blues Bar & Grill

19 South Main Street
Port Deposit, MD 21904
(410) 378-2722
www.backfinblues.com

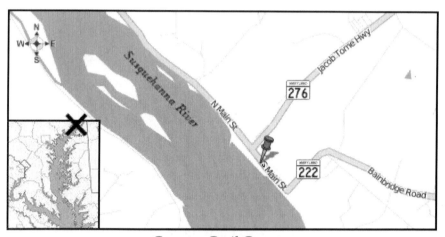

County: Cecil County
Open: Year Round ⚓ Dockage: No
Latitude: N 39° 36' 15" ⟩— Longitude: W 76° 6' 54"
Body of Water: Susquehanna River
Driving Distance: Baltimore 43 miles,
Washington, DC 83 miles, Easton 85 miles

Atmosphere Meter

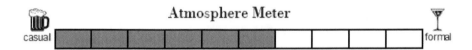

casual .... formal

   Back in the 1800s, Port Deposit served as a junction point
for floating lumber, grain, coal, whiskey, and tobacco down
the Susquehanna River. It was so small that it didn't even
catch the attention of the invading British in 1813, who
skipped over the town and burned down a warehouse across
the river instead. So, who'd expect to find a top-notch

restaurant right on Main Street today? Since 2004, Backfin Blues has served inventive dishes in a casual environment. Service is excellent, and the chef takes risks, giving fresh ingredients a new lease on life. Weekly specials reflect the change in seasons and local farmer's bountiful harvests.

Seafood plays a prominent role on the menu, where you find crab cakes that are massive and made with super lump meat. Jumbo shrimp are stuffed with crab imperial, and pan-seared scallops are finished with a spinach cream sauce. Grilled rib eye steaks are garnished with a Stilton compound butter and crisp onions, and veal medallions are topped with crab, asparagus, and hollandaise sauce.

The intimate dining area's exposed brick walls are decorated with crabs and fish, and the cozy bar shakes up smooth martinis next to regional craft beers. Out on the deck, a yellow cover casts a warm light on guests catching a sunset over the river. Okay, so you have to look over the railroad tracks to get a glimpse of the water, but it's still a lovely view. And you won't regret taking a walk around this charming little town that's eager to show off its gingerbread Victorian houses, unique shops, and stunning scenery.

Crab Decks & Tiki Bars of the Chesapeake Bay, 2015 Maryland Edition

The Wellwood & the River Shack

523 Water Street
Charlestown, MD 21914
(410) 287-6666
www.wellwoodclub.com

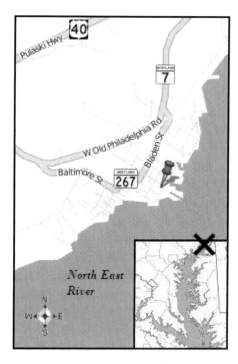

County: Cecil County

Open: Year Round

Dockage: Yes

Latitude: N 39° 34' 22"

Longitude: W 75° 58' 20"

Body of Water: North East River

Driving Distance:
Baltimore 45 miles,
Washington, DC 85 miles,
Easton 76 miles

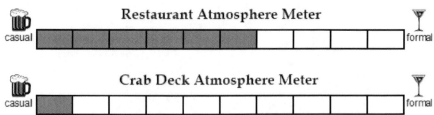

In Cecil County you discover beautiful buildings along the water, and Wellwood is one of the best. Built in 1901, it originally housed a private hunting and fishing club that aimed "to reduce the friction of life to a minimum and increase the pleasure of existence to the maximum." Later it was turned into a country club with a nine-hole golf course, duck pond, gardens, and swimming pool. Noteworthy guests included Teddy Roosevelt and Calvin Coolidge. Be sure to look at the antique collection: a bust of George Washington, lithograph of Lincoln, and a hand-carved eagle donated by President Roosevelt after his visit.

Since 1958, Wellwood has been owned by the Metz family, who host everything from a romantic dinner for two to big family weddings. In the dining room, white linen tablecloths and a fireplace create a soothing ambiance for fine cuisine. The menu showcases local seafood with starters like Oysters Rockefeller and steamed drunken mussels and clams. Crab cakes and fried oysters are Chesapeake classics. Prime rib is slow cooked au jus, and honey-pecan chicken is stuffed with roasted apple-walnut cranberry cornbread. The Club Room encourages casual dining with cozy seating and a big-screen TV. Teak furniture outdoors on the patio gives you a front-row seat for watching the boats sail along the river or listening to a band. Around back awaits the River Shack, where its rustic tiki flare, wooden picnic tables, and sandy beach create the idea spot for all-you-can-eat crabs or Wellwood's legendary bucket of Maryland fried chicken.

Nauti Goose Restaurant

200 Cherry Street
North East, MD 21901
(410) 287-7880
www.nautigoose.net

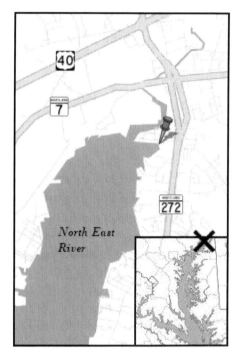

County: Cecil County

Open: Year Round

Dockage: Yes

Latitude: N 39° 35' 34"

Longitude: W 75° 56' 41"

Body of Water: North East
River

Driving Distance:
Baltimore 48 miles,
Washington, DC 88 miles,
Easton 74 miles

Atmosphere Meter

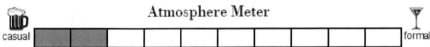

casual ▢▢▢▢▢▢▢▢▢▢ formal

When you explore the headwaters of the Chesapeake, Nauti Goose should top your list of fun places to visit with family and friends. Docking is easy with four long piers to accommodate 50 boats, and a busy marina is conveniently located next door. Parents can let the kids run amok in the park and playground nearby before settling down to a hearty waterfront meal. The upbeat, casual atmosphere extends outdoors to a pair of double-decker decks that span the entire length of the building and offer dazzling views of the water, especially at sunset. Five full-service bars and live bands on weekends keep the energy level high.

The restaurant is best known for seafood and prime rib, and the chef designed a comprehensive menu featuring local ingredients and fresh fruits of the Bay. Hot steamed crabs, shrimp, pizza, burgers, sandwiches, and steaks — there's something for everyone here. Noteworthy fish dishes include crab pretzels, fish tacos, blackened rockfish, and Chesapeake pizza with crab, J.O. Spice, and melted mozzarella. Pecan-encrusted fried shrimp are a crunchy delight.

In this northern region, you can find plenty to see and do using Nauti Goose as home base. Elk Neck State Park has beaches, campsites, excellent fishing spots, and wooded bluffs that overlook the river. You can hike to Turkey Point Lighthouse (built in 1833) and climb 35 feet to the top to catch an unparalleled view of the water. Or you can check out the Upper Bay Museum that celebrates the heritage of fishermen, waterfowl hunting, and art of decoy carving.

Triton Bar & Grill

285 Plum Point Road
Elkton, MD 21921
(410) 350-9943
www.tritonmarina.com

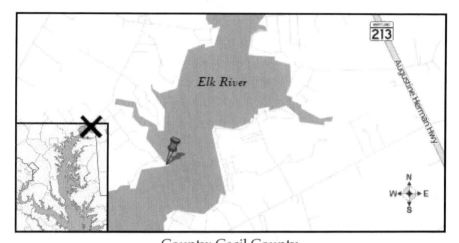

County: Cecil County
Open: Year Round ⚓ Dockage: Yes
Latitude: N 39° 33' 39" ⟩⟩⟩ Longitude: W 75° 51' 26"
Body of Water: Elk River
Driving Distance: Baltimore 56 miles,
Washington, DC 97 miles, Easton 71 miles

Atmosphere Meter

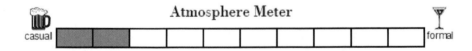

casual | | | | | | | | | | formal

　Triton is the kind of place that makes you want to buy a boat or be glad you have one. It represents the celebration of life on the water that's unique to the Bay region. Restaurants like this and their marinas are the central hub of rural communities — the Chesapeake equivalent to granges in landlocked areas. Parents gather at picnic tables picking crabs while keeping a watchful eye as their children splash in the water. Boaters pull up pink-faced from the sun, opening coolers to show off the day's catch of blues, bass, or rockfish.

The focal point at Triton is the beautiful old gray-and-tan stone building where steamed crabs, fried shrimp, and local seafood is served along with icy pitchers of beer. Casual fare of sandwiches and burgers perfectly matches the laid back way of life. You can go with a traditional New York style pizza with pepperoni and cheese or upgrade to a gourmet pie with jerk BBQ chicken and onions or crab and Old Bay. A kid's menu offers chicken fingers, burgers, and spaghetti.

The atmosphere is addictive: Ancient oak trees cast shade on the wrap-around deck that gives a stellar view of the water or the July 4th fireworks. Friends toss horseshoes or listen to a band on weekends, while their dogs chase squirrels across the wide grassy lawn. The full-service marina claims eight acres of land with three sandy beaches along the Elk River, and its High & Dry Boatel has room for boats up to 47 feet long. In a nutshell, whether you arrive by land or sea, you'll be glad you came to Triton Bar & Grill.

Schaefer's Canal House

208 Bank Street
Chesapeake City, MD 21915
(410) 885-7200
www.schaeferscanalhouse.com

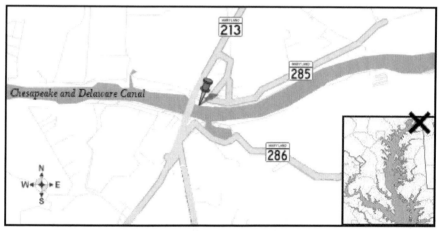

County: Cecil County
Open: Year Round ⚓ Dockage: Yes
Latitude: N 39° 31' 48" ⟷ Longitude: W 75° 48' 46"
Body of Water: Chesapeake and Delaware Canal
Driving Distance: Baltimore 60 miles,
Washington, DC 100 miles, Easton 61 miles

Atmosphere Meter

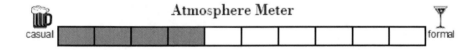

casual   formal

     After a five-year hiatus, Schaefer's reopened in 2012
— much to the delight of folks in Chesapeake City. It had
occupied this prime location along the C&D Canal for as long
as anyone could remember, and its big bold return to the
waterfront is a welcome sight. In 1907, Joseph Schaefer, Sr.
and his wife Winifred opened a grocery and ship chandlery

here. By 1935, his brother John Schaefer added a beer garden, which sold Winifred's crab cakes and hard boiled eggs at the bar. Over the years, the restaurant was expanded and a full-service marina was built. New owners completely renovated the dining rooms, deck, and marina, creating one of the largest waterfront locations on the Bay.

It's a perfect place to watch ocean-bound ships and recreation boats cruise under the towering bridge on the canal. Whether you sit in the spacious dining room or on a patio chair at the veranda, a spectacular view is guaranteed. One of the unique features is the Lighthouse Bar where frozen cocktails and icy beers are served. The climate is family-friendly, fun, and comfortable.

Fresh seafood gets top billing on the extensive menu. Steam pots deliver hefty portions of clams, mussels, snow crab legs, and lobster tail with potatoes and corn on the cob. Crab cakes and friend breaded shrimp are local favorites. Flounder stuffed with crab meat is finished with a lemon butter sauce. Steaks, burgers, pasta, chicken, and garden salads accommodate landlubbers at the table.

The Bayard House Restaurant

11 Bohemia Avenue
Chesapeake City, MD 21915
(410) 885-5040
www.bayardhouse.com

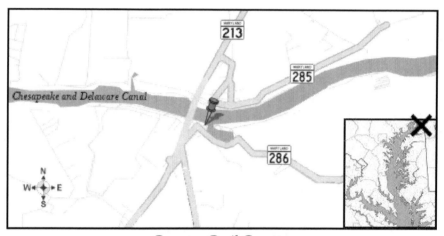

County: Cecil County
Open: Year Round ⚓ Dockage: No
Latitude: N 39° 31' 39" ⚓ Longitude: W 75° 48' 43"
Body of Water: Chesapeake and Delaware Canal
Driving Distance: Baltimore 60 miles,
Washington, DC 100 miles, Easton 61 miles

Atmosphere Meter

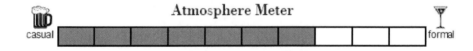

casual .... formal

    Bayard House is the oldest building in Chesapeake City.
Built around 1780 when the town was still called Village of
Bohemia, the house was converted to a pub called Chick's
Tavern in 1829. By 1911, it was christened Harriot Hotel, and
its dubious claim to fame was the Hole in the Wall Bar — so
named because of a hole in the back where "blacks would be

served by reaching their hands in to receive a drink." Allaire DuPont restored the building in 1983 with a keen eye to authenticity, recreating details down to the locks on the doors.

Bayard's visitors today can feast their eyes on the suspension arch bridge over the C&D Canal and watch a grand display of boats pass by. You can unwind in the affable atmosphere of the Hole in the Wall Bar downstairs. Or relax with a cool drink at the bar on the brick patio overlooking the water. The window-lined dining room reflects its architectural and culinary heritage by adding an elegant Old World twist to Chesapeake traditions.

Sunday brunch is a medley of omelets (two with crab meat), french toast, crepes, and steaks. Lunch and dinner offer a cornucopia of seafood: mussels, clams, oysters, and calamari. Crab cakes are topped with a lemon buerre blanc sauce. Seafood fettuccini is creamy bliss with lobster, scallops, and shrimp. Wiener Schnitzel is a treat for meat lovers. Old Wharf Cottage next door is a quaint spot if you want to spend the night in this charming town. Restored Victorian homes, galleries, antique stores, craft shops, boat tours, and summer concerts create an idyllic getaway destination.

The Tap Room Crab House

201 Bohemia Avenue
Chesapeake City, MD 21915
(410) 885-2344 or (410) 885-9873
www.taproomcrabhouse.com

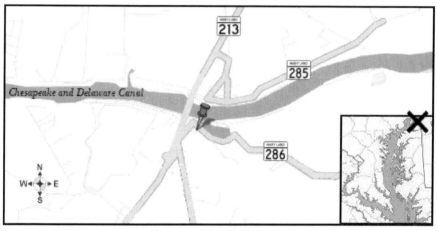

County: Cecil County
Open: Year Round ⚓ Dockage: No
Latitude: N 39° 31' 37" 🐟 Longitude: W 75° 48' 46"
Body of Water: Chesapeake and Delaware Canal
Driving Distance: Baltimore 60 miles,
Washington, DC 100 miles, Easton 61 miles

Atmosphere Meter

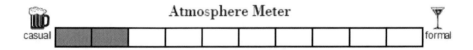

casual | formal

When you walk down the street on a breezy day, you can smell the Tap Room Crab House from a block away. Even with the doors closed, they can't contain the alluring briny aroma of steamed crabs, which starts the stomach rumbling the moment it hits your nose. The restaurant doesn't have an outdoor deck and it's not directly on the water, but it's well worth a visit if you're serious about picking crabs. Since 1982, it's earned the reputation as a traditional Bay crab house.

The place has a charming, old-fashioned vibe, and the staff welcomes you as if you were family. Blue and white walls decorated with vintage pictures of seafood and brown paper neatly laid upon every table are ideal backdrops for trays piled high with red-hot steamed crabs.

On top of the menu is a photo of a crab with claws pointing to appetizers that complement his tender meat. Old Bay fries, catfish fingers, hush puppies, and corn on the cob are among his favorites. You can savor local mussels, clams, and shrimp in steamer pots or in a creamy fisherman's chowder. Maryland crab soup has a classic tomato broth. Crispy fried oysters and soft-shell crabs are nestled inside a fresh kaiser roll. Meat lovers find a pleasant but unexpected Italian option with spaghetti and meatballs. Be sure to ask about daily specials of home-style platters such as fried local seafood combos, all-you-can-eat pasta, 50 cent chicken wings, and Maine lobster fests.

Chesapeake Inn Restaurant

605 Second Street
Chesapeake City, MD 21915
(410) 885-2040
www.chesapeakeinn.com

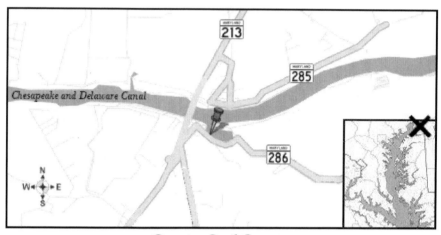

County: Cecil County
Open: Year Round ⚓ Dockage: Yes
Latitude: N 39° 31' 34" ➤ Longitude: W 75° 48' 39"
Body of Water: Chesapeake and Delaware Canal
Driving Distance: Baltimore 60 miles,
Washington, DC 100 miles, Easton 61 miles

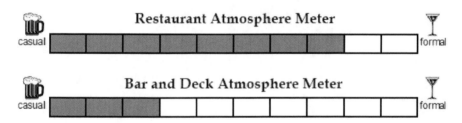

You never know what could happen when you mix classic Bay with tiki, but the Chesapeake Inn pulls it off without a hitch. Its upscale yet comfortable 185-seat dining room puts you at ease with cream-colored linens on the tables, soft lighting, and a piano player on weekends. The Inn's fine cuisine blends classic Bay dishes with a Mediterranean touch. Outside on the veranda, you can enjoy crab cakes and other local seafood, steaks, chicken, or pasta–all garnished with a gentle summer breeze. The lovely banquet room is a popular venue for weddings and events.

The downstairs bar sports a rustic nautical theme with vibrant flags, old boat oars, and model ships accenting the wood and exposed brick walls. The menu here offers light fare, sandwiches, and gourmet sliders. Evenings get kicked up a notch at the tiki bar where giant tiki masks are nailed into palm trees lit with strings of lights. A plastic shark head chews its way through the roof of a bamboo bar. Bands crank up the tunes, and the party shifts into gear.

What makes all this work in one setting? Perhaps the common thread is the water. Young and old alike can't resist gazing at the beautiful backdrop of the canal. History buffs know that it's not your run-of-the-mill waterway. When it opened it 1829, the canal had a monumental impact on the mid-Atlantic region by creating a quick way to transport goods between the Chesapeake Bay and the Delaware River. It's only 14 miles long, but by taking a direct path, the canal reduces the route between Baltimore and Philadelphia by 300 miles. It's the third busiest canal in the world, so when you visit Chesapeake Inn, enjoy the parade of cargo ships, tankers, barges, and sailboats traveling through its waters.

Sunset Café Bar & Restaurant

111 River Road
Chesapeake City, MD 21915
(410) 885-2270
www.sunsetcafemd.com

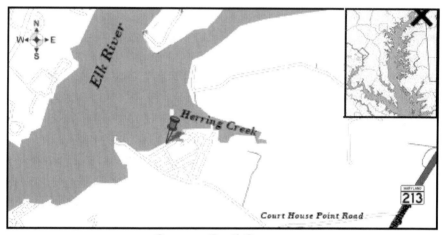

County: Cecil County
Open: Year Round ⚓ Dockage: Yes
Latitude: N 39° 30' 45" ⤙ Longitude: W 75° 52' 34"
Body of Water: Elk River
Driving Distance: Baltimore 65 miles,
Washington, DC 101 miles, Easton 60 miles

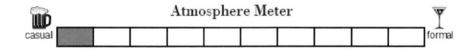

Atmosphere Meter

casual | | | | | | | | | | formal

If you've been out exploring the Bay all day and get hungry for a casual bite to eat, Sunset Café is an easy place to stop. It's located on the water at Harbour North Marina at the west end of the C&D Canal. The flat, one-story building began as the local yacht club in the 1960s and was converted to an eatery for the public in 2011. It's the kind of rustic place where you feel comfortable tossing a T-shirt over your bathing suit or walking inside wearing comfy flip-flops.

The small weather-worn building has an outdoor deck lined with picnic tables that offers a big view of sunsets over the water. Under the low-ceiling inside, you find an electronic dart board, foosball, pool table with new red felt, big-screen TVs for watching Ravens and Orioles games, and vintage snow globes placed on the tables to entertain children who are impatiently waiting for their meal. It feels like a neighborhood watering hole where locals like to kick back with a brew or two after a long day at work.

The Snack Menu has some seafood options: fried shrimp or clam baskets and Yuengling beer battered fish and chips. But most of the choices cover pub fare standards such as nachos, chicken tenders, pizza, and hot dogs. The Sandwich Menu offers more diversity with everything from fried rockfish and crab cake sandwiches to burgers and cheese steak or meatball marinara subs. Daily specials stretch beyond the regular menus with local seafood platters and prime rib that is thick-cut and juicy.

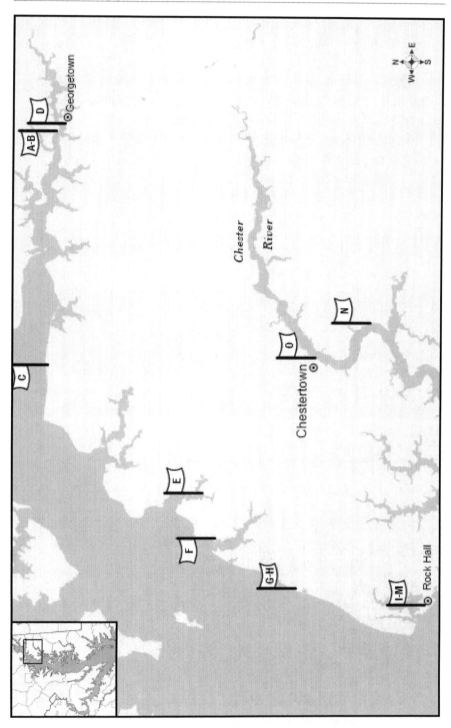

Upper Eastern Shore

Signals Restaurant

150 Skipjack Road
Georgetown, MD 21930
(410) 275-2122
www.skipjackcove.com/restaurant.php

County: Cecil County
Open: Seasonal ⚓ Dockage: Yes
Latitude: N 39° 22' 1" ⟿ Longitude: W 75° 53' 28"
Body of Water: Sassafras River
Driving Distance: Baltimore 76 miles,
Washington, DC 88 miles, Easton 49 miles

Atmosphere Meter

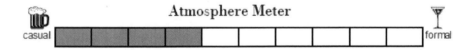

casual   formal

When you sit on the wooden deck on top of the hill at
Signals, you can't help but feel a sense of awe for the fleets of
boaters who love cruising around this part of the Bay and its
tributaries. And who could blame them? The Sassafras River
is famous for its hidden coves and beaches with fresh water
for swimming with reduced fear of jellyfish. The 365-slip

marina below bustles with every imaginable type of water vessel, and families leave stress behind to build memories together. Children are begrudgingly stuffed into puffy life vests, and parents patiently untangle fishing lines.

Whether you're a boater or landlubber, you can begin your day with Signals' breakfast of eggs, bacon, french toast, or hot cakes. Or you can grab salads and sandwiches for a picnic lunch along the water's edge. At dinner, you can enjoy classic Chesapeake dishes. Crab dip and rockfish tenders are tasty beginnings to your meal. The kitchen turns out an array of sumptuous treats: award-winning crab cakes, clams and mussels over pasta, and shrimp fried to a golden brown. Roasted prime rib, steaks, burgers, meatball subs, and chicken parmesan make meat lovers smile.

The blue and white, six-sided building has a casual, relaxing feel. Friends gather for happy hour on the deck to watch the sun set over the river and rolling farmland. When the day is done and little eyelids get heavy, you can start planning your next Chesapeake Bay adventure at Signals Restaurant.

The Granary Restaurant & Sassafras Grill

100 George Street
Georgetown, MD 21930
(410) 275-1603
www.granary.biz

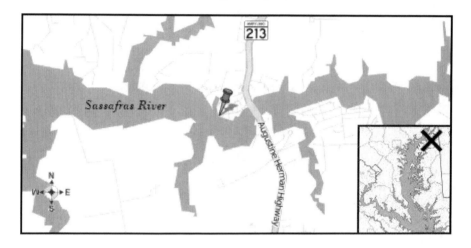

County: Kent County
Open: Year Round ⚓ Dockage: Yes
Latitude: N 39° 21' 49" ⛵ Longitude: W 75° 53' 18"
Body of Water: Sassafras River
Driving Distance: Baltimore 76 miles,
Washington, DC 88 miles, Easton 48 miles

Atmosphere Meter

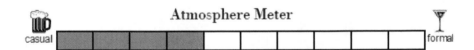

casual | | | | | | | | | | formal

The Granary is located on a spectacular spot that's steeped in local history. During the War of 1812, local residents built Fort Duffy on this site, but the invading Brits burned it to the ground in 1813 along with other neighboring towns. In 1876, a warehouse was erected to store corn and grain slated for shipment to Baltimore. Years later, it housed the Tockwogh Yacht Club, and in the 1940s it became a restaurant that was destroyed by fire in 1985. Some of the original hand-hewn beams were saved and used to construct the building standing here today.

The Granary's two-story building has wrap-around decks on both levels that overlook the river. Picnic tables on the lower deck rest on crushed clam shells bleached white by the sun. A statue of a goose in flight and a real osprey nest on top of a pole remind diners of the abundant waterfowl in the area. The dining room is spacious, and the bar is cozy.

Two framed menus from the 1950s hang on the wall and prove that generations of people have flocked to this place for decades for good seafood. Today's menu shows off regional culinary riches with crab cakes, fried shrimp, and battered fish and chips. You have a variety of other choices ranging from sandwiches and meatloaf to steak and chicken with waffles. On the ground level is the more casual Sassafras Grill that offers steamed seafood platters, Old Bay spiced shrimp, fried oysters, crab cake sandwiches, and fish tacos.

Barbara's on the Bay

12 Ericsson Avenue
Betterton, MD 21610
(410) 348-3079
www.barbarasonthebay.com

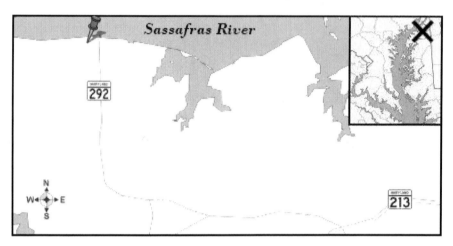

County: Kent County
Open: Year Round ⚓ Dockage: No
Latitude: N 39° 22' 13" 🐟 Longitude: W 76° 3' 51"
Body of Water: Sassafras River
Driving Distance: Baltimore 90 miles,
Washington, DC 92 miles, Easton 53 miles

Atmosphere Meter

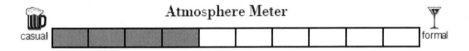

casual | | | | | | | | | | formal

The hill overlooking Betterton Beach is a marvelous location. The magnificent view of the Sassafras River pouring its waters into the Bay, boats pulling up at the dock, and the sun warming the beach seems to stretch for miles. For a long time, an Irish bar held court on high, and then the spot sat vacant for a few years. In 2014, Barbara's on the Bay became king of the hill, and folks around the Eastern Shore began heralding the delightful new restaurant's arrival.

It's a cheerful welcoming place. Bright orange and white walls are decorated with old family photos, cigar boxes, and a patchwork of homespun artwork. The pressed tin and wood bar is constantly abuzz with locals sharing stories about the neighborhood. The deck is covered with white wood lattice that offers some shade yet encourages a soft breeze.

The menu is designed by restaurant owner Barbara Esmonde, a warm and gregarious chef who puts her heart and soul into the food's success. Everything is made from scratch. Maryland crab soup and crab dip lead the appetizer list, but the rare appearance of Scotch eggs on a menu makes these savory bites hard to resist. Tuscan shrimp stew over creamy polenta and teriyaki-glazed salmon over ginger rice are seafood standouts. Meat lovers will relish exceptional dishes such as the homemade lamb gyro with seasoned potato sticks and The Aberdeen Rumble, a dry-rubbed flank steak topped with caramelized onions. And you won't want to leave without trying Barbara's homemade ice cream.

The Kitty Knight House Restaurant

14028 Augustine Herman Highway
Georgetown, MD 21930
(410) 648-5200
www.kittyknight.com

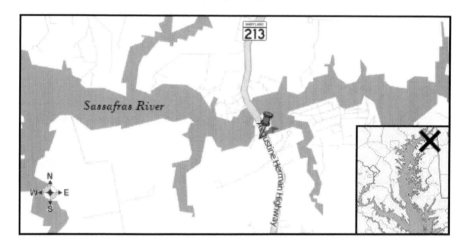

County: Kent County
Open: Year Round ⚓ Dockage: No
Latitude: N 39° 21' 39" ➤ Longitude: W 75° 52' 49"
Body of Water: Sassafras River
Driving Distance: Baltimore 76 miles,
Washington, DC 87 miles, Easton 48 miles

Atmosphere Meter

casual 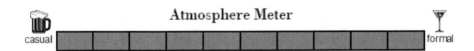 formal

Kitty Knight's fearless efforts to save part of Georgetown ranks among the favorite tales on the Eastern Shore. During the War of 1812, the British burned down towns along the Chesapeake shoreline to curb local resistance against their invading soldiers. After torching Fredericktown and a good portion of Georgetown, British troops set their sights on two brick houses on the hill above the Sassafras River.

But their plans for further destruction were squelched by a defiant Kitty Knight. Neither of the brick homes belonged to her, but she knew that an elderly woman who lived in one house was too sick to flee. When Kitty arrived on the scene, the Brits had already lit the house on fire, but she stomped out the flames and appealed to the commanding officer. He stopped his soldiers on the first house but allowed them to ignite the second. Again, Kitty doused the fires and pleaded to stop the carnage. The officer agreed and ordered his troops back to the ship, sparing the houses and a church nearby.

Those buildings bear Kitty Knight's name as tribute to her heroism. The view from the outdoor deck is spectacular. Inside, the décor is Old World elegance at its best with white linens, candlelight, and pristine oak floors. The menu features upscale regional cuisine and local catch such as crabs, rockfish, and oysters. Must-try entrees: Baked crab imperial and seafood combo scampi with shrimp, scallops, mahi mahi, clams, and mussels. Chicken Chesapeake and grilled pork tenderloin are delightful meat options. Gourmet sandwiches, BBQ ribs, burgers, and salads provide casual fare on the deck.

Harbor House Restaurant

23145 Buck Neck Road
Chestertown, MD 21620
(410) 778-0669

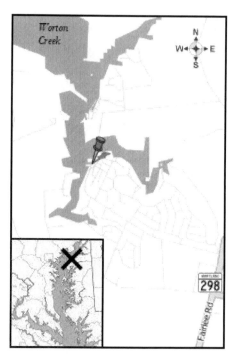

County: Kent County

Open: Seasonal

Dockage: Yes

Latitude: N 39° 16' 31"

Longitude: W 76° 10' 3"

Body of Water: Worton Creek

Driving Distance:
Baltimore 85 miles,
Washington, DC 89 miles,
Easton 44 miles

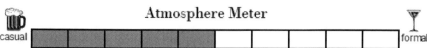

Atmosphere Meter
casual / formal

    Buy locally; think globally. That's the name of the game in the kitchen at Harbor House at Worton Creek Marina. The menu changes weekly, because the chef scours farmers' markets and fishing docks to gather the freshest ingredients in the region and follow the harvest of the seasons. Dishes are paired with the top wines of Maryland vintners.

His efforts pay off royally. Mixing Eastern Shore cuisine with modern influences from around the world results in delicious specialties such as chicken fried soft-shell crab, sesame Asian flat iron steak, scallops pan-seared in truffle oil, and slow-roasted BBQ pork. Signature no-filler crab cakes and crab imperial represent the best of the Bay. Oysters are pulled out of the local waters, and the beef is grass-fed in fields nearby. You're in luck if you get a chance to sample Harbor House's award-winning soup, Bloody Mary crab and corn gazpacho with avocado horseradish purée.

The location underscores the magnificence of the Chesapeake Bay's backwaters. Regal oak trees surround the gray stone building that overlooks boats sailing on Worton Creek. The bar's wood-panel walls are covered with photos of historic Bay lighthouses. A fireplace crackles in the winter, and windows are opened in the spring to let a soft breeze drift in from the water. The small patio out front is a lovely place to relax and enjoy the summer stars. Harbor House is simply a treat to visit any time of year.

Mangroves Restaurant
& Jellyfish Joel's

22170 Great Oak Landing Road
Chestertown, MD 21620
(410) 778-5007
www.mangrovesrestaurantandjellyfishjoels.com

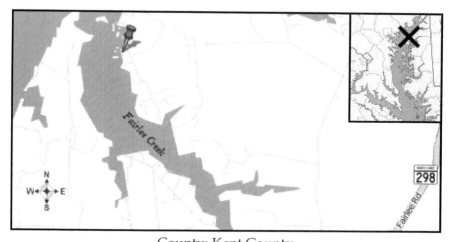

County: Kent County
Open: Year Round ⚓ Dockage: Yes
Latitude: N 39° 15' 48" ➤ Longitude: W 76° 12' 12"
Body of Water: Fairlee Creek
Driving Distance: Baltimore 86 miles,
Washington, DC 90 miles, Easton 45 miles

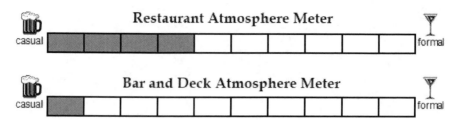

casual **Restaurant Atmosphere Meter** formal

casual **Bar and Deck Atmosphere Meter** formal

You can't swing a dead cat in Kent County without hitting a peaceful B&B or historic inn. They're lovely destinations, but if you want an Eastern Shore retreat with activities to please the entire family, head to Great Oak Landing. This 70-acre marina has 350 slips and 28 waterfront rooms in its lodge. Parents can play a round on the six-hole golf course or master their serve on the tennis courts, and then unwind with a cool beverage from the thatched-roof bar next to the pool and hot tub. Kids can wear themselves out at the playground, moon bounce, water slide, or rec room. Weekend movie nights and campfires bring everyone back together.

Dining at Mangroves is casual and regional. Crab dip, coconut shrimp, fried calamari, and beer-battered clam strips are tasty starters from the sea. Crab cakes and ahi tuna steaks arrive inside a kaiser roll. Meat lovers go bananas over Bubba's jerk chicken, pulled pork BBQ, and cheese steaks.

Jellyfish Joel's celebrates tiki on the beach where you can nibble on snacks under palm trees and bright red umbrellas. Friday night luau parties are famous for mouth-watering Hawaiian barbeque. Gracious bartenders quench your thirst with cold beer or specialty rum drinks while you listen to bands playing under the stars. Yep, this is heaven.

The Shanty Beach Bar

21085 Tolchester Beach Road
Chestertown, MD 21620
(410) 778-1400
www.tolchestermarina.com

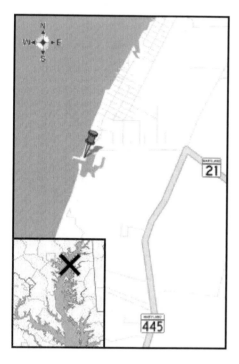

County: Kent County

Open: Seasonal

Dockage: Yes

Latitude: N 39° 12' 49"

Longitude: W 76° 14' 38"

Body of Water: directly on
the Chesapeake Bay

Driving Distance:
Baltimore 88 miles,
Washington, DC 92 miles,
Easton 47 miles

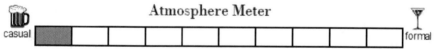

Atmosphere Meter

casual ▮▮▮▮▮ formal

A 20-mile boat ride north of the Bay Bridge can transport you from a stressful, pressed-shirt and high-heel world to the laid-back, T-shirt and flip-flop life at Shanty Beach Bar. Located on the water's edge at Tolchester Marina, this popular watering hole is all about fun in the sun. The building has a thatched roof with tiki flair, and it's surrounded by big wooden decks, wide umbrellas, and plush tropical plants.

You can lie back on a comfy lounge chair at the pool with a frosty drink in your hand and refuse to move until you feel like it. Or you can join in the revelry, because it seems like something's always happening at the Shanty Beach Bar. Pool parties, pirate days, band nights, and an antique car show contribute to the festive vibe. A limited menu offers crab cakes, burgers, pulled pork sandwiches, and wings.

Best of all is the beach. You can lay out a blanket in the sand and watch the sun set over the Chesapeake. Then raise a glass to toast all the folks who go to great lengths trying to protect sandy beaches like this one from disappearing. Rising sea levels and relentless storms erode about 580 acres of Maryland each year. Entire islands, such as James, Holland, and Barren Island, have been abandoned by residents and are slowly sinking into the Bay. Mother Nature ultimately has the final say in these issues, but it never hurts to remember who's behind the scenes trying to preserve beach life on the Bay.

The Channel Restaurant

21085 Tolchester Beach Road
Chestertown, MD 21620
(410) 778-1400
www.tolchestermarina.com

County: Kent County

Open: Seasonal

Dockage: Yes

Latitude: N 39° 12' 48"

Longitude: W 76° 14' 29"

Body of Water: directly on
the Chesapeake Bay

Driving Distance:
Baltimore 88 miles,
Washington, DC 92 miles,
Easton 47 miles

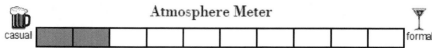

Atmosphere Meter

casual | | | | | | | | | | | formal

The Channel Restaurant is nestled among the boats at Tolchester Marina. It's a low-key kind of place that might be short on menu items but long on Eastern Shore hospitality. Dishes center around seafood brought off the boats that day — crab cakes, shrimp, rockfish — pulled together with a gentle French touch. It's an easy spot for grabbing a quick bite after a long day on the water. The walls are covered with historic photos of an old-fashioned amusement park that once stood on this spot. If you ask why none of it remains, some locals will tell you the story; others will just shake their heads in disappointment.

Tolchester Beach and its sister resort 14 miles north in Betterton were born during the steamboat glory days from the 1880s to 1920s. Tolchester Beach was a popular summer destination for heat-weary Baltimore residents who crossed the Bay on steamboats like the *Louise* and *Bay Belle*. Inspired by Coney Island, the amusement park opened in 1877 with a picnic area, beach, and pavilion with ice cream and dancing. Next came the racetrack, paddleboats, hotel, mini-train, Ferris wheel, and roller coaster. On weekends during its peak, up to 20,000 visitors flocked to the park. Trouble started brewing in the 1920s when paved roads allowed trucks to transport freight from the region more cost-effectively. During the Depression, steamboats' popularity faded, and by the end of World War II, only a few remained. The final nail in the coffin for Tolchester Beach was the Bay Bridge opening in 1952, which gave people easy access to Atlantic beach resorts. The amusement park buildings fell into ruin, were torn down, and eventually were replaced by the marina you see here today.

Passages Bar & Grill

20880 Rock Hall Avenue
Rock Hall, MD 21661
(410) 778-6697 or (800) 506-6697
www.havenharbour.com/destination/bar-and-grill

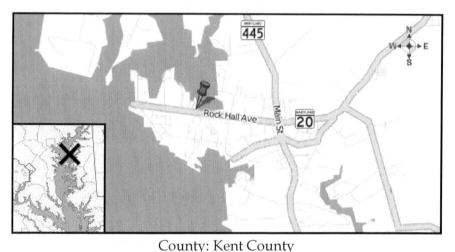

County: Kent County
Open: Seasonal ⚓ Dockage: Yes
Latitude: N 39° 8' 24" ⚓ Longitude: W 76° 14' 59"
Body of Water: The Haven off Swan Creek
Driving Distance: Baltimore 91 miles,
Washington, DC 95 miles, Easton 50 miles

Atmosphere Meter

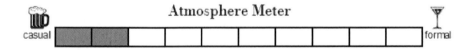

casual | | | | | | | | | | formal

Passages came under new management in 2014, turning operations over to Jeff Carroll, owner of Fish Whistle in Chestertown and enhancing its ties to the Eastern Shore. It's only open Friday through Sunday, but it's among the loveliest little places to catch a sunset on the Bay.

The eatery sits on top of the upper-level deck overlooking beautiful Haven Harbour Marina, which offers full services and a gamut of amenities to boaters. On site are two swimming pools, shaded picnic tables, a children's play area, shuffleboard, horseshoes, and much more.

Cold beer and frozen tropical drinks are the bar's specialty, and the menu keeps things simple. It delivers classic Chesapeake seafood dishes, such as jumbo lump crab cakes, steamed shrimp, and fried fish, as well as grilled burgers and crisp dinner salads.

Another benefit to visiting Passages: It's within walking distance to the main street in Rock Hall, where you can stroll around and explore the craft shops, antique stores, and watermen museum. This picturesque fishing town dates back to 1707. It started as a tobacco port and agricultural hub, but later became a key player in the crab, fish, and oyster industries. Today it's known as a delightful destination with a down-home Fourth of July fireworks celebration and Pirates & Wenches Fantasy Weekend in August.

Osprey Point Restaurant

20786 Rock Hall Avenue
Rock Hall, MD 21661
(410) 639-2194
www.ospreypoint.com

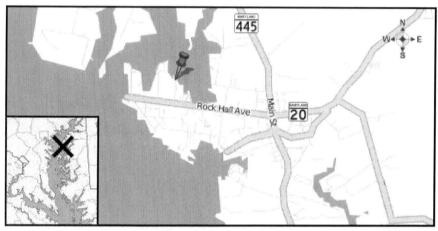

County: Kent County
Open: Year Round ⚓ Dockage: Yes
Latitude: N 39° 8' 36" ⚓ Longitude: W 76° 15' 9"
Body of Water: The Haven off Swan Creek
Driving Distance: Baltimore 91 miles,
Washington, DC 95 miles, Easton 50 miles

Atmosphere Meter

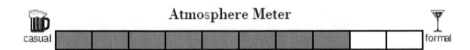

casual | formal

Some folks like to rough it outdoors despite leaky tents, mosquitoes, and tree roots poking your back under the sleeping bag. Others prefer to get their dose of nature in civilized locations like Osprey Point where modern conveniences heighten the experience. The tree-lined driveway harkens back to when country homes were the centerpiece of farms and tobacco plantations along the Bay. Inside the exquisite white and blue inn, you're pampered in rooms with antiques, four-poster beds, and marble bathtubs.

The 30-acre wooded grounds are meticulously groomed, creating a peaceful retreat among old pine trees and sea grass. A gazebo near the marina dares you to come out and watch the sun set over the water. You can have a picnic, hike nature trails, swim in the pool, toss horseshoes, or go fishing. Do whatever you like — as long as you build up an appetite for the epicurean treats coming out of Osprey Point's kitchen.

The atmosphere oozes casual elegance and welcomes you to nibble hors d'oeuvres at the bar or get settled in for a full meal in the dining room. The chef creates seasonal menus that give an upscale touch to regional seafood. Starters include grilled shrimp skewers, local oysters, and drunken mussels. Crab cakes arrive with Old Bay potatoes, and seafood pasta tosses together crab, shrimp, and rockfish in a smooth cream sauce. Meat lovers can sink their teeth into beef tenderloin with broccoli rabe or chicken with prosciutto, buffalo mozzarella, and risotto. In short, it's all about graceful living along the Chesapeake.

Swan Point Inn

20658 Wilkins Avenue
Rock Hall, MD 21661
(410) 639-2500
www.swanpointinn.net

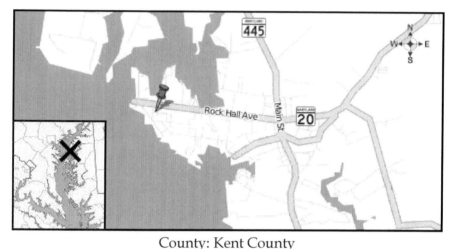

County: Kent County
Open: Seasonal ⚓ Dockage: No
Latitude: N 39° 8' 23" 🐟 Longitude: W 76° 15' 25"
Body of Water: Swan Creek
Driving Distance: Baltimore 91 miles,
Washington, DC 95 miles, Easton 51 miles

Atmosphere Meter

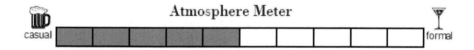

casual   formal

Back in 1929, Swan Point was a waterman's home. Later
it became the Wheelhouse, a local watering hole famous for
cold beer, good food, and lively music. About 20 years ago,
new owners transformed the building into an inn with three
rooms, a cozy bar, and two separate spaces for dining. The
cocktail lounge's walls are painted red and white with black

accents, and that color theme is echoed on the tile floor and barstools. Archways lead to a pizza parlor where regulation red-and-white cloths cover the tables.

The main dining room sports a sophisticated tone with white linens, ruby red napkins, and black chairs. Photographs of the Bay hang on the walls. Outside, trees and big umbrellas cast shade over diners on the large wooden deck.

The menu covers all the Chesapeake basics. Rockfish, shrimp, and scallops gain a smoky flavor from being grilled on cedar planks. Crab soup is rich and creamy. Crab cakes and imperial are made from a traditional Maryland recipe. Cooks have a little fun with local fare by broiling shrimp that's laced with horseradish and wrapped in bacon, or topping croutons with crab meat and melted cheese. Meat eaters will find the prime rib and chicken parmesan irresistible. The pizza parlor lets you cover the dough with anything you like, including crab meat, garlic, and artichokes.

If you had a lucky day on the water, bring your catch to Swan Point's chef and he'll cook your fish and serve it with salad and sides for a minimal fee.

Harbor Shack
Waterfront Bar & Grill

20895 Bayside Avenue
Rock Hall, MD 21661
(410) 639-9996
www.harborshack.net

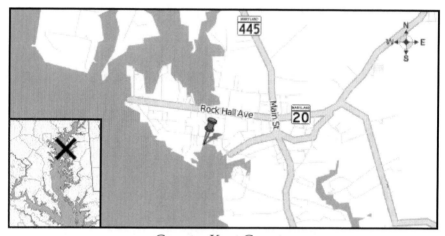

County: Kent County
Open: Year Round ⚓ Dockage: Yes
Latitude: N 39° 8' 4" ⤙ Longitude: W 76° 14' 55"
Body of Water: Rock Hall Harbor
Driving Distance: Baltimore 91 miles,
Washington, DC 95 miles, Easton 50 miles

Atmosphere Meter

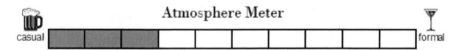

casual / formal

In the dead of winter, Harbor Shack is an oasis of hopeful color amidst the milky gray skies and dry-docked boats wrapped like mummies in white plastic weather protection. Walls painted the yellow and orange of a tequila sunrise promise that summer will return soon. Strings of colorful beer signs will flap in the wind again, and palm trees will get planted in the sand. When the weather turns warm, Harbor Shack becomes the Grand Central Station of Rock Hall — a busy neighborhood hangout where everybody is welcome to join in the revelry.

Charter boats buzz in and out of the marina. Friends and families on the waterfront deck crack open steamed crabs to the rhythm of a rock-and-roll band. This 200-seat restaurant has a casual atmosphere that's reflected in both the décor and menu. Adding to the upbeat vibe are specialty cocktails such as Rock-A-Rita, Shack Attack (orange vodka mixed with an energy drink), and a potent Caribbean rum punch.

The food is creative and inviting. You can warm up your appetite with starters such as Amazing Mussels in alfredo sauce, fried rockfish fingers, or Hawg Legs (grilled BBQ pork shanks). Coconut shrimp and crab dip are pretty tasty, too. Burgers, sandwiches, wraps, and wings provide light fare, and Tex-Mex treats include quesadillas, nachos, and fajitas. Crab soup and garden salads lead the way to seafood entrees. Crab cakes are blended with special seasonings, and ahi tuna is marinated in soy sauce with sesame seeds. Steak, ribs and chicken give savory options to meat eaters.

Waterman's Crab House
Restaurant & Dock Bar

21055 Sharp Street
Rock Hall, MD 21661
(410) 639-2261
www.watermanscrabhouse.com

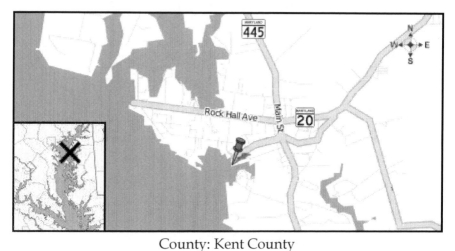

County: Kent County
Open: Seasonal ⚓ Dockage: Yes
Latitude: N 39° 7' 59" ⟶ Longitude: W 76° 14' 36"
Body of Water: Rock Hall Harbor
Driving Distance: Baltimore 91 miles,
Washington, DC 95 miles, Easton 50 miles

Atmosphere Meter

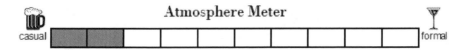

casual   formal

The dynamic duo of crabs and beer reigns supreme at Waterman's classic seafood house. For over 40 years, this Rock Hall landmark has successfully used the briny smell of steaming crabs to lure in diners from all walks of life. Leather-clad bikers, tourists with babies, locals in work shirts, and boaters in Ravens caps sit elbow-to-elbow at long picnic tables covered with mountains of hot red crabs and discarded shells. An air-conditioned dining room keeps you cool and dry, come rain or shine.

The waterfront view is incredible, thanks to one of the largest wooden decks on the Bay. When the sunset fades into night, you can see the distant lights of Baltimore on the horizon across the water. Children toss crackers left over from a bowl of vegetable she-crab soup into the beaks of insistent sea gulls, while a reggae band gets everybody swaying.

The cooks in this family-owned restaurant make crab cakes in the Eastern Shore tradition, with a hint of mustard and Old Bay. You find fresh oysters at the raw bar, fried, or in creamy stew. The Rock Hall Combo piles locally caught crabs, flounder, shrimp, and scallops on a platter with cole slaw and hush puppies. And even though the menu offers burgers, prime rib, chicken, and BBQ ribs, you'll have a hard time taking your eyes off the crabs that your neighbor is picking next to you. Desserts are addictive, especially the hot apple dumpling, red velvet bundt cake, Key lime pie, and Smith Island cake.

The Sandbar at Rolph's Wharf

1008 Rolphs Wharf Road
Chestertown, MD 21620
(410) 778-6389 or (800) 894-6347

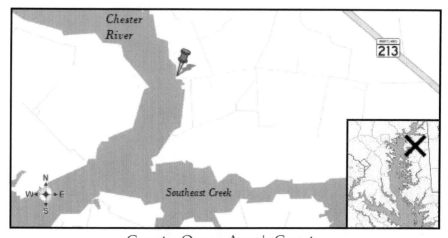

County: Queen Anne's County
Open: Seasonal ⚓ Dockage: Yes
Latitude: N 39° 10' 27" 🐟 Longitude: W 76° 2' 14"
Body of Water: Chester River
Driving Distance: Baltimore 75 miles,
Washington, DC 78 miles, Easton 34 miles

Atmosphere Meter

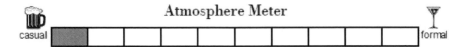

casual · · · · · · · · · formal

What do you do with an old boat that won't float because
of a big hole in its bottom? Rather than chop it up for
firewood, Rolph's Wharf turned it into a unique beach bar.
In its new life as the Sandbar, the boat rests on the shore a few
yards away from the Chester River where it cruised the waters
in its glory days. Cooking appliances, liquor bottles, and
coolers are now in the hull. White barstools around the

outside allow patrons to rest their elbows on the gunwales of the boat, while a bartender inside hands out cold beer. It's the embodiment of Eastern Shore resourcefulness and humor that makes everyone feel at home. A pavilion stands overhead as protection from the rain, and soft white sand spread out on the beach creates a fabulous fun retreat.

The Sandbar's food is simple, pub grub: steamed shrimp, crab cakes, hot dogs, sandwiches, and spicy wings are served on paper plates. Children dig in the sand, while parents relax on beach chairs in the sun. People lounge around the swimming pool, and bands play on weekends.

If a day trip isn't enough, you can spend the night at the River Inn, which is part of the same marina. This beautiful circa 1830 Victorian farmhouse is flanked by ancient holly and pine trees and has a long front porch with a swing bench that's

perfect for lazy summer days. The widow's walk on top stirs up images of anxious women pacing the floor, waiting for their husbands to return from the sea. The inn's rooms are quite comfortable, and they lack that  "no touch" museum feel you find at some B&Bs that makes you worry about breaking an antique crystal vase or porcelain doll that's been handed down for generations. Best of all, the warm hospitality compels you to return to Rolph's Wharf any chance you get.

Fish Whistle

98 Cannon Street
Chestertown, MD 21620
(410) 778-3566
www.fishandwhistle.com

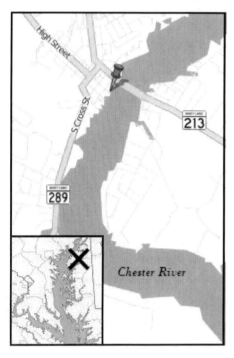

County: Kent County

Open: Year Round

Dockage: Yes

Latitude: N 39° 12' 20"

Longitude: W 76° 3' 50"

Body of Water: Chester River

Driving Distance:
    Baltimore 77 miles,
    Washington, DC 81 miles,
    Easton 36 miles

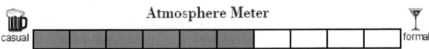

Atmosphere Meter

casual   formal

As you cruise around the Eastern Shore, be sure to stop at Fish Whistle. You'll be glad you did. The restaurant is located at the marina within a stone's throw of the beautiful Chester River Bridge. The building's interior walls are painted warm salmon and pale green and are artfully decorated with carved wooden boats, fish, and other artifacts of the Bay.

The cuisine is upscale nouvelle and features regional seafood such as fried Chesapeake oysters, jumbo lump crab cakes, pan-seared salmon, and sesame-crusted ahi tuna. Meatloaf mashers, Sheppard's pie filled with lamb stew, and roasted chicken Florentine are special treats for meat lovers. Casual fare options include pulled pork BBQ, Cuban sandwiches, Monte Carlo, curried chicken salad, and flash-fried calamari. Daily specials offer irresistible discounted dishes such as Monday's burgers and wings, Taco Tuesdays, and Thursday's all-you-can-eat oysters.

When the kitchen closes on weekends, bands or DJs crank tunes in the bar and music flows out onto the waterfront deck. When dinner's done, take a leisurely stroll around historic Chestertown. Founded in 1705, the town flourished during the shipping boom in the 18th century, which created a wealthy merchant class that built elegant mansions along the river. You can start at the waterfront on High Street, pass the gorgeous Imperial Hotel, and stroll through the historic district until you reach Fountain Park and the quaint shops surrounding the town square. On top of the hill stands Washington College, established in 1782 with support from our nation's first president.

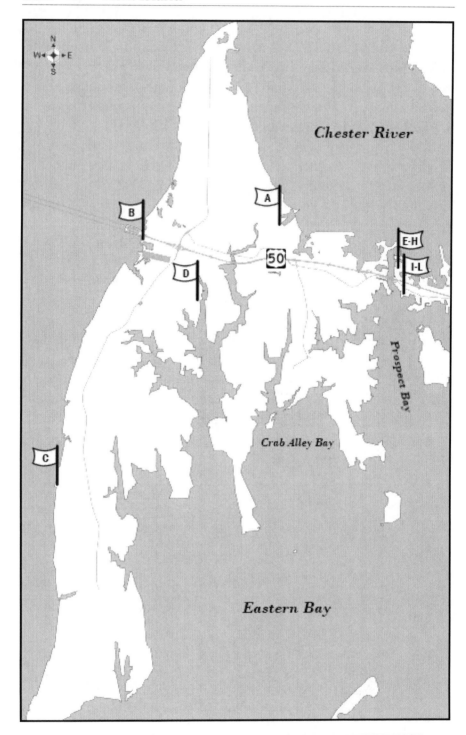

Kent Island

Pour House Pub

205 Tackle Circle
Chester, MD 21619
(443) 249-3242
www.pourhousepubki.com

County: Queen Anne's County
Open: Year Round ⚓ Dockage: Yes
Latitude: N 38° 59' 7" 🐟 Longitude: W 76° 17' 10"
Body of Water: Chester River
Driving Distance: Baltimore 45 miles,
Washington, DC 49 miles, Easton 27 miles

Atmosphere Meter

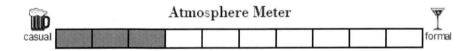

Beer and crabs go hand in hand, but if you want to take a break from the usual domestic brews, then stop by Pour House Pub. It's the latest venture by owners of Good Guys and Pronto Pizza that's appealing to the taste buds of discerning beer connoisseurs. This specialty beer house showcases a wide variety of local and unique suds including

Golden Monkey, Angry Orchard, Guinness, Dogfish Head, Raging Bitch, and Rise Up Coffee Stout.

The new restaurant overlooking Castle Harbor Marina shares a building with a Thai restaurant, so look for the half dozen picnic tables out front to find this quaint neighborhood tavern. The interior décor is casual and cozy with a low pressed-tin ceiling, exposed brick walls with wood trim, and simple wooden tables and chairs. Neon and metal beer signs suffice as artwork. A chalkboard announces daily specials for both beers and food.

The menu starts off with popular standards such as Maryland crab soup, seared ahi tuna crusted with sesame seeds, and fried shrimp with cheesy grits cakes. Seafood entrees include a colossal crab cake, oyster po' boy, shrimp and crab alfredo, and fish and chips. Carnivores are not overlooked with choices such as a Big Daddy porterhouse steak, pot roast, pulled port on a brioche bun, and braised pork shanks with goat cheese mashed potatoes. Salads, soups, and pizza expand the delicious dining options.

Hemingway's Restaurant

357 Pier One Road
Stevensville, MD 21666
(410) 604-0999
www.hemingwaysbaybridge.com

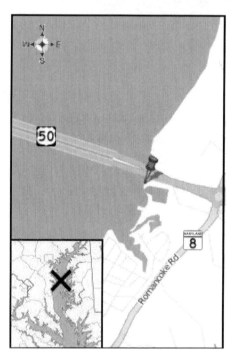

County: Queen Anne's County

Open: Year Round

Dockage: Yes

Latitude: N 38° 58' 50"

Longitude: W 76° 20' 4"

Body of Water: directly
   on the Chesapeake Bay

Driving Distance:
   Baltimore 42 miles,
   Washington, DC 46 miles,
   Easton 29 miles

Atmosphere Meter

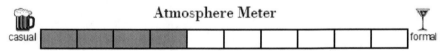

casual ⟶ formal

When the old Hemingway's fell under the wrecking ball in 2010, it felt like something was missing along the Bay. For decades, it was the first thing you'd see as you headed east across the Bay Bridge — a beloved welcome sign that proved you landed safely on the Eastern Shore. In 2011, owners of Bay Bridge Marina pumped a small fortune into renovations and a new Hemingway's appeared. The entire marina is beaming from a complete makeover with spruced up docks, a swimming pool, and other pleasant amenities.

The building makes the most of the spectacular view of the water. You can while away the hours watching boats while relaxing in an Adirondack chair on the lawn, and at a table on the brick patio or double-deck gazebo bar. Sunsets over the Bay Bridge are unforgettable. Inside the restaurant, walls are painted beige and decorated with black-framed vintage photos of watermen and nautical items such as fishnets, ship ropes, and lanterns. The lounge is cozy with overstuffed furniture and a fireplace.

The menu showcases fresh regional seafood. Starters include soups, seared ahi tuna, and a raw bar with local half-shell oysters. Two standout salads make you feel good about eating healthy: spinach with shrimp and crab, and chicken or shrimp fajita salad. Sage-encrusted wild Maryland rockfish is dressed up in jumbo lump crab beurre blanc sauce. Award-winning crab cakes and crab soup are bursting with flavor. Steaks, chicken, ribs, veal meatloaf, and pork chops are on tap for meat lovers.

Kentmorr Restaurant & Crab House

910 Kentmorr Road
Stevensville, MD 21666
(410) 643-2263
www.kentmorr.com

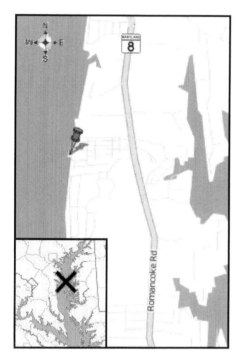

County: Queen Anne's County

Open: Year Round

Dockage: Yes

Latitude: N 38° 54' 54"

Longitude: W 76° 21' 51"

Body of Water: directly
on the Chesapeake Bay

Driving Distance:
Baltimore 47 miles,
Washington, DC 51 miles,
Easton 34 miles

Atmosphere Meter

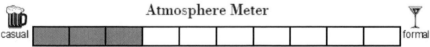

casual — formal

Whether you come by car, boat, or plane, Kentmorr is worth a visit. (Seriously, you really can fly into Kentmorr Airpark and take a short stroll to the restaurant.) What makes this place special? You can stretch out on its beach while kids play in the water and discover treasures of the Bay in its gentle waves. In summer, the opening of Dirty Dave's Tiki

Bar kicks off bikini season when crowds gather around the thatched roof bar with outstretched hands for chilled beer and tropical cocktails. Palm trees and lazy-day hammocks create picturesque sunsets with the Bay Bridge in the distance.

You can watch charter captains load their boats with excited passengers hoping for a lucky day and a bountiful catch. They even post a board with charter information and bragging rights for record catches of the season. It's a bustling little sport-fishing hub that's made folks happy since 1954.

The restaurant sits on the water's edge and wooden picnic tables line up along the dock. The dining area is open and airy, with enough space between tables to ensure you won't get hit by flying shrapnel when other diners crack open their crabs. The kitchen masterfully executes classic Chesapeake fare of local rockfish, shrimp, oysters, and littleneck clams, and steamed crabs and award-winning crab cakes are the centerpiece. Half-and-Half dares to mix cream of crab soup with its red vegetable counterpart. Burgers and chicken breast sandwiches come on sesame seed buns. New York style pizzas, including a pie topped with crab and fresh mozzarella, are baked in a gourmet brick oven. For a few bucks more, you can add a crab cake or shrimp to steak entrees.

Kent Manor Inn
& Restaurant

500 Kent Manor Drive
Stevensville, MD 21666
(410) 643-5757
www.kentmanor.com

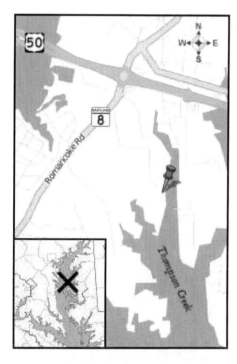

County: Queen Anne's County

Open: Year Round

Dockage: Yes

Latitude: N 38° 57' 51"

Longitude: W 76° 18' 56"

Body of Water: Thompson
Creek off Cox Creek
off Eastern Bay

Driving Distance:
Baltimore 43 miles,
Washington, DC 46 miles,
Easton 34 miles

 Atmosphere Meter

casual ▭▭▭▭▭▭▭▭▭▭ formal

Fine dining accented with Old World elegance and natural beauty await you at Kent Manor Inn & Restaurant. The beautiful Victorian building (circa 1820) and gorgeous grounds set the stage for an upscale culinary experience. Italian marble fireplaces and classic English décor create a serene atmosphere in the dining rooms. An outdoor deck overlooks the garden house and Thompson Creek.

American nouvelle cuisine is infused with Eastern Shore influences, offering presentations so lovely that the most discriminating chefs would nod their heads in approval. The menu changes often to capture the seasons' harvests and fresh ingredients. Local crab, shrimp, and rockfish get the gourmet spa treatment in the kitchen. When you walk in the door for Sunday brunch, the aroma of smoky bacon and just-baked pastries make your stomach rumble with excitement.

The estate's grounds are gorgeous. The land was granted to Thomas Wetherall in 1651, only 17 years after Lord Calvert set foot in Maryland. In 1843, Alexander Thompson inherited the property and built an addition on the house right before the Civil War broke out. Local historians describe old A.T. as quite the character — rich, flamboyant, cigar-smoking, and fond of women. He married three times but had no children, and was famous for his charming ways and love of horses. Some say Thompson's ghost still gallops around the place on his white steed and roams the halls of the inn, mysteriously turning on lights or opening locked doors. When you visit, perhaps you'll get a chance to meet him.

Annie's Paramount
Steak & Seafood House

500 Kent Narrows Way North
Grasonville, MD 21638
(410) 827-7103
www.annies.biz

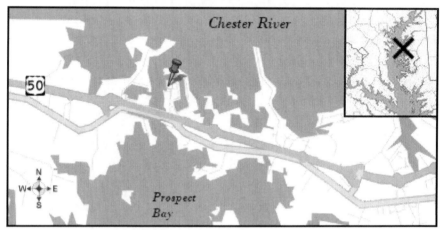

County: Queen Anne's County
Open: Year Round ⚓ Dockage: Yes
Latitude: N 38° 58' 27" ⚓ Longitude: W 76° 14' 41"
Body of Water: Kent Island Narrows off the Chester River
Driving Distance: Baltimore 46 miles,
Washington, DC 50 miles, Easton 24 miles

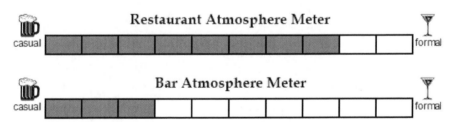

Annie's is the Chesapeake's way of saying, "Look how
we do surf and turf." Since 1982, it's held center court at

Mears Point Marina. You won't find outdoor deck seating, but tall windows around the building open out to a gorgeous view of Kent Narrows and the bridge. The lounge sports a casual neighborhood pub feel with a pool table, 20+ TVs lined up along the walls, and time-worn wood floors. Carpeted and more upscale dining rooms blush with hushed pink lighting. Here you find feminine touches like fresh floral arrangements near the black grand piano and bud vases with clusters of petite flowers on tables covered with pink and white linens.

The restaurant takes pride in its select cuts of beef, dry aged and hand-cut on the premises, complemented by an extensive wine menu. Texas bone-in rib eye (The Famous Cowboy Steak), prime rib, and marinated tenderloin tips served sizzling (Bull in the Pan), are guaranteed to make your mouth water in anticipation.

"Toast of the Town" crab cakes, jumbo breaded oysters, sesame-crusted ahi tuna, and stuffed shrimp imperial are the pride and joy of the seafood side on the menu. Annie's cream of crab soup is so good that it's sold at specialty markets in Annapolis and other Bay locations. Crab melts and burgers, along with shrimp salad and Philly cheese steak subs are among light fare dishes. Pastas in marinara sauce, shrimp scampi, and other Mediterranean house specials are delicious.

Red Eye's Dock Bar

428 Kent Narrows Way North
Grasonville, MD 21638
(410) 827-EYES
www.redeyedockbar.com

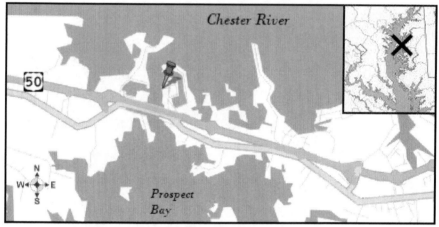

County: Queen Anne's County
Open: Year Round ⚓ Dockage: Yes
Latitude: N 38° 58' 24" Longitude: W 76° 14' 44"
Body of Water: Kent Island Narrows off the Chester River
Driving Distance: Baltimore 46 miles,
Washington, DC 50 miles, Easton 24 miles

Atmosphere Meter

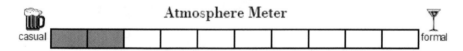

casual .... formal

If you look all the way up at the top of the building, you'll notice a large eyeball painted on the wall, and you might wonder why that eye is so red. Maybe it's tired? For decades, The Red Eye has been the last stop for a final view of the Bay and a sunset cocktail before heading home to Washington or

Baltimore. It's a welcoming port for a little hair of the dog after a memorable weekend at the beach.

Maybe the eye turned red because it doesn't dare to blink for fear of missing the merriment happening down below. Neon palm trees and colorful tiki masks carved on pylons stand guard along the water's edge, and boaters pull up ready to rumble. Rock and country bands crank tunes on the stage.

Perhaps the famous Sunday bikini contests made that eye blood-shot? Probably not. At best it might raise its eyebrow with amusement. The redness could be from cold easterly winds that blow across the Bay during the off-season, when locals camp out in the newly renovated and heated second-story dock bar called The View to watch sports on 16 HD TVs. Hot Maryland crab soup, zesty Buffalo wings, grilled steaks, and steamed mussels take the bite out of a blustery winter day. Pork BBQ and crab cakes are flawless comfort foods.

We may never solve the mystery of what turned that eyeball red, but it's worth the trip to investigate — even if you wake up the next morning with eyes of a similar hue.

Harris Crab House
& Seafood Restaurant

433 Kent Narrow Way North
Grasonville, MD 21638
(410) 827-9500
www.harriscrabhouse.com

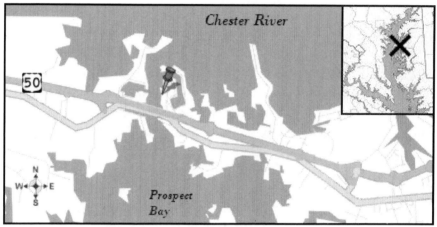

County: Queen Anne's County
Open: Year Round ⚓ Dockage: Yes
Latitude: N 38° 58' 22" ⟜ Longitude: W 76° 14' 44"
Body of Water: Kent Island Narrows off the Chester River
Driving Distance: Baltimore 46 miles,
Washington, DC 50 miles, Easton 24 miles

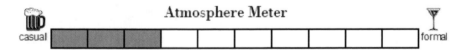

When asked about Harris' secret for making perfect fried oysters, the waitress leaned in close and whispered, "Shake off the excess flour, make sure your grease is good and hot, and pull 'em out fast right when they turn crispy golden brown." Before tending to the rest of her tables, she winked and added,

"And don't you dare settle for anything less than fresh Bay oysters! The rest ... well, why bother?" She's right about the oysters and everything else you pop into your mouth at Harris Crab House. Only the best of the Chesapeake and True Blue Maryland crabs land on your table. As proof, you can sit on the outside decks and watch local watermen unload just-caught seafood and haul them into the kitchen. Next door to the restaurant is one of the few remaining oyster shucking houses on the Bay.

All you can eat steamed crabs are cooked in the traditional Maryland way. Rockfish sandwiches and soft-shell crabs stuffed with crab imperial are sure hits for seafood fans. Vegetable and cream of crab soups are legendary for robust flavors. And regional seafood — crabs, shrimp, mussels, and clams — regularly win awards for freshness and special house seasonings. Harris' long-term commitment to local seafood is on display in the restaurant. The walls are covered with antique oyster cans and vintage posters of dancing bivalves and crabs. Dedicated local patrons keep this cozy seafood house bustling day and night, all year round. Watching swans and ducks quack around the dock and catching a sunset over Kent Narrows Bridge are the finishing touches to a terrific evening at this classic Chesapeake crab house.

The Big Owl Tiki Bar

3015 Kent Narrows Way South
Grasonville, MD 21638
(410) 827-6523
www.thebigowl.com

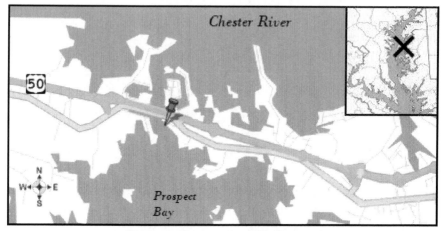

County: Queen Anne's County
Open: Seasonal ⚓ Dockage: Yes
Latitude: N 38° 58' 8" 🐟 Longitude: W 76° 14' 44"
Body of Water: Kent Island Narrows off Prospect Bay
Driving Distance: Baltimore 46 miles,
Washington, DC 50 miles, Easton 24 miles

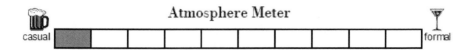

Atmosphere Meter
casual | formal

When you hear the sounds of contagious laughter, clinking glasses, and Jimmy Buffet tunes out on the pier at Big Owl Tiki Bar, you know right away that they take the business of having fun very seriously. Perched on the water at Kent Narrows, the building and pylons are painted neon Key West orange and turquoise, with hand-carved tiki masks grinning from their posts on the walls and bar. Bright blue and yellow umbrellas offer relief from the heat on the long wooden deck. You can capture memories of your visit by taking a photo with your arm around a giant cut-out of Big Owl wearing Ray Bans, a Hawaiian shirt, and flip-flops.

The menu is simple: "Nothing fancy, no fine china, just good eat'n with an island breeze." Caribbean-influenced pub food features steamers of clams, mussels, and Yucatan shrimp in a garlic butter broth. Munchies present light fare of coconut shrimp, clam strips, rockfish tenders, and wings. Sandwich platter highlights: Paradise Cheeseburger, Jamaican jerk chicken, and Momma Owl's crab cakes. The wide selection of cold beer takes the edge off a hot summer night.

At Big Owl's, it's easy to sit back, catch an amazing sunset, and let the reggae music lull you into a blissful relaxed state. On your way out when you first step on land again, check out two cemetery stone markers. They serve as memorials to Hazel and Mamma Cass, a pair of visionary women who were instrumental in fostering business development on the southern part of Kent Narrows.

The Narrows Restaurant

3023 Kent Narrows Way South
Grasonville, MD 21638
(410) 827-8113
www.thenarrowsrestaurant.com

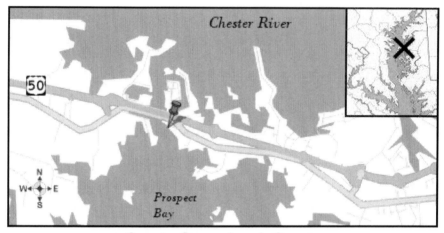

County: Queen Anne's County
Open: Year Round ⚓ Dockage: Yes
Latitude: N 38° 58' 8" Longitude: W 76° 14' 43"
Body of Water: Kent Island Narrows off Prospect Bay
Driving Distance: Baltimore 46 miles,
Washington, DC 50 miles, Easton 24 miles

Atmosphere Meter

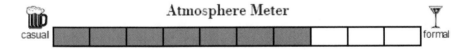

casual   formal

If a restaurant is built upon the foundation of an old
oyster-shucking house, there's almost an obligation to serve
top-quality local seafood. That's been happening since 1983
at The Narrows. In 2015, the restaurant underwent major
renovations resulting in a new, airy, contemporary look with
pale gray walls, wood-top tables with black chairs, and a

bright red bar top made of concrete and oyster shells. Modern art and an occasional mounted fish hang on the walls. Wow is the best word to describe the transformation. A long row of windows over the water completes the stunning new vibe.

For years, Narrows' chefs have taken home prizes for the best crab cake, crab soup, and romantic restaurant. The menu shows a thoughtful marriage of traditional Bay cuisine with innovative cooking. You'll have a hard time choosing between enticing appetizers such as the crab tart with feta, provolone, spinach, and tomato on a flatbread crust or smoked salmon Napoleon layered between wonton pastries with caper dill cream.

Fried oyster Caesar and seared tuna salad elevate mixed greens to a whole new level. Seafood takes the lead among the entrees: crab imperial topped with applewood-smoked bacon, pecan-crusted catfish, and grilled freshwater trout in a lemon buerre blanc sauce. Savory meat dishes — braised pork shank, filet mignon over garlic mashed potatoes, and rosemary-crusted rack of lamb — make sure everyone leaves full and happy.

Fisherman's Inn & Crab Deck

3116 Main Street
Grasonville, MD 21638
(410) 827-8807 Inn, (410) 827-6666 Crab Deck
www.crabdeck.com

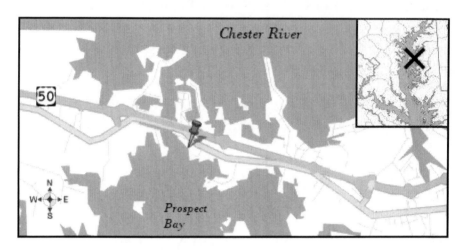

County: Queen Anne's County
Open: Year Round ⚓ Dockage: Yes
Latitude: N 38° 58' 3" ➤ Longitude: W 76° 14' 37"
Body of Water: Kent Island Narrows off Prospect Bay
Driving Distance: Baltimore 46 miles,
Washington, DC 50 miles, Easton 24 miles

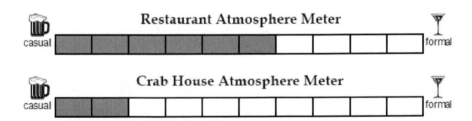

If you're looking for a one-stop shop to fulfill all your
Chesapeake dreams, then head for Fisherman's Inn. Since
1930, this Kent Narrows landmark has survived everything

from tough economic times to Hurricane Isabel. Somehow it keeps growing bigger and better. The Inn's main restaurant shows its nautical roots with an aquarium at the entrance, a collection of more than 300 antique oyster plates decorating the walls, and a bar shaped like a boat. A toy train chugs overhead on its track. The menu presents an impressive array of regional seafood, pasta, beef, salads, and sandwiches.

The newly renovated Nauti Mermaid Bar features a long wood bar, inlaid blue glass with waves and fish, and metal mermaid artwork hung on exposed brick walls. The crab deck offers a casual waterfront experience where cooks steam, grill, or fry crabs, shrimp, rockfish, oysters, clams, and other catch that local fishermen deliver daily. Rolls of paper towels, brown paper on the tables, and the aroma of Old Bay in the air leave no doubt that this place is the real deal for a traditional crab-picking experience.

Waiters at Cappy's Tiki Bar quickly place a cool beverage in your hand while you watch a band or inspect boats passing by the dock. And that's not all. If you want to bring home a sampling of the Bay, you can fill a cooler with fresh seafood and ice at the seafood market.

Bridges Restaurant

321 Wells Cove Road
Grasonville, MD 21638
(410) 827-0282
www.bridgesrestaurant.net

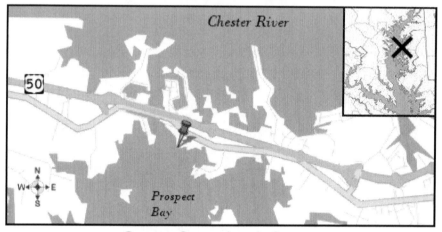

County: Queen Anne's County
Open: Year Round ⚓ Dockage: Yes
Latitude: N 38° 57' 57" ⤖ Longitude: W 76° 14' 35"
Body of Water: Kent Island Narrows off Prospect Bay
Driving Distance: Baltimore 46 miles,
Washington, DC 50 miles, Easton 24 miles

Atmosphere Meter

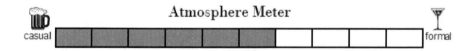

casual ⟵⟶ formal

When Bridges opened in 2010, sidestepping the traditional crab deck vibe was the plan. Now that they've had time to get settled into the Kent Narrows neighborhood, they offer a lovely alternative to old-school Bay eateries. The atmosphere is upscale comfortable, and the space has a bistro-style open kitchen serving a nice variety of dishes. It's the kind of place where you might take a date, rather than find one. Plus you can't beat the location, right on the water's edge with two tiers of spacious decks offering a heavenly view of Prospect Bay. Live music on Friday and Saturday nights promotes local jazz and blues artists.

Its yellow-and-white striped awnings, red roof, and mustard-color walls glow golden at sunset. Inside, the blond wood and black chairs are accented by French café artwork. The massive chandelier made out of wine bottles foreshadows an extensive wine list that tempts you to indulge in anything from a crisp chardonnay to a bold cabernet. Specialty drinks feature champagne, martinis, and sangria.

The menu presents an innovative fusion of local ingredients with a contemporary twist. Crab cakes and rockfish are served with sweet potato mash and lemon hollandaise. Lobster and shrimp penne are tossed in a basil cream sauce, and don't be shy to ask for extra bread to soak up every last drop of mussels in pesto cream. Gourmet pizza, BBQ pork shank, steak, and Mediterranean chicken are among the dishes for meat eaters. It all boils down to exploring a new spin on regional dishes while uncorking a bottle of fun.

The Jetty Restaurant & Dock Bar

201 Wells Cove Road
Grasonville, MD 21638
(410) 827-4959
www.jettydockbar.com

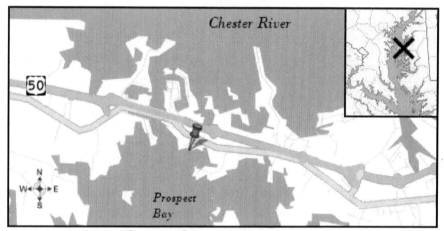

County: Queen Anne's County
Open: Year Round ⚓ Dockage: Yes
Latitude: N 38° 57' 57" ⤐ Longitude: W 76° 14' 30"
Body of Water: Wells Cove off Kent Island Narrows off
Prospect Bay
Driving Distance: Baltimore 46 miles,

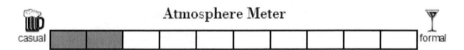

A cacophony of color — electric blue, green, yellow, and a touch of magenta — paint a fun-inspiring tropical landscape at The Jetty. Clusters of palm trees, thick green foliage and rustling sea grass make you feel like you landed on a little slice of paradise. Vintage Harleys parked out front imply that good times have just rolled in. There's a laid-back feel to this place, almost as if you're required to check your worries at the door before entering. Children dig in the beach area, while parents steal a moment to relax with a cool cocktail and a crimson sunset. Seating right above the waves guarantees a gentle Bay breeze at night.

Friends linger at the tables washing down mountains of hot steamed crabs with icy beer. The menu infuses Bay ingredients with Caribbean flavors, creating food that is simple, fresh, and delicious. Local seafood standards of crabs, shrimp, and fried soft-shells are served with creamy cole slaw and salty fries. Hearty sandwiches, jerk chicken, steaks, rack of ribs, pasta, and salads round out your dining options.

Live local bands entertain patrons after the sun goes down. On summer evenings, the energy level and crowd size picks up considerably, so parking can be a challenge. But never fear, The Jetty Bus thoughtfully shuttles people to and from nearby hotels and parking lots to make sure everyone can enjoy this casual Bay destination.

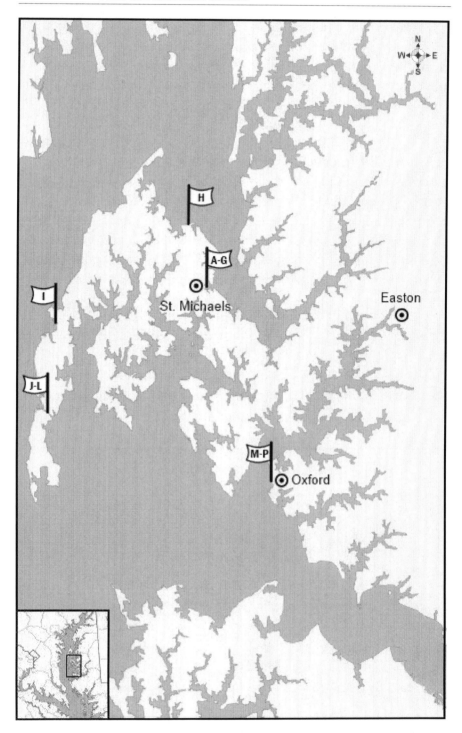

Middle Eastern Shore

Harbourside Grill

101 North Harbor Road
St. Michaels, MD 21663
(410) 745-9001 or (800) 955-9001
www.harbourinn.com/dine/harbourside-grill

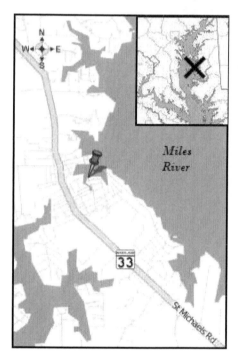

County: Talbot County

Open: Year Round

Dockage: Yes

Latitude: N 38° 47' 7"

Longitude: W 76° 13' 11"

Body of Water: St. Michaels
Harbor off the Miles River

Driving Distance:
Baltimore 78 miles,
Washington, DC 82 miles,
Easton 10 miles

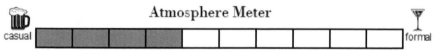

Atmosphere Meter

casual — formal

When you visit Harbourside Grill, you have two good options: spend a few hours enjoying a pleasant meal at the waterfront or stay overnight getting pampered at a luxury resort. Both choices reward you with a gorgeous view of the Miles River and historic St. Michaels. Harbourside Inn's 49 guest rooms provide a luxurious retreat for weary travelers and its full-service 52-slip transient marina offers a convenient port to boaters. Heated massage tables and hot towels in the spa await your aching muscles. The seasonal outdoor pool invites you to grab a cool martini and wash away all the stress from your workweek.

In 2014, the hotel renovated its restaurant, creating a more laid-back atmosphere and casual menu. The cozy lounge encourages guests to linger with board games, comfy seating, and specialty craft beers. Black cast-iron tables and chairs are arranged on the new dining area on the outdoor deck. Flaps roll up to let in a gentle breeze in warm weather.

The new menu marries Chesapeake favorites with southern cuisine. You can start with shrimp and grits cakes, low-country mussels with andouille sausage, or fried green tomatoes. Standout seafood entrees include crab cakes with bacon and sweet corn succotash, shrimp with angel hair pasta, and the Harbourside seafood feast. Meat eaters also get their fill with selections such as char-grilled flatiron steak, fried chicken cordon bleu, and hot country ham and cheese with honey mustard and cheddar.

St. Michaels
Crab & Steak House

305 Mulberry Street
St. Michaels, MD 21663
(410) 745-3737
www.stmichaelscrabhouse.com

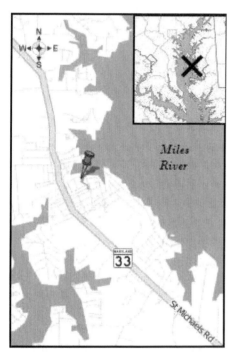

County: Talbot County

Open: Seasonal

Dockage: Yes

Latitude: N 38° 47' 6"

Longitude: W 76° 13' 15"

Body of Water: St. Michaels
Harbor off the Miles River

Driving Distance:
Baltimore 78 miles,
Washington, DC 82 miles,
Easton 10 miles

Atmosphere Meter

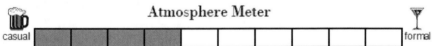

casual ◻◻◻◻ formal

Did you know that when you walk up to St. Michaels
Crab & Steakhouse, the patio bricks under your feet were
kilned in the 1800s? And did you realize that the building was
home to one of the area's earliest oyster-shucking houses? The

thick wooden ceiling joists holding up the tavern serve as proof of its age and authenticity.

History is all around you here, and so is really good food that's prepared to order. For 22 years, the chefs have taken guests on a culinary tour of regional treasures — succulent crab cakes, briny half-shell oysters, steamed mussels and clams, Chesapeake chicken, and more. Crowd pleasers include Crab Benedict (crab imperial with tomato on an English muffin), crisp soft-shell crabs, and a seafood platter with a crab cake, flounder, shrimp, and scallops. The house special for sipping: Bloody Marys with vegetable-infused vodka and Old Bay clinging to the rim of the glass. Yum!

The waterfront deck is often packed with local watermen who proudly tell how their town fooled the British. In 1813, British ships planned to attack St. Michaels. Forewarned, the quick-thinking residents hoisted lanterns to the masts of ships and tops of trees, causing the cannons to overshoot the town. Only one house was hit when a cannonball cut through the roof and rolled down the staircase as a mother carried her infant daughter to safety downstairs. The town was saved. Want to learn more? Walk to the Chesapeake Bay Maritime Museum that celebrates the region's culture and history.

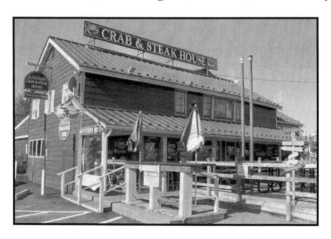

Town Dock Restaurant

125 Mulberry Street
St. Michaels, MD 21663
(410) 745-5577
www.towndockrestaurant.com

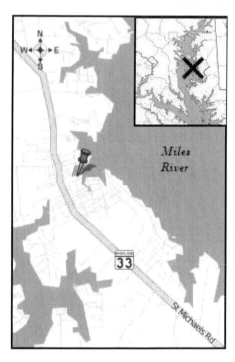

County: Talbot County

Open: Year Round

Dockage: Yes

Latitude: N 38° 47' 7"

Longitude: W 76° 13' 16"

Body of Water: St. Michaels
Harbor off the Miles River

Driving Distance:
Baltimore 78 miles,
Washington, DC 82 miles,
Easton 10 miles

Atmosphere Meter

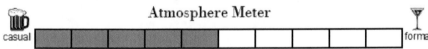

casual   formal

Town Dock closed for a while to repair damage from a fire in 2010. Thank heavens, it reopened in April 2011 to complete the cluster of classic Bay dining on the harbor, along with The Crab Claw and St. Michaels Crab & Steakhouse. The two-tiered building hovering above the harbor presents an unobstructed and dazzling view of the water from every seat in the house. Tables inside are covered with white linens, but the atmosphere is still comfortable and welcoming. The outdoor deck offers a casual spot to enjoy cocktails and watch the boats parade on a summer evening. Right in the heart of St. Michaels harbor, its ideal location is frequented by locals and tourists alike.

Town Dock's specialty is seafood, but it also delivers delicious land-based alternatives. Folks rave about the crab cakes and oysters, and you find plenty of other treasures from the sea on the menu. Shrimp, scallops, fish, and mussels simmer nicely in a spicy tomato broth. Scallops are lightly blackened and served with a red pepper polenta. Grilled pork chops over redskin smashed potatoes, filet mignon, and slow-cooked BBQ ribs are star attractions for meat eaters. You won't leave a crumb on the plate if you order crab and artichoke dip or bacon and cheese enriched oysters casino.

Bands play tunes at the Union Jack Pub and Fireside Lounge. And if you're looking for a venue to accommodate a big crowd or special event, Town Dock has two waterfront banquet rooms with ample seating for large groups.

Foxy's Harbor Grille

125 Mulberry Street
St. Michaels, MD 21663
(410) 745-4340
www.foxysstmichaels.com

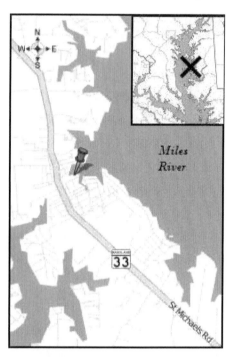

County: Talbot County

Open: Seasonal

Dockage: Yes

Latitude: N 38° 47' 7"

Longitude: W 76° 13' 17"

Body of Water: St. Michaels
Harbor off the Miles River

Driving Distance:
Baltimore 78 miles,
Washington, DC 82 miles,
Easton 10 miles

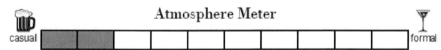

Atmosphere Meter

casual | formal

Captain John Smith cruised through St. Michaels in 1608. If Foxy's Harbor Grille had been on the shore at that time, he probably would have stayed longer, because world explorers know a terrific dock bar when they see one.

This vibrant waterfront spot opened in 1999 and is named after Foxy's Island Bar in the British Virgin Islands. Today's voyagers discover a welcoming port with an energetic Key West vibe and a phenomenal view of the harbor. Sunsets are guaranteed to inspire awe. A mosaic made of metallic glass portrays palm trees, parrots, and the restaurant logo, while a rainbow of colorful beach umbrellas covers tables on the wooden deck.

It's only open in the warm weather season, so drinks and dishes are designed to cool a sweaty brow. Just watch how the temperatures drop when you sip famous giant martinis, icy rum cocktails, or the house special Key West Lemonade. You can also pick from an extensive list of American craft beers, many of which are brewed locally.

The menu is intentionally uncomplicated, blending Bay standards with Caribbean treats. Crab cakes, gazpacho topped with crab meat, steamed shrimp, and clam buckets hit the spot for Chesapeake cuisine lovers. You've got plenty of options if you've got an island groove going: Cuban cobb salad and jerk chicken breast. Landlubber specials include skirt steak, Buffalo chicken wrap, and bison burgers. It's good food in a great location, and you'll want to linger for hours.

Marcoritaville Tiki Bar & American Grille

105 North Talbot Street
St. Michaels, MD 21663
(410) 745-5557
www.marcosbar.com

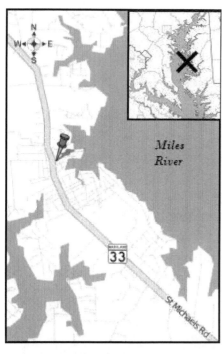

County: Talbot County

Open: Year Round

Dockage: No

Latitude: N 38° 47' 13"

Longitude: W 76° 13' 27"

Body of Water: St. Michaels
   Harbor off the Miles River

Driving Distance:
   Baltimore 78 miles,
   Washington, DC 82 miles,
   Easton 10 miles

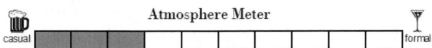

Atmosphere Meter

casual .... formal

When St. Michaels was established in the 1770s, its founding fathers probably didn't envision a tiki bar on the main street. But there stands Marcoritaville like a Polynesian renegade among the 18th century buildings, serving up a cheerful dose of tiki. It's not located on the water, but it sure is making a big splash in this historic little town.

Thatched umbrellas rustle above wooden patio furniture, and palm trees glow with white sparkly lights wrapped around their trunks. Green cushioned seats are turned toward the deck railing, giving a better angle for people watching. The interior décor continues the tropical theme. Super-sized sharks and trophy fish hang on sky-blue walls covered with murals of sunny Caribbean beaches. Tropical plants stand at attention among the tables. Woven bamboo mats edged with grassy thatch cover the roof of the bar. Live bands on the deck trumpet the opening of summer on this island-inspired oasis.

The Vietnamese owner/chef and his wife have crafted a menu that honors their heritage and new home on the Bay. An eclectic mix of seafood, meat, and vegetarian dishes is inspired by flavors from around the globe. The sushi bar cranks out rolls with fresh fish, seaweed, and sticky rice. A steaming bowl of Vietnamese pho soup fights off the chill from a rainy day. American cuisine has equal footing in the kitchen. Oysters are billed as "Viagra on the Half Shell." Crab cakes, soft-shell clams, Maine lobster, and prime rib are big hits at dinner, and icy rum drinks transport you to the islands.

The Crab Claw Restaurant

304 Burns Street
St. Michaels, MD 21663
(410) 745-2900
www.thecrabclaw.com

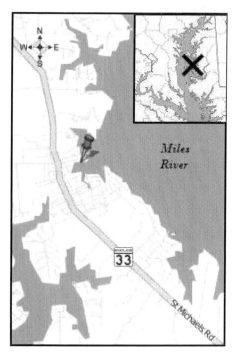

County: Talbot County

Open: Seasonal

Dockage: Yes

Latitude: N 38° 47' 13"

Longitude: W 76° 13' 14"

Body of Water: St. Michaels
Harbor off the Miles River

Driving Distance:
Baltimore 78 miles,
Washington, DC 82 miles,
Easton 10 miles

Atmosphere Meter

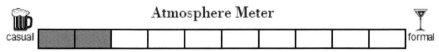

casual   formal

Crabs, clams, oysters, and shrimp. Steamed, fried, broiled, or raw. You name it, they've got it, because The Crab Claw is all about fresh Chesapeake seafood. How fresh? "If he don't kick, we don't cook!" promises the kitchen staff. And they've upheld this high standard for 50 years. The restaurant evolved from a clam-shucking and crab-harvesting business in the 1950s to a seafood eatery in 1965. You can feel the sense of tradition as you climb the stairs inside the rustic two-story wood and clapboard building to get a sea gull's view of the harbor. Down on the expansive outdoor decks at the water's edge, waitresses scurry among crowded picnic tables and deliver frosty beers to thirsty crab-pickers.

You can get the party started with clams casino, crab balls, and spicy chicken wings, or settle in with a bowl of creamy oyster stew or Maryland crab soup. The raw bar list reads like a Who's Who of Chesapeake favorites: fresh clams, fried shrimp, steamed mussels, and half-shell oysters. Entrees range from seafood samplers to soft-shells, and Maryland fried chicken is the envy of many Eastern Shore kitchens.

If you finish your last bite and want to experience more Chesapeake Bay living, go next door and get on board the *St. Michaels Patriot*. For 90 minutes, you can cruise the water on the tour boat, taking in views of the unique wildlife that lives along the Miles River and the historic mansions that date back to Colonial and Victorian eras.

Stars at the Inn at Perry Cabin

308 Watkins Lane
St. Michaels, MD 21663
(410) 745-2200
www.belmond.com/inn-at-perry-cabin-st-michaels

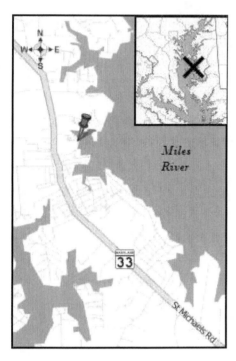

County: Talbot County

Open: Year Round

Dockage: Yes

Latitude: N 38° 47' 26"

Longitude: W 76° 13' 18"

Body of Water: Miles River

Driving Distance:
Baltimore 78 miles,
Washington, DC 82 miles,
Easton 10 miles

 Atmosphere Meter

casual · · · · · · · · · · · · formal

The exquisite Inn at Perry Cabin was built in 1816 by Samuel Hambleton, the aide-de-camp to Commodore Oliver Hazard Perry during the War of 1812. The inn is named after Perry, and its design replicates the graceful lines of his cabin on the flagship *U.S.S. Niagara*. Over the years, the property changed hands, becoming a private residence, farm, and riding academy. The co-founder of Laura Ashley bought the place in 1989 and expanded it into a 41-room luxury hotel. It is currently owned by Belmond, a collection of high-end hotels, trains, and river cruises.

Perry Cabin is Maryland's only four-star, four diamond hotel, and it truly is beautiful. The stately colonial mansion is surrounded by meticulously groomed gardens, and the view of Miles River is breathtaking. Afternoon tea is served in the serene Morning Room, and you can recline in leather chairs by the fireplace while sipping cocktails at Purser's Pub. Fine dining takes place at Stars restaurant, which is the epitome of rural elegance. Subtle décor celebrates the Eastern Shore's heritage and nautical life. Candles in ship lamps cast gentle light, and blue pastel murals depict Baltimore clippers sailing across the water. A baby grand plays softly in the corner.

Through partnerships with local farmers and watermen, the chef crafts a menu that is fresh and laced with seafood. Top picks: Imperial crab cakes, oysters two ways (raw and baked with sauerkraut and hollandaise), and the seafood collection of shrimp, crab, and lobster. Other noteworthy entrees include seared diver scallops, butter-poached Maine lobster, and lamb porterhouse chop.

Bayview Restaurant & Duck Blind Lounge

9784 Martingham Drive
St. Michaels, MD 21663
(410) 745-9066 or 800-446-9066
www.harbourtowne.com

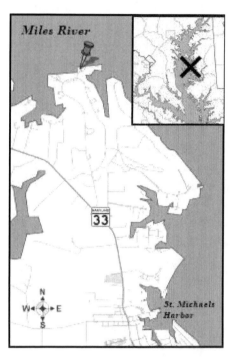

County: Talbot County

Open: Year Round

Dockage: Yes

Latitude: N 38° 49' 15"

Longitude: W 76° 13' 58"

Body of Water: Miles River

Driving Distance:
    Baltimore 81 miles,
    Washington, DC 82 miles,
    Easton 12 miles

Atmosphere Meter

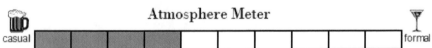

casual — formal

Sometimes the quest for crabs takes us to unlikely places. In this instance, Chesapeake seafood emerges amidst the fairways and putting greens of Harbourtowne Waterfront Golf Hotel. It's a pleasant getaway destination with 111 guest rooms, tennis courts, swimming pool, and family activities such as bike rentals, horseshoes, and basketball. Plus this lovely resort is a quick drive to downtown St. Michaels shops.

Bayside Restaurant and Duck Blind Lounge is where golfers recover from 18 holes and local visitors are welcome to enjoy the recently upgraded dining and drinking spot on the water. Upstairs in the spacious building is the Chesapeake Lounge with a pool table and casual conversation furniture. The main floor hosts the bar and dining room. White cloths are spread across tables, and nautical items and ship models hang on the walls. The large outside brick patio gives diners a spectacular view of the river.

The menu tees off with appetizers such as cream of crab soup, poached mussels, salt and pepper calamari, and coconut crusted shrimp. Lighter side items include shrimp and chicken salads. The cooks hit a hole in one for seafood fans with traditional jumbo lump crab cakes, Old Bay scallops, and honey Dijon salmon. Dishes with meat eaters' preferences in mind include grilled burgers and steaks, chicken breasts with marinated tomatoes and mozzarella, and blackened pork steak topped with fried oysters.

Lowes Wharf Marina Inn

21651 Lowes Wharf Road
Sherwood, MD 21665
(410) 745-6684 or (888) 484-9267
www.loweswharf.com

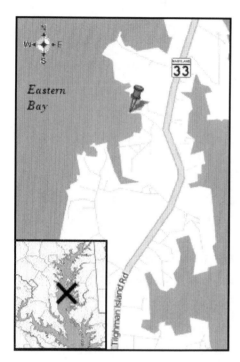

County: Talbot County

Open: Seasonal

Dockage: Yes

Latitude: N 38° 45' 57"

Longitude: W 76° 19' 42"

Body of Water: Ferry Cove

Driving Distance:
    Baltimore 88 miles,
    Washington, DC 92 miles,
    Easton 20 miles

Atmosphere Meter

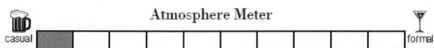

casual | | | | | | | | | | formal

One of the best-kept secrets on the Eastern Shore is Lowes Wharf. As you travel south on Route 33 from St. Michaels to Tilghman Island, keep your eyes peeled near the town of Sherwood. Upon arrival, you see a two-story inn, tavern, and beach that make you almost feel like you're in Key West. Bathing suit-clad guests kick back in red, blue, and yellow

Adirondack chairs and picnic tables with cool beverages clenched in their hands. The wind playfully tugs at colorful umbrellas that try to cast a little protective shade.

A two-foot retaining wall encircles the beach area — tall enough to prevent waves from washing away the sand, short enough to allow a spectacular view of the Bay, and just the right height for children to jump off into the water. The entire place is flanked by two scenic coves that offer hours of entertainment for kids to explore the shores at low tide. Bicycle rentals, fishing boats, kayaks, volleyball, and bonfires open up possibilities for outdoor fun.

As the sun sets, you might get the sinking feeling that it's time to go home. Keep in mind, the inn can solve your problem and delay the return to civilization. Rooms are comfortable, but you might not spend much time in them, because of the lure of a summer breeze, tasty seafood treats in the restaurant, and the temptation to play darts or billiards in the bar. During a recent visit, the bartender confessed, "The best thing about my job is when I get hot, I jump into the water, cool off, and then come back to serving drinks dripping wet." After decades in business, Lowes sure knows how to help you enjoy life at the Bay.

Characters Bridge Restaurant

6136 Tilghman Island Road
Tilghman, MD 21671
(410) 886-1060
www.charactersbridgerestaurant.com

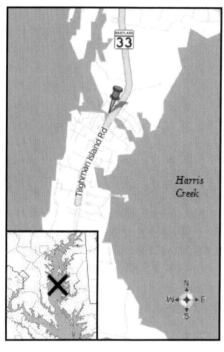

County: Talbot County

Open: Year Round

Dockage: Yes

Latitude: N 38° 43' 10"

Longitude: W 76° 19' 59"

Body of Water: Knapps Narrows

Driving Distance:
Baltimore 91 miles,
Washington, DC 95 miles,
Easton 23 miles

Atmosphere Meter

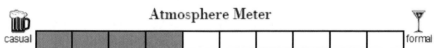

casual | | | | | | | | | | formal

You have two excellent choices at Characters Bridge Restaurant. You can grab a table on the building's upper floor to get a bird's-eye view of the busy boat traffic making its way under Tilghman Island Bridge. Or you can venture down to the water's edge, take a seat on the deck, and relish a

waterman's perspective. Either way, you can't go wrong.
This place embodies traditional Bay cuisine and merriment.

Everyone who eats here is grateful that the owners of this
family-owned restaurant share their family's recipe for
delicious crab cakes and carry traditional Chesapeake cooking
style into all of the dishes. Rockfish bites, smoked bluefish,
and hot crab dip represent tasty regional fare on the appetizer
list. Classic entrees such as soft-shell platter, fried oysters, and
shrimp stuffed with crab imperial are big crowd pleasers.
Veal marsala, half-pound burgers, braised short ribs, and
prime rib au jus satisfy the most ravenous meat eaters.

While you're here, take an up-close look at Tilghman
Island Bridge. Since the 1840s, various types of bridges have
spanned Knapps Narrows. Built in 1998, the current one is
called a bascule bridge and it is Maryland's only overhead
counterweight bridge (others have counterweights
underneath). It's also the nation's busiest bridge, opening up
over 10,000 times annually to let nautical traffic pass through.
So, chances are pretty good that you'll get to witness a little
local history as the bridge raises its moveable span.

Mike & Eric's Bay Hundred Restaurant at the Tilghman Island Inn

21384 Coopertown Road
Tilghman, MD 21671
(410) 886-2141 or (800) 866-2141
www.tilghmandining.com

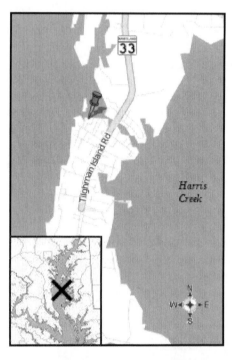

County: Talbot County

Open: Year Round

Dockage: Yes

Latitude: N 38° 43' 12"

Longitude: W 76° 20' 14"

Body of Water: Knapps
    Narrows

Driving Distance:
    Baltimore 91 miles,
    Washington, DC 95 miles,
    Easton 23 miles

Atmosphere Meter

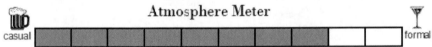

casual   formal

    Mike & Eric's Bay Hundred has created a lovely marriage of elegant contemporary and traditional style. It hosts a gorgeous waterfront dining room with oriental rugs, walls painted the color of the sea, and tables set with white linens. The outdoor deck bar, walls speckled with gray oyster shells, presents two Bay views: To the left is an expanse of open water and to the right is a grassy nature preserve that offers sanctuary to fledgling crabs, shrimp, and other aquatic life.

Sunsets are amazing, lodging at the inn is beautiful and roomy, and the restaurant's fine cuisine is an innovative experience. The chef alters menus to match the seasons. Seafood starters range from mussels in a garlic cream sauce, oysters Rockefeller, and sautéed calamari, to a sushi volcano roll with shrimp and lava sauce. Special entrees include crab jubilee with mango salsa and raspberry balsamic compote and miso-glazed salmon with coconut rice. Meaty treats: lamb chops with tabbouleh and grilled asparagus and chicken roulade filled with vegetables and goat cheese. An extensive in-house wine collection complements the flavors of the dishes, and desserts made in-house finish the meal nicely.

"Bay Hundred" refers to the land between Oak Creek and the tip of Tilghman Island. Talbot County was divided into "hundreds" for administrative purposes in the 1670s. The term "hundred" comes from medieval England when shires were parceled into segments that could yield 100 fighting men. This area is named after the Tilghman clan who owned this land for almost 100 years, starting in 1752. Tench  Tilghman, an aide-de-camp to George Washington, made his mark on U.S. history. In 1781, he rushed through the Bay on the way from Yorktown to Philly to tell the Continental Congress that Cornwallis had surrendered.

Harrison's Chesapeake House Restaurant

21551 Chesapeake House Drive
Tilghman, MD 21671
(410) 886-2121
www.chesapeakehouse.com

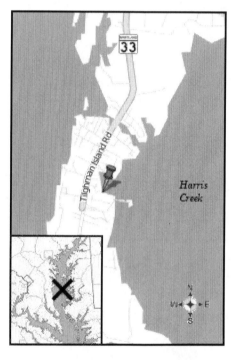

County: Talbot County

Open: Year Round

Dockage: Yes

Latitude: N 38° 42' 39"

Longitude: W 76° 20' 8"

Body of Water: Dogwood
Harbor off Choptank River

Driving Distance:
Baltimore 91 miles,
Washington, DC 95 miles,
Easton 23 miles

Atmosphere Meter

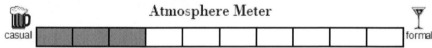

casual / formal

Ten years after the Civil War ended, Captain Levin Harrison opened his doors to entertain guests with sport fishing, duck hunting, and classic seafood at Harrison's Chesapeake House. The tradition continues at this waterfront inn and restaurant where the kitchen serves "no apologies, lots of butter" country cooking. Here's how the owners describe their place: "If you like chrome and glass high-rise hotels, hot tubs, and sushi bars, we're not the place for you. On the other hand, if your taste tilts toward waterfront decks with picnic tables that groan under the weight of huge platters of hot steamed crabs and sweating pitchers of icy beer and brewed tea, we're for you."

The restaurant and inn have an old-fashioned charm that makes you want to kick back and enjoy Bay life. To enhance the waterfront experience, Harrison's has been busy with modern upgrades. Everything has a fresh coat of paint, especially the dining rooms which now sport a bright and open feel. Legends Sports Bar has pool tables, dartboards, and flat-screen TVs. The Crab Deck, which hovers over the water and has a giant crab hanging from the rafters, serves hot steamed crabs and shrimp on classic wooden tables.

Family-style dinners are fresh and hearty, with show-stoppers like crab cakes, fried oysters, and Betty's shrimp salad. Fish specialties: Bay rockfish and wild salmon. Land favorites include ham steak, fried chicken, and roasted duck. Warm biscuits, buttered corn on the cob, and cole slaw make you feel like you're at a picnic in the country. Tip for arriving safely: Bring a map. Cell phone coverage gets spotty, and you don't want to miss this gem because you relied on a GPS.

Pope's Tavern at the Oxford Inn

504 South Morris Street
Oxford, MD 21654
(410) 226-5220
www.oxfordinn.net/dining.html

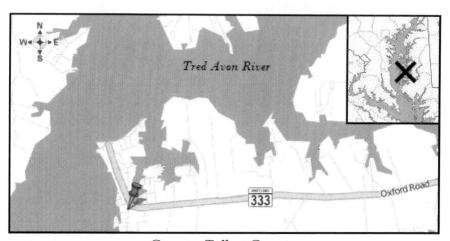

County: Talbot County
Open: Year Round ⚓ Dockage: No
Latitude: N 38° 41' 3" ⚓ Longitude: W 76° 10' 15"
Body of Water: Town Creek off the Tred Avon River
Driving Distance: Baltimore 72 miles,
Washington, DC 84 miles, Easton 10 miles

Atmosphere Meter

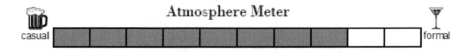

casual   formal

When an anniversary or Valentine's Day roll around, it doesn't hurt to have a romantic destination already picked out. So, keep Pope's Tavern in mind when you want to impress that special someone with a memorable getaway. Its location is dreamy — overlooking the water in a circa 1880 historic home among the picturesque streets of Oxford. In

2005, the building was renovated but retained its old-world charm while creating an elegant European-style bistro.

The front porch has white wicker and Adirondack chairs stationed on a red brick floor. Crimson printed swags of fabric hang lazily over windows in amber-colored walls of the intimate 40-seat dining room. The cozy library lounge is a perfect setting for whispering over cocktails or dessert. And the 12-seat bar features domestic and European wines and spirits, as well as special brandies from Spain. If you don't feel like driving, the house "Popemobile" will shuttle you to the dock or other spots in town.

Field green salads and cheeses are made with fresh local ingredients. Seafood favorites include jumbo lump crab cakes, Pope-style local oysters, linguini with shrimp in carbonara sauce, pan-seared swordfish, and just-caught rockfish. The kitchen also likes to court meat lovers with dishes such as chicken breast with wild mushrooms in marsala sauce, duck with bleu cheese potato croquette, and grilled beef tenderloin with truffle potato canoli. Homemade desserts infuse a little sugar into an evening with your sweetheart.

Schooner's on the Creek

314 Tilghman Street
Oxford, MD 21654
(410) 226-0160
www.schoonersonthecreek.com

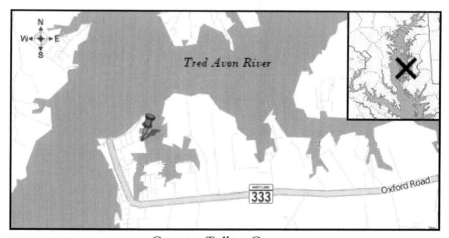

County: Talbot County
Open: Seasonal ⚓ Dockage: Yes
Latitude: N 38° 41' 34" ⊶ Longitude: W 76° 10' 6"
Body of Water: Town Creek off the Tred Avon River
Driving Distance: Baltimore 80 miles,
Washington, DC 84 miles, Easton 11 miles

Atmosphere Meter

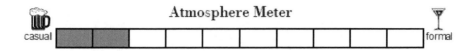

Whether you come by land or sea to Schooner's, you know you found a real Chesapeake jewel. The building was an oyster-shucking plant in the early 1900s. Today, a big plastic shark greets landlubbers entering from the parking lot, and a welcoming red sign above the deck invites you to sip a Schooner's Squeeze after you dock the boat. It's the local hangout for enjoying laid-back atmosphere and a spectacular waterfront view. Bands liven up the mood on weekends. Orange, yellow, and green picnic tables brighten up the deck.

Featuring classic Eastern Shore and American cuisine served inside or on a large outdoor deck, this crab house specializes in seafood caught daily by fishermen on the Bay and Tred Avon River. Hot steamed crabs, fried oysters, and seared sea scallops are big hits on the menu. Key West-style smoked fish dip is a blissful start to a meal. Southern garlic and cheddar cheese grits are topped with jumbo shrimp. Not in a fishy mood? Then opt for dishes such as bison burgers, BBQ pulled pork sandwiches, steak, or jambalaya with chicken, ham, and andouille sausage.

If you're lucky, you might hear folks tell tales of their historic town. Established in 1683, Oxford was a major trading center on the Bay. British ships unloaded goods imported from Europe in exchange for tobacco grown on local plantations. After the Civil War and completion of the local railroad in 1871, Oxford grew into a hub for canning local seafood. And a stone's throw away from your cold beer and hot crabs is the historic Oxford Boatyard, founded in 1866, which still provides services for seafarers.

The Robert Morris Inn

314 North Morris Street
Oxford, MD 21654
(410) 226-5111
www.robertmorrisinn.com

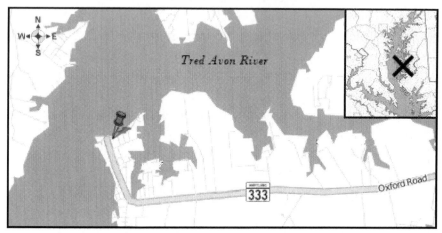

County: Talbot County
Open: Year Round ⚓ Dockage: No
Latitude: N 38° 41' 34" ➤ Longitude: W 76° 10' 27"
Body of Water: Tred Avon River
Driving Distance: Baltimore 80 miles,
Washington, DC 83 miles, Easton 10 miles

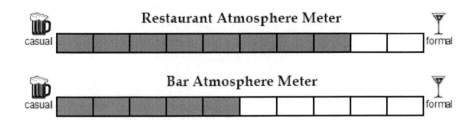

Some history buffs believe that we might still be bowing
our heads to the Queen of England if it weren't for Robert
Morris. He signed the Declaration of Independence, hung out
with George Washington, and was a major player in early

American politics. His vast fortune from shipping and banking greased the wheels of the Revolutionary Army and earned him the title "Financier of the American Revolution." He personally paid for 80% of all the bullets shot during the war and used $14 million of his own credit to move Washington and his troops from New York State to Yorktown. He never asked for reimbursement from the new government.

This inn was his home when he arrived from Liverpool to live with his father. A sense of history radiates from its very foundation. Built in 1710, the inn has been expanded over the years in keeping with its graceful Colonial design. The flooring is Georgia white pine. Antique murals in the elegant dining room depict key events from America's early days. Brick walls, slate floors, and fireplaces with antique carved swans set a relaxed tone in the tavern, where the atmosphere is more casual. Tables on the front porch and river terrace let guests watch the Oxford Ferry cross the water.

The chef taps into local farmers and fishermen for fresh ingredients and creates a superb dining experience. Classic starters: cream of crab soup, spicy shrimp salad, and fried Chesapeake oysters. Award-winning crab cakes, seared jumbo scallops, and beer and cheddar cheese encrusted rockfish are signature entrees. Desserts are heavenly.

The Masthead
at Pier Street Marina

104 West Pier Street
Oxford, MD 21654
(410) 226-5171
www.themastheadatpierstreetmarina.com

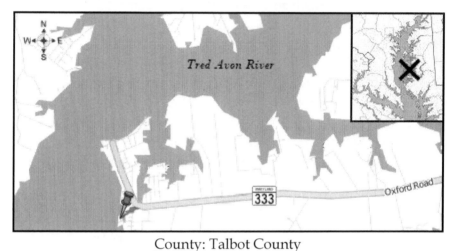

County: Talbot County
Open: Seasonal ⚓ Dockage: Yes
Latitude: N 38° 40' 58" ⬌ Longitude: W 76° 10' 25"
Body of Water: Tred Avon River
Driving Distance: Baltimore 80 miles,
Washington, DC 83 miles, Easton 10 miles

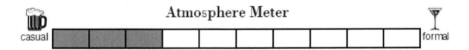

If you want to experience sensational sunsets and seafood
in a quaint historic town, head for The Masthead at Pier Street
Marina. The location is perfect. Jutting out where the Tred
Avon River pours into the Bay, this place tempts you to grab

a cold beverage at its outdoor gazebo bar and take in the 360-degree waterfront view from its massive wooden deck.

The stars of the menu are steamed crabs, shrimp, and cherrystone clams. Chesapeake crab dip and Caribbean conch fritters are excellent starters. The rest reads like a seafood lover's fantasy: Crab cakes, blackened shrimp tostada with mango, roasted corn, and cilantro salsa, steamed mussels topped with crisp fries, and lobster rolls piled high on toasted buns. Meat lovers are not forgotten: grilled burgers, a full pound of wings laced with Buffalo sauce, and sliced beef tenderloin sandwiches topped with melted Brie cheese.

The owners completely rebuilt the restaurant in 2004 after extensive damages from Hurricane Isabel and created seating for 250 guests on the deck and 85 indoors. Although it's tempting to linger in this idyllic spot, save time to cruise into downtown Oxford for its colonial architecture and charm. The best part is riding the ferry between Oxford and Bellevue. Started in 1683, it's the oldest privately owned ferry in the United States. The 20-minute round-trip ride gives you a duck's-eye view of the water and harkens back to a time when life was less hectic and hurried.

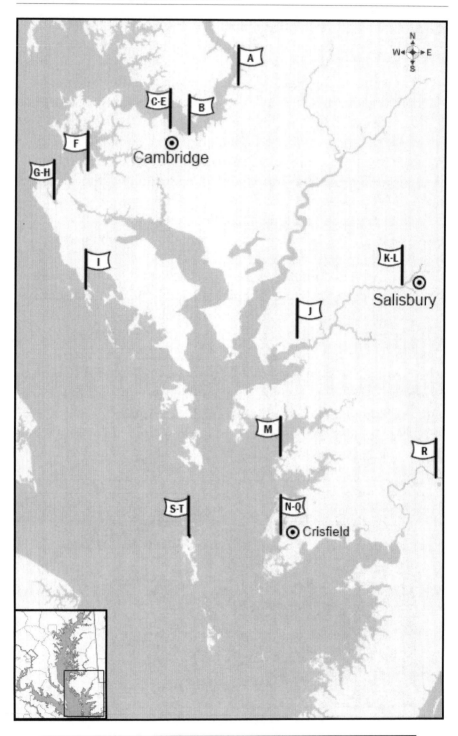

Lower Eastern Shore

Suicide Bridge Restaurant

6304 Suicide Bridge Road
Hurlock, MD 21643
(410) 943-4689
www.suicide-bridge-restaurant.com

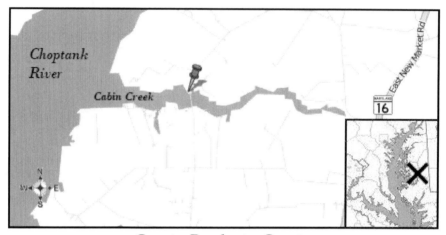

County: Dorchester County
Open: Year Round ⚓ Dockage: Yes
Latitude: N 38° 38' 0" ⟶ Longitude: W 75° 56' 49"
Body of Water: Cabin Creek off the Choptank River
Driving Distance: Baltimore 87 miles,
Washington, DC 91 miles, Easton 20 miles

Atmosphere Meter

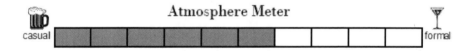

casual   formal

There's something about a name like Suicide Bridge
that makes you want to ask questions. Has anyone really...?
When? How? Depending on the size of the crowd, the
bartender in the Light House Lounge will either patiently
answer or hand you a piece of paper with enough local lore
to satisfy an inquiring mind. The original wooden bridge was

erected in 1888; another took its place in 1910. The current 21-foot high structure was erected in 1968. Nearly a dozen people chose this location as the place to meet their maker. Several shot themselves, then toppled into the river below. After one man jumped off the bridge and hit his head on a piling, locals suspected foul play and performed an autopsy on his body at a nearby picnic table.

But there's more to this place than stories of unfortunate demise. The restaurant's two-story clapboard building offers a waterfront view of a beautiful setting. Walls of knotty pine and stone are decorated with super-sized metallic crabs and wildlife. Menus offer an extensive selection of fresh seafood, beef, chicken, and pasta. Backfin crab cakes, stuffed flounder, grilled rockfish, and shrimp and scallops a la Suicide (cream sauce over pasta) are dinner favorites. Landlubbers cut into prime rib, lamb chops, BBQ ribs, and veal parmesan. Sandwiches and baskets are available for smaller appetites.

Want some vintage fun? Take a cruise on two reproductions of turn-of-the-century paddlewheel riverboats, named *The Dorothy & Megan* and *The Choptank River Queen*, located next door. Restaurant staff will prepare meals for you to take along or you can enjoy a crab feast on board.

Blue Point Provision Company & Water's Edge Grill

100 Heron Boulevard
Cambridge, MD 21613
(410) 901-6410
www.chesapeakebay.hyatt.com

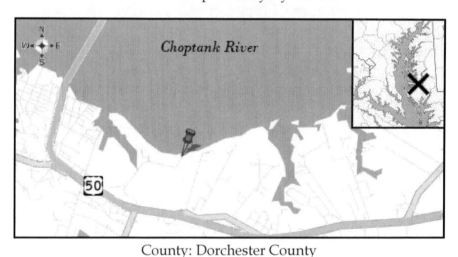

County: Dorchester County
Open: Year Round ⚓ Dockage: Yes
Latitude: N 38° 33' 41" 🐟 Longitude: W 76° 2' 32"
Body of Water: Choptank River
Driving Distance: Baltimore 86 miles,
Washington, DC 90 miles, Easton 17 miles

Atmosphere Meter

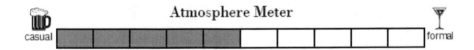

casual ┊┊┊┊ formal

In pursuit of the authentic Bay experience, a Hyatt Regency resort doesn't usually top the priority list. So, if you're a Bay purist with visions of crusty boat captains and rusty crab pots, then Blue Point Provision Company might not be right for you. But if you're willing to keep an open mind and look beyond the manicured golf course, swimming pool, and big-hotel backdrop, then you will be pleasantly surprised at what you discover here.

Blue Point Provision Co. has a panoramic view of the Choptank at River Marsh Marina, and it's tucked away in a far corner of the resort. The grounds' 400 acres of gorgeous waterfront property should give you plenty of room to avoid the resorty stuff. Plus, the restaurant has a good Bay attitude and appreciation for Chesapeake traditions, food, and heritage. Oyster tongs and a crab dredge hang on the entry wall, and somebody with a sense of humor uses an oversized fishing lure for a mailbox.

The dining room has an open contemporary look with vintage nautical décor. The menu carries a wide selection of Chesapeake seafood that's delivered daily by local watermen. Regional favorites include grilled rockfish, smoked oyster salad, and crab cakes. Dishes that show the cooks know their way around the Bay: BBQ shrimp with grits, steamed mussels, and the special "Waterman's Balls," or fritters made with crab and scrapple. Old Bay rubbed Delmarva chicken, smoked ribs, and grilled skirt steaks are simply delicious.

Portside Seafood Restaurant

201 Trenton Street
Cambridge, MD 21613
(410) 228-9007

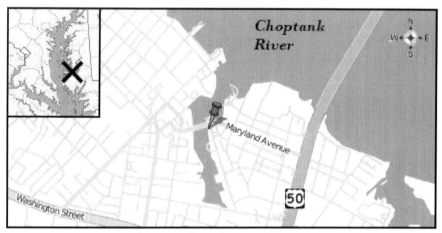

County: Dorchester County
Open: Year Round ⚓ Dockage: Yes
Latitude: N 38° 34' 13" ➤ Longitude: W 76° 4' 23"
Body of Water: Cambridge Creek off the Choptank River
Driving Distance: Baltimore 84 miles,
Washington, DC 88 miles, Easton 16 miles

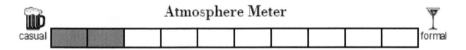

Atmosphere Meter

casual — formal

You get the best of both worlds at Portside Restaurant —
indoor and outdoor good times at the Eastern Shore. When
the weather's warm, bright blue and red umbrellas mark the
way to a two-tiered wooden crab deck. That's where you find
relaxed waterfront tables overlooking the bridge that spans
Cambridge Creek just shy of the Choptank River.

The inside sports haven gives you a front-row seat to autumnal football frenzy as zealous fans toast the Maryland Terps or Baltimore Ravens (Steelers fans beware!). Whether you work up an appetite from the fresh air or an intercepted touchdown pass, Portside aims to please. Snacks include wings, crab dip, nachos, and cheese and bacon potato skins.

Crab soup is award winning and creamy smooth. Soft-shell sandwiches and crab melts are perfect for lunch, along with garden-fresh salads. Steamed shrimp, clams, and mussels like to get dipped in warm drawn butter, and oysters are available raw, steamed, casino, or Rockefeller. Lump crab cakes are the size of baseballs. Landlubbers can opt for burgers, Delmonico steaks, chicken Chesapeake, or pasta. And it's all available for a reasonable price.

Since the 1950s when it was called Eastside, this restaurant became as a favorite watering hole for local residents. When you're finished eating, spend some time exploring this one of the oldest towns in Maryland that is home to festivals, skipjack races, museums, and quaint streets lined with historic buildings.

Jimmie & Sook's Raw Bar & Grill

527 Poplar Street
Cambridge, MD 21613
(410) 228-0008
www.jimmieandsooks.com

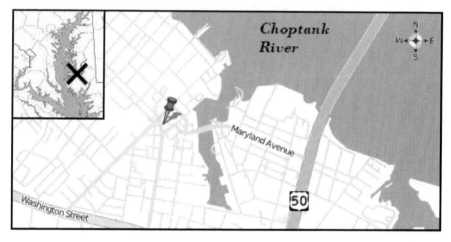

County: Dorchester County
Open: Year Round ⚓ Dockage: No
Latitude: N 38° 34' 14" ➤ Longitude: W 76° 4' 39"
Body of Water: Cambridge Creek off the Choptank River
Driving Distance: Baltimore 84 miles,
Washington, DC 88 miles, Easton 16 miles

Atmosphere Meter

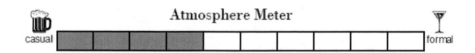

casual   formal

     If you're itching to explore the Eastern Shore, the perfect starting point is Jimmie & Sook's. It's the go-to place to experience an authentic taste of this side of the Bay. While it's not on the water, it is located in historic downtown Cambridge on a street laden with unique shops and pubs.

The inside is decorated with working tools and relics used by local watermen and photos presenting a visual history of the Bay. The front porch offers wooden rocking chairs for whiling away an afternoon. On the right side of the restaurant is a bar and lounge with exposed brick walls and plush leather couches. To the left, a mural portrays fishing boats and aquatic life for dining room guests. In the back is a raw bar where Chesapeake delicacies are shucked. The outdoor patio, plush with potted flowers and herbs, offers a calm escape for an evening. Bands play inside on weekends.

You won't see frozen or pre-packaged food on your plate, because the kitchen is committed to real food and fresh ingredients. The raw bar's Buck a Shuck deal lets you sample regional oysters, mussels, clams, and shrimp for a reasonable price. With a name like Jimmie & Sook's (male and female crabs), how could you walk out the door without sampling a bite of Maryland crab? Both cream and tomato versions of crab soup are delicious, and the lump crab and goat cheese salad is a sure hit. Pan-fried crab cakes are served on a potato roll, and you can get crab and shrimp on nachos. Other hot seafood and meat dishes: stuffed rockfish, fried oysters, prime rib, and chicken stuffed with spinach and tomatoes.

Snappers Waterfront Café

112 Commerce Street
Cambridge, MD 21613
(410) 228-0112
www.snapperswaterfrontcafe.com

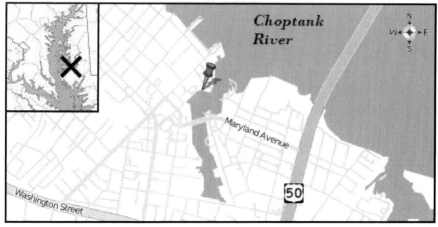

County: Dorchester County
Open: Year Round ⚓ Dockage: Yes
Latitude: N 38° 34' 21" ⤏ Longitude: W 76° 4' 24"
Body of Water: Cambridge Creek off the Choptank River
Driving Distance: Baltimore 85 miles,
Washington, DC 88 miles, Easton 16 miles

Atmosphere Meter

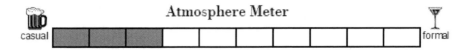

casual · formal

At first glance from the parking lot, Snappers looks like a garden-variety crab deck. But once you cruise around, you discover this 20-year old location has something special to make everybody happy. For a blast of fun, belly up to the tiki bar, toss back an oyster shooter, wiggle your toes in the sand, and sip an icy margarita. You can't resist the temptation to kick back on an Adirondack chair under a palm tree and soak up the tropical setting. Bands on weekends take the laid-back beach groove to a whole new level.

When you're ready for a bite to eat, head for the dining areas where you can go alfresco with a waterfront view or take a seat inside where subtle tiki touches garnish the walls. The casual atmosphere is quite pleasant, and the service is friendly. The menu blends Caribbean flavors with Eastern Shore cuisine by offering a mix of local seafood, BBQ ribs, steaks, Tex-Mex dishes, burgers, pasta, and salads. House specialties include jumbo shrimp fajitas, Eastern Shore fried chicken, and filler-free crab cakes. Chicken Chesapeake is topped with crab imperial and baked golden brown. Jamaican jerk chicken soars with island spices.

When you're ready to rumble, climb upstairs to The Rave Cave. It's billed as a "Real Sports Fan's Ultimate Hide-Away," and it hits the mark. Wide-screen TVs, overstuffed leather sofas, La-Z-Boy recliners, and low-set coffee tables encourage you to kick up your feet and let waitresses deliver cold beer. It's a manly retreat for sneaking away from visiting in-laws or watching a game with fellow football fans.

Madison Bay Restaurant Bar & Grill

4814 Madison Canning House Road
Madison, MD 21648
(410) 228-1108

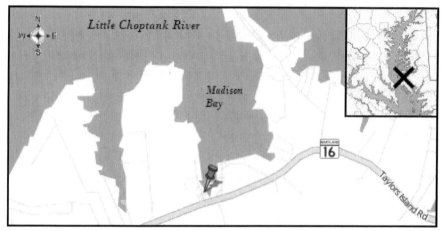

County: Dorchester County
Open: Year Round ⚓ Dockage: Yes
Latitude: N 38° 30' 30" Longitude: W 76° 13' 26"
Body of Water: Madison Bay off the Little Choptank River
Driving Distance: Baltimore 97 miles,
Washington, DC 101 miles, Easton 28 miles

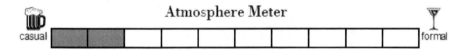

Madison Bay is only 11 miles southwest of Cambridge, but you feel like you are transported into an entirely different world. It's tucked between a campground and marina, so you see more boats and campers than cars and brick buildings. People enjoy the slowed-down pace of rural living with excellent sports fishing, hiking trails, and crabs galore.

The white one-story building is topped with a red roof. The atmosphere is rustic casual. Locals strike up a game of pool while country music plays on the radio. People convene at the outdoor bar to sip chilled drinks and watch boats shuffle into the marina. Steamed crab and shrimp bucket parties get everybody hopping.

The kitchen serves Eastern Shore home-style cooking. Appetizers include crab dip, fried oysters, and steamed shrimp or clams. Filler is not allowed in the jumbo lump crab cakes. Tables are crowded with sandwiches, burgers, seafood platters, ribs, and fried chicken. Crisp beer-battered onion rings garnish plates painted with blue crabs around the rim.

Originally this area was called Tobacco Stick Bay. According to local lore, an Indian fleeing from white settlers used a tobacco stick to jump across the channel at the mouth of the cove and ran away into the woods. The name stuck until 1881 when it was changed to Madison Bay. During the War of 1812, British ships entered the harbor to ransack the countryside. They torched vessels, including a ship owned by Thomas Linthicum. But that wasn't enough to satisfy the Brits' thirst for destruction. They carted off Linthicum and held him prisoner for months. Then they dumped him off in a remote corner of the Bay, half-clad and barefoot, leaving him to walk all the way home to Dorchester County.

Palm Beach Willie's
Fine Food & Spirits

638 Taylors Island Road
Taylors Island, MD 21669
(410) 221-5111

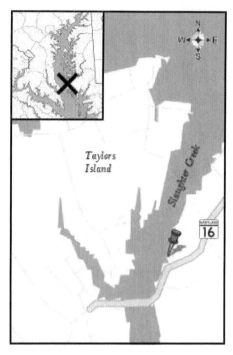

County: Dorchester County

Open: Seasonal

Dockage: Yes

Latitude: N 38° 28' 34"

Longitude: W 76° 17' 11"

Body of Water: Slaughter
Creek off the Little
Choptank River

Driving Distance:
Baltimore 101 miles,
Washington, DC 105 miles,
Easton 32 miles

Atmosphere Meter

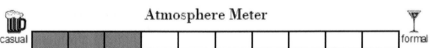

casual | | | | | | | | | | formal

Along the Bay it's common to hear places named after historic figures, family ancestors, or crusty ship captains. But Palm Beach Willie's gets kudos for naming its restaurant after the owner's dog. Apparently a Labrador Retriever, originally called plain-old "Willie," developed a strong preference for warm water rather than icy cold waves and became known as "Palm Beach Willie." That's not the only unique feature of this delightful place on the banks of Slaughter Creek. The restaurant resides on top of a floating houseboat that rests on the water. Sunsets are spectacular. An enclosed deck with tall windows opens to catch a breeze off the water. Tropical plants are placed out front, and thatched umbrellas rustle above wooden picnic tables. The island motif is carried inside with portraits of parrots staring down at tables covered in colorful Polynesian prints. Twine rope and lights shaped like flip-flops are wrapped around poles at the bar with a few coconuts dangling near the ceiling.

If you're looking for fresh seafood, you've come to the right place. Jumbo crab cakes, steamed shrimp, and crab pretzels are cooked just right. Willie's Seafood Stew is a savory cauldron of the daily catch, homemade clam strips offer a delicate crunch, and Poncho's Club Sandwich is a multi-layer feast of crab cakes, grilled shrimp, bacon, ham, cheese, lettuce, and tomato. Burgers, fried chicken, prime rib, and egg salad with bacon satisfy every appetite. Desserts made in-house are scrumptious. Palm Beach Willie's is a boater's dream, because the marina recently had a facelift that updated the facilities and amenities such as a swimming pool, showers, and overnight transient slips.

Crab Decks & Tiki Bars of the Chesapeake Bay. 2015 Maryland Edition

The Island Grille

514 Taylors Island Road
Taylors Island, MD 21669
(410) 228-9094

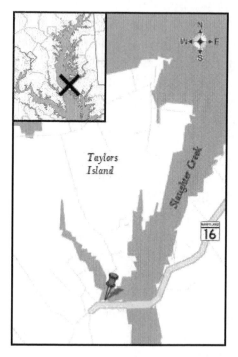

County: Dorchester County

Open: Seasonal

Dockage: No

Latitude: N 38° 28' 11"

Longitude: W 76° 17' 51"

Body of Water: Slaughter
Creek off the Little
Choptank River

Driving Distance:
Baltimore 102 miles,
Washington, DC 106 miles,
Easton 33 miles

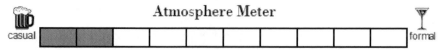

Atmosphere Meter

casual ▐▐▐ formal

If the Island Grille looks like an old-fashioned general store, that's because it used to be one. Around 1816, the building was erected to replace a store that burned down. As time passed, it became the post office, gathering place, and market for this remote neck of the Bay. When Hurricane Isabel stormed through in 2003, she flooded Taylors Island and the store. After extensive renovations, the building began a new life as the local café and watering hole. Chapel Cove Marina office and tackle shop are located next door.

Island Grille's exterior walls are painted pale green, and its sign out front shows a heron wearing a chef's hat and bow tie serving beverages. The inside still feels like a general store. On the walls and shelves are vintage knickknacks, maps, deer heads, ships, carved waterfowl, books, and old photos. Tables are covered with red oilcloths, and a full service bar is located in the back. The atmosphere is relaxed and accented with a lovely view of the water. The kitchen dishes out casual fare of spicy wings, beer-battered shrimp, burgers, sandwiches, salads, and terrific local seafood.

History buffs might be interested in seeing a relic from the War of 1812 a few yards from the restaurant. The Becky Phibbs Cannon was captured from the British warship, *Dauntless,* in 1815 by Joseph Stewart and local militiamen near James Island. Freezing winter temperatures and ice along the shore allowed the men to get within firing range of the ship and make off with the cannon. Its name is a combination of the ship's commander, Matthew Phibbs, and a black woman named Becky, who had been captured and forced to work as a cook on the English vessel.

Old Salty's Restaurant

2560 Hoopers Island Road
Fishing Creek, MD 21634
(410) 397-3752
www.oldsaltys.com

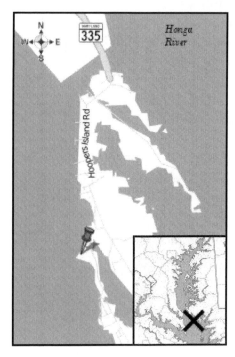

County: Dorchester County

Open: Year Round

Dockage: No

Latitude: N 38° 19' 27"

Longitude: W 76° 13' 51"

Body of Water: Back Creek
off the Honga River

Driving Distance:
Baltimore 110 miles,
Washington, DC 114 miles,
Easton 42 miles

Atmosphere Meter

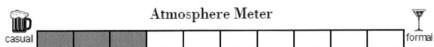

casual   formal

    If you're looking for an authentic Bay adventure, put
Old Salty's on your must-see list. It's in a remote location
about 45 minutes south of Cambridge, but the rural landscape
is so dramatically beautiful, you'll be sorry when the ride is
over. You drive past crab-picking plants, white-washed
Methodist churches, workboats tied up to rickety docks, and

miles of marshland interrupted by clusters of loblolly pines. You pass Blackwater Wildlife Refuge, home to egrets, eagles, and a menagerie of wildlife. Eventually you arrive at Hoopers Island, which is a string of three islands connected by a narrow causeway that divides the Chesapeake Bay and Honga River. Old Salty's is located in the former schoolhouse of Fishing Creek (population 163). In this historic fishing village, watermen have harvested crabs and oysters for generations. The vibe at Old Salty's is casual and timeless. Dining room chairs are upholstered in nautical fabric, and duck decoys rest quietly on window ledges. On wood panel walls, paintings of ship captains smoking long-stem pipes watch your back as you sip a drink at the bar.

The food is traditional home-style. Steaks and pork tenderloin are on the menu, but it's hard to resist seafood when you just drove past fishermen hauling it out of the water. House specialties include crab cakes, fried oysters, steamed shrimp, sautéed soft-shells, and fried seafood platters. The service is friendly and peppered with stories told by folks who are proud of their heritage. John Smith first discovered the islands in the early 1600s. Local legend says European settlers bought the land from the Yaocomaco Indian tribe for five woolen blankets. The island was named after a friend of the Calverts, Henry Hooper, who purchased a large parcel of land in 1668. His descendants still live in the area.

The Red Roost

2670 Clara Road
Whitehaven, MD 21856
(410) 546-5443
www.theredroost.com

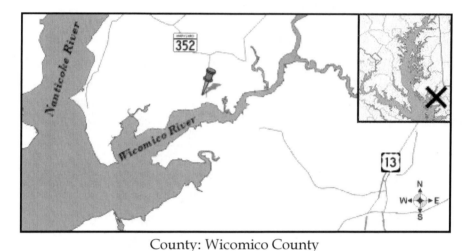

County: Wicomico County
Open: Seasonal ⚓ Dockage: No
Latitude: N 38° 16' 4" 🐟 Longitude: W 75° 49' 18"
Body of Water: Wicomico River
Driving Distance: Baltimore 126 miles,
Washington, DC 127 miles, Easton 57 miles

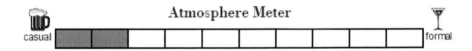

Atmosphere Meter

casual ▮▮▮▮ formal

You arrived with a hearty appetite and placed your order. Now you're tapping a wooden mallet on the table covered with brown paper, waiting with a cold one in hand for the first bite of Maryland blue crabs. If this happens at the Red Roost, you won't be disappointed. This all-you-can-eat crab house is worth the wait to fulfill your crab-picking dreams.

The building began as a chicken house in the 1940s and was later converted to a campground's recreation room and general store. In the early 1970s, Frank Palmer and his wife Peggy used it for steaming crabs and frying chicken that their neighbors couldn't resist. In 1974, it was officially christened the Red Roost Restaurant.

This traditional Bay crab house is not on the water, but it has wooden picnic tables in the center of the dining room and orange vinyl booths around the edges. Exposed wooden beams on the ceiling are lit by crab bushels hung upside down as light fixtures. The irresistible aroma of Old Bay permeates the building.

Fresh local seafood rules this roost, with crabs as the centerpiece of the menu. The tender meat is stuffed into mushrooms, patted into crab cakes, and folded into creamy dip. Stuffed shrimp, oysters Rockefeller, and clams casino add to the celebration of Chesapeake cuisine. Southern fried chicken is the most popular choice for meat eaters, followed by savory smokehouse dishes such as pulled pork BBQ, beef brisket, and hickory-smoked St. Louis ribs. Corn on the cob, baked beans, corn fritters, and cole slaw are served on the side.

When Red Roost closes for bit in the off-season, you can still get your crab cakes shipped right to your door thanks to a partnership with Crab Country Gourmet.

Brew River Restaurant & Bar

502 West Main Street
Salisbury, MD 21801
(410) 677-6757
www.brewriver.com

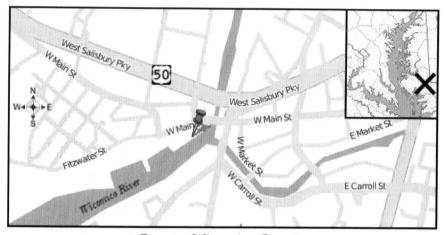

County: Wicomico County
Open: Year Round ⚓ Dockage: Yes
Latitude: N 38° 21' 52" ⋟ Longitude: W 75° 36' 21"
Body of Water: Wicomico River
Driving Distance: Baltimore 115 miles,
Washington, DC 119 miles, Easton 47 miles

Atmosphere Meter

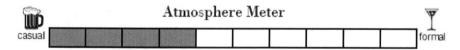

casual — formal

Can you believe there's a crab deck so far up the
Wicomico River that you could throw a rock from one bank
to the other? Well, it's true. Brew River Restaurant carries
the spirit of the Bay about 16 miles inland to a marina in
downtown Salisbury. It opened in the spring of 2000 by a

family that's worked in the restaurant biz since 1974 and also owns Harpoon Hanna's on Fenwick Island, DE.

Brew River is casual and comfortable with knotty pine walls decorated with pictures of Chesapeake crabs, oyster boats, and watermen. Wooden barrels and hand-painted fish hang from the ceiling, and antique stained glass windows serve as dividers between the booths. A massive stone fireplace warms the air during the winter. In the summer, head outside to the expansive deck and dock bar where cold beer, frozen concoctions, and crisp martinis are plentiful. Live music, tiki torches, and fire pits spice up the waterfront. Watching sunsets in the cozy setting is delightful.

When your stomach rumbles, order inside or outside from the full menu. Seafood leads the charge with crab dip, coconut shrimp, bacon-wrapped scallops, and a raw bar for appetizers. Crab cakes, seafood alfredo, and fried oysters are delicious. Prime rib, burgers, pizza, and chicken carbonara cater to hearty appetites, while sandwiches and salads offer lighter fare. After dinner, you can end the evening by dancing at the nightclub or taking a moonlit stroll along the river.

Market Street Inn

130 West Market Street
Salisbury, MD 21801
(410) 742-4145
www.marketstreetinnsalisbury.com

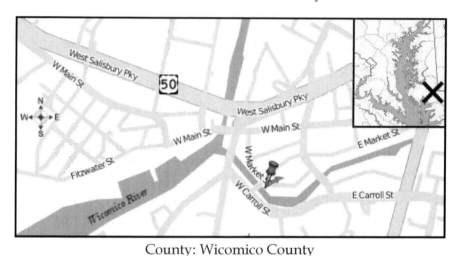

County: Wicomico County
Open: Year Round ⚓ Dockage: No
Latitude: N 38° 21' 48" 🐟 Longitude: W 75° 36' 8"
Body of Water: Wicomico River
Driving Distance: Baltimore 115 miles,
Washington, DC 119 miles, Easton 47 miles

Atmosphere Meter

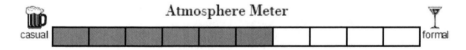

casual   formal

The building where Market Street Inn now resides has gone through almost as many lives as a cat. Built in 1941, it was originally a seafood market, and in the 1960s it became a sports bar owned by a couple of Baltimore Colts players. It got painted bright pink in the '70s while serving margaritas and burritos. In the '80s, owners covered up the pink paint, added a floating dock, and turned it into an open air sandwich shop. In 2001, the current owner transformed Market Street into an upscale casual dining establishment with gourmet food and an exceptional wine selection.

You see clues that it doesn't take itself too seriously. The giant red martini glass sculpture and a mailbox shaped like a big beer tap out front say people are having fun here. And the cheery blue umbrellas on the outdoor waterfront BARge are clear signs of merriment. Depending on your beverage of choice, you can join clubs with comrades seeking good wine, beer, or martinis. The pub's low ceiling is decorated with a huge martini glass and mini glasses around it.

The dining room walls are covered in rich earth tones with beautiful hand-painted murals of village landscapes. Black-and-tan wooden chairs are accented with gray tables and soft lighting. Menus change with the seasons. For lunch, you can go light with jerk chicken Caesar or tropical salmon salad, or be more ambition with the black-and-bleu burger or pulled BBQ beef sandwich. At dinner, the kitchen shines with well-prepared crab cakes, coconut shrimp, Eastern Shore seafood pasta, roasted pork loin, rack of lamb, seared rib eye steaks, and Tuscan chicken marsala.

Hide Away Grill

25763 Rumbley Road
Westover, MD 21871
(410) 651-1193
www.goosecreekmarina.com

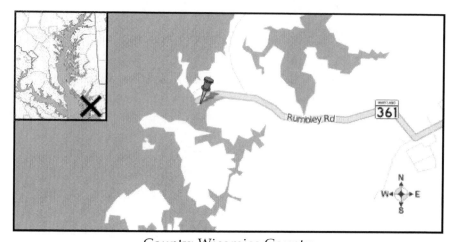

County: Wicomico County
Open: Seasonal ⚓ Dockage: Yes
Latitude: N 38° 5' 33" 🐟 Longitude: W 75° 51' 40"
Body of Water: Goose Creek off Tangier Sound
Driving Distance: Baltimore 150 miles,
Washington, DC 154 miles, Easton 81 miles

Atmosphere Meter

casual ▨▨▨▨▨ | | | | | | | | formal

Tucked away in a remote part of Somerset County awaits one of the sweetest hidden jewels of the Bay, appropriately called Hide Away Grill. To get there, boaters relish the uncrowded open waters of Tangier Sound, and drivers are treated to scenic country roads lined with loblolly pines and golden marshlands that serve as incubators for infant crabs and marine creatures. The restaurant is located at Goose Creek Marina in the quaint fishing village of Rumbley where life revolves around water, boats, and crabs. A campground is nearby if you want to linger for a day or two.

Hide Away is "rustic tiki" at its best. The tiny building is painted tropical turquoise and rosy pink, and its sign is made of letters nailed to a gnarly piece of driftwood. Sand covers the ground outside near the boats, and a "palm tree" made of blue and green wine bottles stuck on an old tree trunk adds a unique island touch. The view is unobstructed and gorgeous. Neighbors toss horseshoes while children splash in the waves.

Inside walls are painted with palm trees and a pastel Caribbean sunset. Chrome and black vinyl bar stools line up along a thatched roof bamboo bar. The dining room holds about a dozen tables, but crowds of diners often overflow onto the picnic tables outside. The bathrooms, labeled Sooks and Jimmies, forewarn that crabs are major players here. Food is simple and caught locally. The aroma of Old Bay fills the air. Steamed crabs, clams, rockfish, and shrimp are menu all-stars. Flounder stuffed with crab imperial and chicken Chesapeake are bursting with flavor. Burgers with fries, garden salads, and wraps with creamy cole slaw are yummy summer treats.

The Crab Place

504 Maryland Avenue
Crisfield, MD 21817
(877) 328-2722
www.crabplace.com

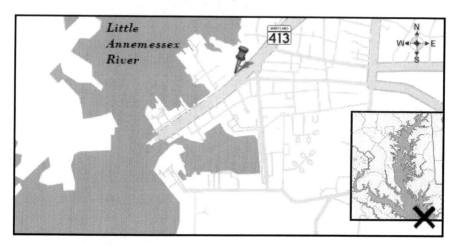

County: Somerset County
Open: Year Round ⚓ Dockage: No
Latitude: N 37° 58' 55" ⚓ Longitude: W 75° 51' 24"
Body of Water: Little Annemessex River off Tangier Sound
Driving Distance: Baltimore 153 miles,
Washington, DC 157 miles, Easton 84 miles

Atmosphere Meter

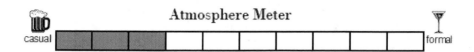

casual — formal

Whether you like to pick crabs at a lively deck or prefer to eat them in the comfort of your home, The Crab Place is ready for your order. About 15 years ago, it started shipping crabs from Crisfield and has grown into the country's largest retail supplier of Maryland crabs. The business continues to expand

and provides other local seafood, including clams, oysters, fish, shrimp, and crawfish. So, if you strike out on your next fishing trip, you can fill your cooler here.

For years, the location only offered take-out until spring 2013 when this national retailer added a new restaurant and bar out front. It's hard to miss the big sign with a grinning crab waving his claw at traffic on Crisfield's main street or the bright red and orange paint trimming the building that's flanked with palm trees and tropical greens. In keeping with Bay traditions, wooden picnic tables are placed in rows while fans hum overhead. Bands play on weekends, and the mood is upbeat and jovial.

Seafood is the name of the game at this location, and you can count on everything being fresh and having the True Blue certificate for using only Maryland crabs. If you're a fan of Old Bay, melted butter, or vinegar, everything you need is on the table for a genuine Chesapeake feast. Breaded, fried, or broiled — they make seafood the way you like it. They also sponsor a Crab & Cruise in late June. This event begins with a food and wine tasting, offers all-you-can-eat crabs, and ends with a boat trip around Tangier Sound.

Chesapeake Brewing Company

801 West Main Street
Crisfield, MD 21817
(410) 783-5705
www.chesbrewco.com

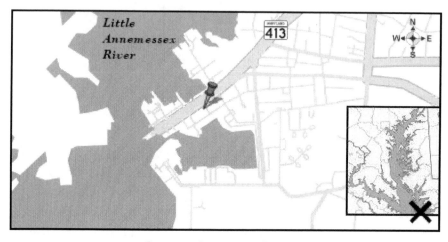

County: Somerset County
Open: Year Round ⚓ Dockage: No
Latitude: N 37° 58' 47" ⟶ Longitude: W 75° 51' 33"
Body of Water: between Somers Cove and
the Little Annemessex River off Tangier Sound
Driving Distance: Baltimore 153 miles,
Washington, DC 157 miles, Easton 84 miles

Atmosphere Meter

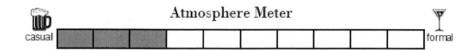

casual   formal

What began as the little Blue Crab Café has grown into a
restaurant and craft beer haven called Chesapeake Brewing
Company. Conveniently located on Crisfield's main drag near
the town's attractions, this new place successfully pairs two
beloved elements of the Bay — hot crabs and good beer. The

owners welcome visitors with warmth and enthusiasm about their new venture and are eager to help you discover their specialty brews. Beer names show a strong connection to their home: Crab Shanty Pale Ale, Soul of a Waterman Double IPA, and Marsh Mud Oyster Stout (150 Tangier Island oysters are in every batch).

Coastal home cooking and fresh local ingredients create ideal dishes to accompany microbrew tastings. Savory starters include shrimp skewers with vegetables, and crab in parmesan dip or on nachos. And who doesn't love warm soft pretzels when sampling beer? Cole slaw and pasta salad accompany entrees such as crab cake platter with shrimp and soft-shells, lamb chops grilled with garlic, and blackened chicken pasta alfredo. Seafood specials reflect the daily catch.

If you need more than one day to experience Crisfield, the brewery's owners can accommodate guests at Marquis Manor, a lovely Victorian home that they've spent years painstakingly renovating. They put together weekend packages so you can tour regional points of interest, take a crabbing tour with watermen, or go kayaking at a local state park. Extra bonus: They can hook you up with Smith Island Cake to help savor memories of your trip to their sweet part of the Bay.

The Watermen's Inn

901 West Main Street
Crisfield, MD 21817
(410) 968-2119
www.crisfield.com/watermens

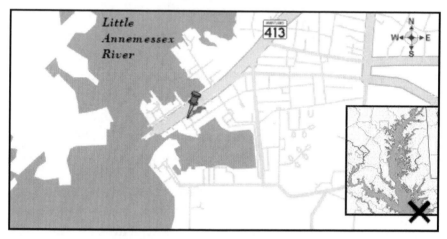

County: Somerset County
Open: Year Round ⚓ Dockage: No
Latitude: N 37° 58' 45" ⚓ Longitude: W 75° 51' 38"
Body of Water: between Somers Cove and
the Little Annemessex River off Tangier Sound
Driving Distance: Baltimore 153 miles,
Washington, DC 157 miles, Easton 84 miles

Atmosphere Meter

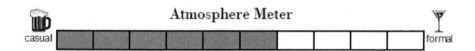

casual   formal

    Fine dining mixed with local folklore awaits you at Watermen's Inn. The building is painted burnt orange, and above the front porch rests a mural of a sailboat coasting toward the sunset. The interior walls have a soft glow of amber and beige, and tall windows give an open airy feel.

Pictures of Chesapeake boats and wildlife hang on the walls, and etched glass depictions of herons separate the dining area from the kitchen. The taproom bar has an old-fashioned saloon feel, accented by vintage photos.

Since 1988, the owners have created a gourmet experience that makes the most out of regional and seasonal ingredients. Menu highlights include shrimp, scallops, and crab in a cream sauce topped with puff pastry, crab cakes, oysters on the half shell or bacon roasted, filet mignon with béarnaise sauce, and chicken cordon bleu. Homemade desserts, artfully displayed on an antique desk, tempt you to indulge your sweet tooth.

Long known for its abundance of seafood, Crisfield hit an economic boom in the mid-1800s thanks to the railroad's arrival and the invention of refrigeration for transporting perishable items. Seafood processing plants sprang up all around the area. Workers from nearby plants liked to hang out at the honky-tonk where Watermen's now resides. During breaks they'd dash over and put back a few. Coaxing them back to work wasn't easy, so plant managers sounded steam whistles to mark the end of the break. But the workers didn't always listen. To fix the problem, each plant developed a unique whistle with its own pitch. When workers heard theirs blow, they had no excuse but to return to their jobs.

Chesapeake Crabhouse & Tiki Bar

923 Spruce Street
Crisfield, MD 21817
(410) 968-1131

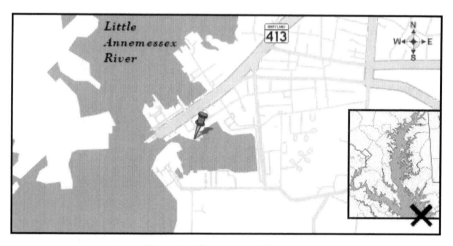

County: Somerset County
Open: Year Round ⚓ Dockage: Yes
Latitude: N 37° 58' 40" ⟜ Longitude: W 75° 51' 35"
Body of Water: between Somers Cove and
the Little Annemessex River off Tangier Sound
Driving Distance: Baltimore 153 miles,
Washington, DC 157 miles, Easton 84 miles

Atmosphere Meter

casual 🍺 ▮▮▮ formal 🍸

Chesapeake Crabhouse is the type of place that devoted crab pickers dream about when they want an authentic destination. Long rows of wooden picnic tables line up on the outdoor deck waiting for orders of steamed crabs and cold beer. Fans hanging from a lofty ceiling keep a constant breeze along the waterfront. Sunsets are glorious. The new thatch and wood tiki bar is a home away from home for local watermen. Pale blue and white are the house colors inside, accented by fishnets and photos of the Bay and oyster boats.

The home-style cooking is hearty, and meals are served in ample portions. Crab cakes are the size of a fat man's fist, and rockfish is sautéed to a golden brown. Steamed shrimp and fried oysters are adorned with creamy cole slaw and fries.

In the background, the crab-emblazoned water tower stands watch over a town that has played a key role in Chesapeake history. Crisfield was called Somers Cove to honor Benjamin Somers, who settled the area in 1663. That name might have stuck if it hadn't been for John W. Crisfield, a local lawyer and Congressman who was instrumental in bringing the railroad to this region and sparking a zenith in the seafood industry. One day in the mid-1860s, Mr. Crisfield was inspecting the docks near the steamboat landing. While walking across a section of rotten boards, he crashed through the planks and toppled into the frigid water. After fishing him out, officials named the town after him in a gesture of apology and appreciation to their benefactor. Learn more at Tawes Historical Museum down the street.

Riverside Grill

2 Riverside Drive
Pocomoke City, MD 21851
(410) 957-0622
www.riversidegrillpocomoke.com

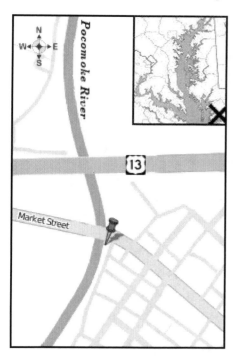

County: Worcester County

Open: Year Round

Dockage: Yes

Latitude: N 38° 4' 34"

Longitude: W 75° 34' 14"

Body of Water: Pocomoke
River

Driving Distance:
Baltimore 147 miles,
Washington, DC 151 miles,
Easton 79 miles

Atmosphere Meter

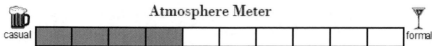

casual   formal

Pocomoke City's nickname is "The Friendliest Town on the Eastern Shore." A few years ago, it got a lot friendlier thanks to a new restaurant called Riverside Grill. It was developed by the city, is run by the folks who own Back Street Grill in Salisbury, and they got it right when they built this place. The location is idyllic — right along the river next to a graceful historic drawbridge with lights that cast a lovely reflection on the water at night. Ducks paddle around the river while dodging boats that tie up to the dock. The dining room's design is contemporary and open, drawing everyone's attention to the row of windows facing the water. Walls are painted various shades of sky blue, accented with pastel pictures of crabs and waterfowl. Booths with tall wooden backs offer privacy during meals, but the most coveted seats are on the outdoor deck and patio overlooking the river.

The menu looks like a multiple choice test with no wrong answers. If you want a sandwich, burger, or salad, put a mark next to the type of bread, meat, and extras you like and hand your selection to the waiter. Appetizers cover the basics: crab dip, wings, crab pizza, and seafood skins. Entrees are divided between the land and the sea. Featured dishes: seafood platter, ale-battered fried shrimp, crab cakes, and grilled 10-ounce rib eye. Jerk chicken and island-style fish bring a pinch of spice to the table. The kids menu offers essentials such as PB&J, chicken fingers, grilled cheese, and hot dogs.

To make a day out of your visit, go next door to the Delmarva Discovery Center to learn about the region's heritage. Then stroll around the charming streets of Pocomoke City to find out what makes this town so friendly.

Bayside Inn Restaurant

4065 Smith Island Road
Ewell, MD 21824
(410) 425-2771

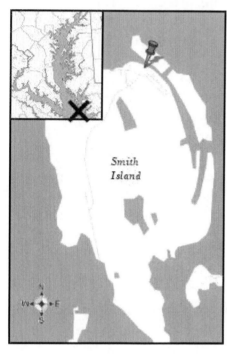

County: Somerset County

Open: Seasonal

Dockage: Yes

Latitude: N 37° 59' 46"

Longitude: W 76° 1' 57"

Body of Water: Big Thorofare
Channel off Tangier Sound

Driving Distance to ferry:
Baltimore 153 miles,
Washington, DC 157 miles,
Easton 84 miles

Atmosphere Meter

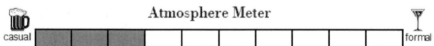

casual   formal

The arrival of crabs in the spring is grounds for celebration at Bayside Inn and all around Smith Island. It marks the opening of a new season when visitors venture out to Maryland's only inhabited island that is not attached to the mainland by bridge or causeway. Daily ferry boats from Crisfield and Point Lookout offer the only means to get there. The island was originally mapped by Captain John Smith in

1608 and named after Henry Smith, a Jamestown man who was granted 1,000 acres of land there in 1679. At its peak, nearly 800 residents lived on the island, but the number has dwindled to 276 people who live in the three villages of Ewell, Rhodes Point, and Tylerton. Erosion has reduced its size, so folks get around by foot or golf cart. Nearly 8,000 acres of marshland surround the island, giving sanctuary to fledgling sea creatures and waterfowl.

Bayside Inn is located in Ewell near the Smith Island Heritage Center and the pier where boats unload the mail, supplies, and tourists. It's a favorite hang-out for locals who like to bring down wooden mallets on steamed crabs or peel succulent shrimp. Tomato-based or creamy crab soup is on tap, and fried oysters are plump and crispy. Given the location, it's hard to imagine ordering anything other than seafood, but baked ham and turkey breast sandwiches are on the menu, and the kitchen offers specials like prime rib, steak, and BBQ ribs. At the rear of the restaurant, the carry-out shop scoops hand-dipped ice cream and sells Smith Island Cake, made of 10 pencil-thin layers of moist cake separated by icing. It was originally only four layers high until women started competing over who could stack it higher. In 2008, Maryland voted to make this cake the state's official dessert.

Ruke's Seafood Deck

20840 Caleb Jones Road
Ewell, MD 21824
(410) 425-2311
www.rukesgeneralstore.com

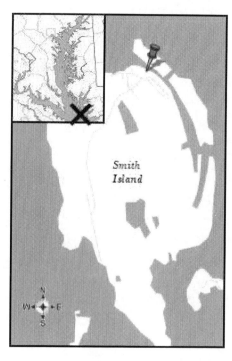

County: Somerset County

Open: Seasonal

Dockage: Yes

Latitude: N 37° 59' 46"

Longitude: W 76° 1' 57"

Body of Water: Big Thorofare
Channel off Tangier Sound

Driving Distance to ferry:
Baltimore 153 miles,
Washington, DC 157 miles,
Easton 84 miles

Atmosphere Meter

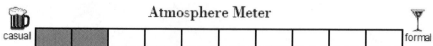

casual ▢▢▢ ▢ ▢ ▢ ▢ ▢ ▢ ▢ formal

If you travel by boat, getting to Ruke's Seafood Deck isn't a problem. But if you explore the Bay by car or motorcycle, arriving at this hideaway requires some advance planning. It's located on Smith Island, about 12 miles offshore from the mainland, and ferry service is the only way to reach this destination. You board the boat in Crisfield, and it departs every day promptly at 12:30 in the afternoon. Many people visit the island to hear the unique American English dialect that has been preserved through isolation.

Why make the trip? Ruke's began serving patrons more than 55 years ago. The eatery/general store combo takes you back to a simpler time when neighbors gathered at diners, curled their fingers around hot cups of coffee, and exchanged news about fishing, friends, and family. Items in the general store underscore that yesteryear feeling. The shelves are filled with antique collectibles, old photos, model ships, miniature lighthouses, and decorative art and glassware. Colorful vintage signs hang on the walls.

The food is simple and easy. Soft-shell crabs are fried to a pleasant crisp, crab cakes are mixed with hardly any filler and shrimp baskets come with cole slaw and fries. Burgers, grilled cheese sandwiches, hot dogs, cold cut subs, pizza, and fried chicken say comfort food is never out of style. Milkshakes and chocolate sundaes resurrect uncomplicated childhood memories.

Bodies of Water Index

Cities Index

Restaurant Names Index

C

Cabana Bar (see Mango's Bar & Grill, page 116)

Cabanas is now Nick's Riverside Grill, page 4

Café 7 is now Coconut Joe's Hawaiian Bar & Grill, page 104

Calypso Bay Boatyard Bar & Grill is now Dockside Restaurant & Sports Bar, page 110

Calypso Bay Crab House is now Charles Street Brasserie, page 92

Cantina Marina 16

Cantler's Riverside Inn (see Jimmy Cantler's Riverside Inn, page 130)

Canton Dockside (see Hamilton's Canton Dockside, page 226)

Cappy's Tiki Bar (see Fisherman's Inn & Crab Deck, page 354)

Captain Billy's Crab House..........32

Captain George's at Harbor Sounds is now Charles Street Brasserie, page 92

Captain James Seafood Palace...220

Captain John's Crabhouse...........36

Captain Tyler's Crab House is now Chesapeake Crabhouse & Tiki Bar, page 428

Captain White's Seafood City (see Maine Avenue Fish Market, page 14)

Captain's Galley Restaurant (Crisfield)................................☠

Captain's Table is now Anglers Seafood Bar & Grill, page 76

Carrol's Creek Waterfront Restaurant 154

Carson's Creekside Restaurant & Lounge...............................234

Catamarans Restaurant is now The Striped Rock at Solomons, page 82

Cat's Eye Pub 216

Channel Restaurant.....................318

Chappelear's Place (Benedict) ....☠

Characters Bridge Restaurant 380

Charles Street Brasserie 92

Chart House Restaurant............. 158

Chesapeake Brewing Company 424

Chesapeake Crabhouse & Tiki Bar.. 428

Chesapeake House Restaurant (see Harrison's Chesapeake House Restaurant, page 384)

Chesapeake Inn Restaurant 298

Cheshire Crab Restaurant 272

Chester River Inn is now Pour House Pub, page 336

City Lights Seafood Restaurant (Baltimore)..............................☠

Clarke's Landing Restaurant is now Stoney's Seafood at Clarke's Landing, page 72

Clearview at Horn's Point (Cambridge) ....☠

Coconut Joe's Hawaiian Bar & Grill.. 104

Courtney's Restaurant & Seafood.. 54

Cove Restaurant (Crisfield) ....☠

Crab Cake Café............................. 22

Crab Claw Restaurant 372

Crab Place.................................... 422

Crab Shanty is now The Big Owl Tiki Bar, page 350

Crabby Dick's at Port Tobacco Marina is now Port Tobacco Restaurant, page 30

Crazy Tuna Bar & Grille............ 238

Crisfield Crab House & Grill (Crisfield)..............................☠

Crooked I Sports Bar & Grill (Chesapeake Beach).....................☠

Crown & Anchor Pub (Annapolis).............................☠

D

Davis' Pub 162

Dead Eye Saloon is now Nick's Fish House, page 260

Deep Creek Restaurant............. 128

S

T

V

W

Y

Z

Tiki Tracker

*As you head out on Bay adventures, use this Tiki Tracker
to keep track of your favorite crab decks and tiki bars.*

Name: _____

Location: _____

Date: _____

Rating: ○ ○ ○ ○ ○

Checklist of things consumed

☐ Steamed Crabs   ☐ Oysters

☐ Crab Cake   ☐ Crab Soup

☐ Beer   ☐ Rum

☐ Other: _____

Comments: _____

_____

_____

_____

_____

_____

Name: _____

Location: _____

Date: _____

Rating: ○ ○ ○ ○ ○

Checklist of things consumed

☐ Steamed Crabs   ☐ Oysters

☐ Crab Cake   ☐ Crab Soup

☐ Beer   ☐ Rum

☐ Other: _____

Comments: _____

_____

_____

_____

_____

_____

Name: _____

Location: _____

Date: _____

Rating: ○ ○ ○ ○ ○

Checklist of things consumed

☐ Steamed Crabs   ☐ Oysters

☐ Crab Cake   ☐ Crab Soup

☐ Beer   ☐ Rum

☐ Other: _____

Comments: _____

_____

_____

_____

_____

_____

Name: _____

Location: _____

Date: _____

Rating: ○ ○ ○ ○ ○

Checklist of things consumed

☐ Steamed Crabs   ☐ Oysters

☐ Crab Cake   ☐ Crab Soup

☐ Beer   ☐ Rum

☐ Other: _____

Comments: _____

_____

_____

_____

_____

_____

Tiki Tracker

Name: _____
Location: _____
Date: _____
Rating: ○ ○ ○ ○ ○
Checklist of things consumed
☐ Steamed Crabs   ☐ Oysters
☐ Crab Cake   ☐ Crab Soup
☐ Beer   ☐ Rum
☐ Other: _____
Comments: _____
_____
_____

Name: _____
Location: _____
Date: _____
Rating: ○ ○ ○ ○ ○   —
Checklist of things consumed
☐ Steamed Crabs   ☐ Oysters
☐ Crab Cake   ☐ Crab Soup
☐ Beer   ☐ Rum
☐ Other: _____
Comments: _____
_____
_____

Name: _____
Location: _____
Date: _____
Rating: ○ ○ ○ ○ ○
Checklist of things consumed
☐ Steamed Crabs   ☐ Oysters
☐ Crab Cake   ☐ Crab Soup
☐ Beer   ☐ Rum
☐ Other: _____
Comments: _____
_____
_____

Name: _____
Location: _____
Date: _____
Rating: ○ ○ ○ ○ ○
Checklist of things consumed
☐ Steamed Crabs   ☐ Oysters
☐ Crab Cake   ☐ Crab Soup
☐ Beer   ☐ Rum
☐ Other: _____
Comments: _____
_____
_____

Name: _____
Location: _____
Date: _____
Rating: ○ ○ ○ ○ ○
Checklist of things consumed
☐ Steamed Crabs   ☐ Oysters
☐ Crab Cake   ☐ Crab Soup
☐ Beer   ☐ Rum
☐ Other: _____
Comments: _____
_____
_____

Name: _____
Location: _____
Date: _____
Rating: ○ ○ ○ ○ ○
Checklist of things consumed
☐ Steamed Crabs   ☐ Oysters
☐ Crab Cake   ☐ Crab Soup
☐ Beer   ☐ Rum
☐ Other: _____
Comments: _____
_____
_____

Tiki Tracker

Name: _____
Location: _____
Date: _____
Rating: ○ ○ ○ ○ ○
Checklist of things consumed
☐ Steamed Crabs   ☐ Oysters
☐ Crab Cake   ☐ Crab Soup
☐ Beer   ☐ Rum
☐ Other: _____
Comments: _____
_____
_____

Name: _____
Location: _____
Date: _____
Rating: ○ ○ ○ ○ ○
Checklist of things consumed
☐ Steamed Crabs   ☐ Oysters
☐ Crab Cake   ☐ Crab Soup
☐ Beer   ☐ Rum
☐ Other: _____
Comments: _____
_____
_____

Name: _____
Location: _____
Date: _____
Rating: ○ ○ ○ ○ ○
Checklist of things consumed
☐ Steamed Crabs   ☐ Oysters
☐ Crab Cake   ☐ Crab Soup
☐ Beer   ☐ Rum
☐ Other: _____
Comments: _____
_____
_____

Name: _____
Location: _____
Date: _____
Rating: ○ ○ ○ ○ ○
Checklist of things consumed
☐ Steamed Crabs   ☐ Oysters
☐ Crab Cake   ☐ Crab Soup
☐ Beer   ☐ Rum
☐ Other: _____
Comments: _____
_____
_____

Name: _____
Location: _____
Date: _____
Rating: ○ ○ ○ ○ ○
Checklist of things consumed
☐ Steamed Crabs   ☐ Oysters
☐ Crab Cake   ☐ Crab Soup
☐ Beer   ☐ Rum
☐ Other: _____
Comments: _____
_____
_____

Name: _____
Location: _____
Date: _____
Rating: ○ ○ ○ ○ ○
Checklist of things consumed
☐ Steamed Crabs   ☐ Oysters
☐ Crab Cake   ☐ Crab Soup
☐ Beer   ☐ Rum
☐ Other: _____
Comments: _____
_____
_____

Tiki Tracker

Name: _____
Location: _____
Date: _____
Rating: ○ ○ ○ ○ ○
Checklist of things consumed
☐ Steamed Crabs   ☐ Oysters
☐ Crab Cake   ☐ Crab Soup
☐ Beer   ☐ Rum
☐ Other: _____
Comments: _____
_____
_____

Name: _____
Location: _____
Date: _____
Rating: ○ ○ ○ ○ ○
Checklist of things consumed
☐ Steamed Crabs   ☐ Oysters
☐ Crab Cake   ☐ Crab Soup
☐ Beer   ☐ Rum
☐ Other: _____
Comments: _____
_____
_____

Name: _____
Location: _____
Date: _____
Rating: ○ ○ ○ ○ ○
Checklist of things consumed
☐ Steamed Crabs   ☐ Oysters
☐ Crab Cake   ☐ Crab Soup
☐ Beer   ☐ Rum
☐ Other: _____
Comments: _____
_____
_____

Name: _____
Location: _____
Date: _____
Rating: ○ ○ ○ ○ ○
Checklist of things consumed
☐ Steamed Crabs   ☐ Oysters
☐ Crab Cake   ☐ Crab Soup
☐ Beer   ☐ Rum
☐ Other: _____
Comments: _____
_____
_____

Name: _____
Location: _____
Date: _____
Rating: ○ ○ ○ ○ ○
Checklist of things consumed
☐ Steamed Crabs   ☐ Oysters
☐ Crab Cake   ☐ Crab Soup
☐ Beer   ☐ Rum
☐ Other: _____
Comments: _____
_____
_____

Name: _____
Location: _____
Date: _____
Rating: ○ ○ ○ ○ ○
Checklist of things consumed
☐ Steamed Crabs   ☐ Oysters
☐ Crab Cake   ☐ Crab Soup
☐ Beer   ☐ Rum
☐ Other: _____
Comments: _____
_____
_____

Tiki Tracker

Name: _____
Location: _____
Date: _____
Rating: ○ ○ ○ ○ ○
Checklist of things consumed
☐ Steamed Crabs   ☐ Oysters
☐ Crab Cake   ☐ Crab Soup
☐ Beer   ☐ Rum
☐ Other: _____
Comments: _____
_____
_____

Name: _____
Location: _____
Date: _____
Rating: ○ ○ ○ ○ ○
Checklist of things consumed
☐ Steamed Crabs   ☐ Oysters
☐ Crab Cake   ☐ Crab Soup
☐ Beer   ☐ Rum
☐ Other: _____
Comments: _____
_____
_____

Name: _____
Location: _____
Date: _____
Rating: ○ ○ ○ ○ ○
Checklist of things consumed
☐ Steamed Crabs   ☐ Oysters
☐ Crab Cake   ☐ Crab Soup
☐ Beer   ☐ Rum
☐ Other: _____
Comments: _____
_____
_____

Name: _____
Location: _____
Date: _____
Rating: ○ ○ ○ ○ ○
Checklist of things consumed
☐ Steamed Crabs   ☐ Oysters
☐ Crab Cake   ☐ Crab Soup
☐ Beer   ☐ Rum
☐ Other: _____
Comments: _____
_____
_____

Name: _____
Location: _____
Date: _____
Rating: ○ ○ ○ ○ ○
Checklist of things consumed
☐ Steamed Crabs   ☐ Oysters
☐ Crab Cake   ☐ Crab Soup
☐ Beer   ☐ Rum
☐ Other: _____
Comments: _____
_____
_____

Name: _____
Location: _____
Date: _____
Rating: ○ ○ ○ ○ ○
Checklist of things consumed
☐ Steamed Crabs   ☐ Oysters
☐ Crab Cake   ☐ Crab Soup
☐ Beer   ☐ Rum
☐ Other: _____
Comments: _____
_____
_____

WASHINGTON
DISTRICT OF COLUMBIA ✦ USA

ANNAPOLIS
U.S. NAVAL ACADEMY ✦ MARYLAND

BALTIMORE
BICENTENNIAL 1812–1815 ✦ MARYLAND

Who is Citizen Pride?

There's a special pride each of us take in our hometown and iconic symbols that are unique to where we live. We call it "Citizen Pride" and our artwork in print, on canvas, flags and note cards offer an original and meaningful way to share and display it.

Joe and Eva Barsin at the Maryland Bay Plate's unveiling ceremony.

Illustrations by Joe Barsin are well known since he created the **Maryland Bay license plate** and the recent series of posters promoting the *Annapolis Film Festival*, along with numerous magazine and commissioned artwork.

Living abroad in Italy during his formative years developed his understanding of an artist's role in defining a community's culture and history. Being an Eagle Scout developed his sense of community, patriotism and appreciation for the natural world.

Joe is a native of Akron, Ohio, who graduated from Kent State University with a degree in graphic design. He and his wife, Eva, started their own design firm, JEB Design, Inc., in 1998, and continue to work from home while raising their two boys.

Take a look at Joe's work at *CitizenPride.com* to see what stirs your sense of Maryland pride. We have a full line of gifts and products featuring Joe Barsin's work.

CitizenPride.com
facebook.com/CitizenPrideUSA

**CITIZEN®
PRIDE**

Show your Pride!

Citizen Pride art products offer you a unique way to express your pride of Maryland and the places you visit.

Our Products Include:
**Garden & House Flags • Door Mats
Canvas Wall Art • Prints • Notecards
Postcards • Magnets • Stickers**

Visit **CitizenPride.com** *to see our full line of gifts and products.
Featured here are some of the illustrations offered.*

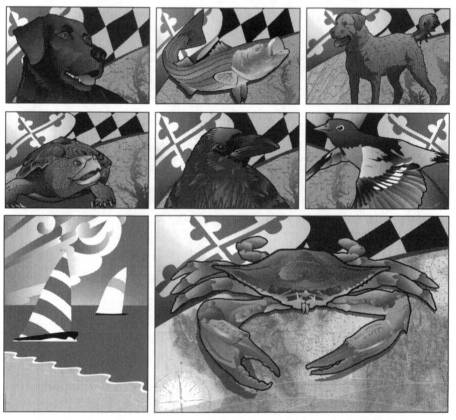

Illustration by local artist, Joe Barsin.
Barsin created the Maryland Bay license plate.

CitizenPride.com
facebook.com/CitizenPrideUSA

CITIZEN® PRIDE

Made in the USA
Charleston, SC
10 June 2015